FAMILIES
AND
AGING

Recent Titles in
Bibliographies and Indexes in Gerontology

Suicide and the Elderly: An Annotated Bibliography and Review
Nancy J. Osgood and John L. McIntosh, compilers

Human Longevity from Antiquity to the Modern Lab: A Selected, Annotated
Bibliography
William G. Bailey, compiler

Federal Public Policy on Aging since 1960: An Annotated Bibliography
William E. Oriol, compiler

European American Elderly: An Annotated Bibliography
David Guttmann, compiler

Legal Aspects of Health Care for the Elderly: An Annotated Bibliography
Marshall B. Kapp, compiler

Crime and the Elderly: An Annotated Bibliography
Ron H. Aday, compiler

Jewish Elderly in the English-Speaking Countries
David Guttmann, compiler

Women and Aging: A Selected, Annotated Bibliography
Jean M. Coyle, compiler

Fundamentals of Geriatrics for Health Professionals: An Annotated
Bibliography
Jodi L. Teitelman and Iris A. Parham, compilers

Geriatric Nursing Assistants: An Annotated Bibliography with Models to
Enhance Practice
George H. Weber

Anthropology of Aging: A Partially Annotated Bibliography
Marjorie M. Schweitzer, general editor

FAMILIES AND AGING

A Selected, Annotated Bibliography

Compiled by
JEAN M. COYLE

Bibliographies and Indexes in Gerontology, Number 14
Erdman Palmore, Series Adviser

GREENWOOD PRESS
New York • Westport, Connecticut • London

Library of Congress Cataloging-in-Publication Data

Coyle, Jean M.
   Families and aging : a selected, annotated bibliography / compiled
by Jean M. Coyle.
     p. cm.—(Bibliographies and indexes in gerontology, ISSN 0743-7560 ;
no. 14)
   Includes bibliographical references and index.
   ISBN 0-313-27211-5
   1. Aged—Family relationships—Bibliography. 2. Aged—United
States—Family relationships—Bibliography.   I. Title.   II. Series.
Z7164.O4C67 1991
[HQ1061]
016.6467'8—dc20   91-29593

British Library Cataloguing in Publication Data is available.

Library of Congress Catalog Card Number: 91-29593
ISBN: 0-313-27211-5
ISSN: 0743-7560

First published in 1991

Greenwood Press, 88 Post Road West, Westport, CT 06881
An imprint of Greenwood Publishing Group, Inc.

Printed in the United States of America

The paper used in this book complies with the
Permanent Paper Standard issued by the National
Information Standards Organization (Z39.48-1984).

10 9 8 7 6 5 4 3 2 1

Dedicated to my nieces,
Jeana Maria, Ericka Elizabeth, and Sara Ann Mayne,
and to the memory of my grandparents,
John and Anna Maria Lay

Contents

Series Foreword by Erdman B. Palmore   ix

Preface   xi

Acknowledgments   xiii

Introduction   xv

1. Middle-aged Families   1

2. Singlehood   7

3. Older Couples   15

4. Widowhood   25

5. Grandparents   47

6. Adult Children   59

7. Intergenerational Relationships   71

8. Family Caregiving   83

9. Racial and Ethnic Minority Groups   123

10. Living Arrangements of Older Persons   143

11. General   161

    Author Index   183

    Subject Index   195

Series Foreword

The annotated bibliographies in this series provide answers to the fundamental question, What is known? Their purpose is simple, yet profound: to provide comprehensive reviews and references for the work done in various fields of gerontology. They are based on the fact that it is no longer possible for anyone to comprehend the vast body of research and writing in even one sub-specialty without years of work.

This fact has become true only in recent years. When I was an undergraduate (Class of '52) I think no one at Duke University had even heard of gerontology. Almost no one in the world was identified as a gerontologist. Now there are over 6,000 professional members of the Gerontological Society of America. When I was an undergraduate there were no courses in gerontology. Now there are thousands of courses offered by most major (and many minor) colleges and universities. When I was an undergraduate there was only one gerontological journal (the Journal of Gerontology, begun in 1945). Now there are over forty professional journals and several dozen books in gerontology published each year.

The reasons for this dramatic growth are well known: the dramatic increase in numbers of aged, the shift from family to public responsibility for the security and care of the elderly, the recognition of aging as a "social problem," and the growth of science in general. It is less well known that this explosive growth in knowledge has developed the need for new solutions to the old problem of comprehending and "keeping up" with a field of knowledge. The old indexes and library card catalogues have become increasingly inadequate for the job. On-line computer indexes and abstracts are one solution, but they make no evaluative selections or organize sources logically as is done here. These annotated bibliographies are also more widely available than on-line computer indexes.

These bibliographies will obviously be useful for researchers who need to know what research has (or has not) been done in their field. The annotations contain enough information so that the researcher usually does not have to search out the original articles. In the past, the "review of literature" has often been haphazard and was rarely comprehensive, because of the large investment of time (and money) that would be required by a truly comprehensive review. Now, using these bibliographies, researchers can be more confident that they are not missing important previous research; they can be more confident that they are not duplicating past efforts and "reinventing the wheel." It may well become standard and expected practice for researchers to consult such bibliographies, even before they start their research.

The families of elders are the single most important group affecting their health and welfare. Most elders live with their spouse or other family members. Surveys show that elders are most concerned about their families, spend more time with them, give and get more aid from them, and are more likely to be cared for by them than by any other type of person. Thus, this is a most important field in gerontology. This book is needed not only by academics, students, and researchers, but also by professionals who work with elders, by elders themselves, and by anyone who wants better to understand elders.

Dr. Coyle has done an outstanding job of covering all the relevant literature and organizing it into easily accessible form. Not only are there 778 annotated references organized into 11 sections, but there are also an introductory chapter, an author index, and a subject index with many cross-references for the items in the bibliography.

Thus, one can look for relevant material in this volume in several ways: (1) look up a given subject in the subject index; (2) look up a given author in the author index; (3) turn to the section that covers the topic; or (4) look over the introduction for a basic orientation to the topic.

Dr. Coyle is unusually qualified to author this bibliography because she is a recognized expert in the field, having provided expert consultation on several national programs dealing with families of elders, and having taught at universities in Indiana, Texas, Louisiana, Illinois, Washington, D.C., Virginia, and now in New Mexico. Her annotations are concise and clear so that one can easily use this bibliography and so that one can determine whether the original is worth pursuing. Dr. Coyle is also the author of a previous, annotated bibliography in this series titled "Women and Aging."

So it is with great pleasure that we add this bibliography to our series. We believe you will find this volume to be the most useful, comprehensive, and easily accessible reference work in its field. I will appreciate any comments you care to send me.

Erdman B. Palmore
Center for the Study of Aging and Human Development
Box 3003, Duke University Medical Center
Durham, North Carolina, 27710

Preface

This book provides an extensive, selected bibliography on the topic of families and the aging process. The focus is on the diverse types of family relationships which exist for older Americans--from singlehood to older couples to widowhood to grandparenthood. Both pragmatic and theoretical publications are included.

Over 700 annotations are included in the book. On some topics it is apparent that there are fewer references that were discovered, which would seem to indicate areas where research is needed. Most references, with some exceptions, were published from 1980 through 1990. The objective was to provide the most current information available on these topics.

These annotated references are provided as guides to relevant materials on families and the aging process. The primary goal is to direct readers to relevant and appropriate documents on these topics.

Within each chapter, annotations are divided into books, articles, films, government documents, and dissertations. All materials identified are accessible through basic library systems.

The major areas covered herein include middle-aged family members', singlehood, older couples, widowhood, grandparenthood, adult children, intergenerational relationships, family caregiving, racial and ethnic minority groups, and living arrangements of older families. Also included is an extensive collection of general items that did not fit exactly into any of the aforementioned chapters.

Acknowledgments

I would like to acknowledge the assistance of Erdman Palmore, series editor, and Loomis Mayer and George F. Butler, past and present editors, behavioral and social sciences, Greenwood Press, for their help in the preparation of this annotated bibliography.

Assistance in identifying appropriate materials for this manuscript was provided by staff members in several divisions of the Library of Congress and the Resource Center of the American Association of Retired Persons, both located in Washington, D.C., the New Mexico State University Library, located in Las Cruces, New Mexico, and the University of New Mexico libraries, located in Albuquerque, New Mexico. Librarian Donnelyn Curtis of New Mexico State University Library was especially helpful. Angela Sandoval provided advice on computerization.

Among those who have provided support and encouragement over the years are Sara Rix, Carl and Helen McGeehon, Elizabeth Brown, Marie Fuller, Kay Wood, Herb Weiss, Carolyn Ward, Heather and Norman Louat, Gertrude Leich, and Mary Grizzard.

Among those who have provided role models for various family structures and ways of dealing with the aging process are Frank and Louise Parsons, Dorothy and Merrill Kreipke, Anne McCarrick, Elmer and Elizabeth Dean, Kay Wood, Gertrude Leich, Elizabeth and Steve Brown, Bill and Selma Trautvetter, Aldina and Jack Cabrera, Elizabeth Weiss, Margaret MacLeish, Christine Echols, Rudy and Eulalee Anderson, Ed and Louise Tiedemann, Vardine Moore, and John Julia McMahan.

Introduction

New challenges exist for today's families in facilitating intergenerational relationships across the lifespan. The increasing number of four- and five-generation families is adding to the complexity of these family relationships. The smaller numbers of children in the "baby boomer" families contributes to new concerns about caregiving for those baby boomer parents as they age.

The many and diverse types of families that exist in middle age and old age are examined in the multiple citations and annotations included herein. A general chapter of references that did not fit readily into the aforementioned chapters is included, also.

Middle-aged Families

The transitions faced by women in their middle years are explored in several references, with such themes as the impact of social change and the heterogeneity of midlife women. The traditional family life cycle has been changed by trends such as the postponement of marriage and childbearing, divorce and separation, and early career entry. The trends lead to continuities and discontinuities in individual women's lives and in the experiences of different age cohorts of women over a period of time (O'Rand, A., and Henretta, J., 1982, 57-64).

The middle-aged family is seen as a support system for its aging parents (Tappen, 1980), with the amount of help given most influenced by the distance between the family and its parents. Findings of another study (Snow, 1980) indicate that middle-aged wives had the highest degree of emotional bondedness with their mothers and their fathers, and middle-aged husbands had the highest degree of emotional bondedness with their mothers and their fathers.

Singlehood

The status regarding never married, divorced, and separated persons is included in this section on singlehood. In the literature there is support for the thesis that married elderly, compared to unmarried older persons, have higher levels of morale, life satisfaction, mental and physical health, economic resources, social integration and social support, and lower rates of institutionalization (Bengston, V., Rosenthal, C., and Burton, L., 1990). A model of singleness in later life shows how the social context may influence the personal and social resources of older, unmarried persons (Keith, P., 1986b). Keith (1986a) also discusses role transitions of the unmarried over the life course, finances, health, and social relationships of older, single persons. Data from two studies reported by Rubinstein (1987 and 1989) suggest that "never married elderly are not necessarily socially isolated, may experience some loneliness, do not have a uniform attitude concerning the possibility of marriage, and do suffer from the effects of loss in late life" (1987).

Another study that predicts a rapid increase in divorce in the next several decades (Uhlenberg, P., and Myers, M., 1986) predicts, as well, a possible deterioration in the economic and social welfare of the elderly that may also produce other changes--such as coping skills in dealing with widowhood, and more unattached men over the age of 65, leading to increased non-marital sexual activity among the elderly. Those persons divorced in late life generally are urban residing, with low occupational status, few assets, and weak religious and kinship ties (Wilson, 1983). In Wilson's study, divorce was found to result from a longstanding lack of emotional gratification aggravated by some type of precipitating event. Overall, females were found to have more negative divorce experiences and to suffer greater negative consequences than did males.

Older Couples

Ade-Ridder and Brubaker (1983) review research on marital quality across the life cycle and during retirement, finding that marital quality includes variables such as happiness, success, satisfaction, and adjustment. Another study states: "As they enter their older years, husbands and wives may need to reexamine their own behavior and balance their relationships in light of the new definitions they encounter" (Dobson, 1983). For the Terman study subjects (studied for more than 40 years from 1940 to 1984), cited in Holahan, there was found significant change in the direction of increased egalitarianism in marital attitudes--"these changes are in accord with the trend toward greater sex role equality in our society" (Holahan, 1986).

It is better to be married than not be married in old age is the conclusion of Hess and Soldo (1985), since married, older persons have higher incomes, more primary group ties, sexual access, companionship, residential privacy, sufficient nutrition, and better physical and mental health than persons who are not married. "The marital dyad is associated with a number of positive outcomes, particularly for husbands--longer life, lower morbidity, higher standard of living, greater life satisfaction, and homebased care when disabled" (Hess and Soldo, 1985).

Cole's (1984) central perspective is that marriage provides elderly couples with many life-sustaining resources that add to the quality of retirement life. Cole indicates that "retirement offers unique opportunities for married couples to enhance their relationship and to develop support systems for the continued growth of their full marital potential." The reward for years of companionship and mutual interests "is the caring and nurturing of each other in the later years of life. . . . Commitment, companionship, care, and concern are found to be strengths in the relationship" (Darnton, 1977).

Widowhood

Widowhood seems to be a universal problem (Palmore, 1987). Palmore suggests that the problems associated with widowhood are replacing the functions of the dead spouse/parent and determining who should inherit the property of the dead spouse and where the surviving family should live. Palmore presents various solutions to these problems based on demographic characteristics of developing and developed countries.

General stability among the recently widowed with regard to family relations was found by Ferraro and Barresi (1982), with lower levels of social interaction with family members for persons widowed more than four years. Heinemann (1983) also found that relatives provided much initial help for bereaved individuals, but that, as the widowed person "adapts to the loss, roles and relationships with relatives are renegotiated from the perspective of a single person." However, Morgan's 1984 study showed that there was an increase in the average frequency of interaction with available kin over time. "Widows' past experiences and attitudes toward independence influence the amount of overall help they receive, whereas income, number of children, and perceived willingness of children to help affect the proportion of help that comes from children" (O'Bryant, S., and Morgan, L., 1990).

The transition from wife to widow was found to be orderly and congruent with their previous lifestyles for the widows in Barrell's 1980 study. The women in this sample had experienced major losses throughout their lives. The most successful of these widows were "personally strong, self-confident women with necessary knowledge, skills, and abilities to continue satisfying lives alone when their husbands died."

In the Biggers (1981) study, the most important factor in resolving the grief process was the widows' perceived financial status. An inverse relationship was found between "the grief reaction of older widows and their level of ego development; the length of widowhood, length of the husband's illness prior to his death, the widow's perceived financial status, and her level of ego development were the combination of factors most important in resolution of the grief process in older widows." Bright (1985) found that factors that were significantly associated with the normal grief pattern were higher education, a close relationship to one's husband, an action-oriented coping style, having received professional intervention, high family inclusion, and an active relationship with friends. Characteristics that had an impact on atypical grief included increased age, a long work history, a pink-collar job, less education, more than one marriage, not being close to one's husband, a shared family decisionmaking process, a dependent coping style, an early move after the husband's death, less family communication, and fewer activities with friends.

Grandparents

In their edited book (1985), Bengston and Robertson and the respective authors explore the nature and importance of the grandparent role. Data from the first, representative, nationwide study of grandparents are reported by Cherlin and Furstenberg (1986). The authors found strong sentimental ties and loose bonds of obligation.

There are few rules constraining grandparent roles, according to Funder (1989). Another study states: "As a family relationship, grandparenthood represents a series of ongoing, longstanding bonds. As a role, it comprises a unique range of behaviors, meanings and satisfactions" (Kivnick, 1984). Troll concludes that grandparents often play an important role in central family dynamics; grandparental roles are more diverse than parental ones and differ by social class, ethnicity, and sex, as well as with individual preferences; the developmental status of both grandparent and grandchild influences their interactions and feelings; and "the most important role of the grandparents may be that of maintaining the family system as a whole" (Troll, 1983).

Adult Children

Family members often provide the primary support for older persons living in the community (Wright, 1986). Among findings of Wright's study were that single caregivers found a caring role hard to continue, caring had more effect on the daughter's employment than on the son's, friends and volunteers did not provide significant support, there is little participation by the wider community in the caring process, social workers were the least evident of caring professionals, the most widely used services were Meals on Wheels and home help services, there was no appropriate support for persons who had given up outside employment because of the need to care for their parents, there was a loss of personal freedom (for the caregiver), and day care was not very evident.

Other publications examine sibling relationships in old age, parenting, filial expectations, and social interaction between adult children and older parents.

Intergenerational Relationships

Cohler's and Grunebaum's (1981) quantitative study of the modified, extended family focuses on the psychological significance of contact and support of family members across generations for the continued adult development of these family members. Browne and Onzuka-Anderson (1985) examine the perspectives of three generations of a caregiving family about their interdependence. Furstenberg (1981) looks at whether and how the divorce and remarriage patterns in this country are likely to restructure ideas of kinship and the functioning of the kinship system in American society. Hagestad (1981) predicts that "a social psychology of intergenerational bonds holds a rich promise of new insights into the shaping of individual lives, the mediation of social change, and the maintenance of long-term primary ties." A number of multigenerational families testifying before the U.S. House Select Committee on Aging (1980) discuss how older family members can help strengthen family bonds, establish pride in heritage, care for younger family members, and contribute to the productive force of the family unit, as well as assist with services which could help family caregivers.

Educational programs emphasizing intergenerational relationships are cited, as well as publications about intergenerational relationships in other countries.

Family Caregiving

Jarvik and Small (1988) provide pragmatic responses for major problems associated with caring for aging parents, such as dealing with the anger and stress of caregiving, managing financial resources, and facing dying and death. Using data from interviews with 131 older spouse caregivers to compare gender differences in reporting the caregiving burden, Barusch and Spaid (1989) found that the most important predictor of burden, was the patient's cognitive and behavioral difficulties, followed by caregiver age, unpleasant social contacts, sex of caregiver, and overall coping effectiveness. Age differences contributed to observed differences in burden.

In the Brody et al. study, three generations of women were surveyed on their opinions of appropriate filial behavior toward elderly parents and on their preferences for service-provision that they might need in old age. Women preferred adult children providing emotional support and financial management, but not income (Brody, Johnsen, and Fulcomer, 1984). In another aspect of that study (Brody, Johnsen, Fulcomer, and Lang, 1983), the oldest generation was most accepting of the idea of formal services for elderly persons and the youngest the least interested in such services. All three generations agreed that older people should be able to depend on adult children for help.

Finch and Mason (1990) found that "relationships between parents and children are founded on a sense of obligation up to a point, but assent for this is not universal and such obligations are seen as having definite limits."

Older caregivers and respite programs for caregivers are among the other family caregiving-related topics included in this chapter.

Racial and Ethnic Minority Groups

Publications focusing on various racial and ethnic minority group elderly comprise this chapter.

Block (1979) considers the status of the American Indian aged and the role played by family in their culture. Bastida (1978) summarizes a study of 210 elderly Mexican-Americans, Puerto Ricans, and Cubans, with special consideration of the family and of intergenerational exchange. Gibson (1986) predicts that "the renowned strengths of the black family will be put to a severe test as our society ages, and as larger and more powerful groups compete for limited resources."

Mindel (1983) describes patterns and variations that are distinctive to ethnic minority families and their relationships with the elderly, and presents the special family patterns of the two largest ethnic minority groups--American blacks and Hispanics. Mutran's (1986) study considers racial differences in family helping behavior and whether the difference results from socioeconomic variables or cultural factors. Black families appear to be more involved in exchanging help across generations.

Included in this chapter are congressional reports on the status of various minority elderly groups, as well as materials on racial and ethnic minorities from an international perspective.

Living Arrangements of Older Persons

Diverse housing options for older persons are cited in this chapter, from life care communities to shared housing to single-room occupancy hotels. Brody and Leibowitz (1981) present information on innovative living arrangements for older people, such as group homes or residences, cooperatives, and communes. Rubinstein (1989) describes the meaning with which older people endow the home environment. In a review of the literature, Soldo and Brotman (1981) show that living arrangements are the outcome of a life cycle process. "Because living arrangements are the end product of a process, the effects of intervention strategies are likely to rebound through the system. . . . Previous research strongly suggests that efforts to modify existing patterns of living arrangements will be successful only if they reflect a comprehensive life-course perspective."

General

And in the final, general chapter, publications include books on family relationships in later life (Brubaker, 1983) and later life families (Brubaker, 1985) as well as how older people and their families cope with stress and conflict (Gwyther et al., no date) and the social networks of men and women (Lein and Sussman, 1983).

Other topics include changes in household composition of the elderly (Fillenbaum and Wallman, 1986), career impact on independence of the elderly (Eisler, 1984), a typology of sibling relationships in later life (Gold, Woodbury, and George, 1990), women and grandparents as kin-keepers (Hagestad, 1986), guardianship (Iris, 1988), the elderly as network members (Stueve, 1983), a structural analysis of men and women in retirement (Hatch, 1986), and poverty over the family life cycle (Tuttle, 1987).

Family issues, especially intergenerational relationships and support networks, will continue to be a topic of growing importance in the study of and service to today's and tomorrow's older Americans. The references included herein represent an attempt to develop a thorough delineation of recent publications focusing on some of the most crucial issues affecting family relationships among older individuals.

REFERENCES

Ade-Ridder, Linda, and Brubaker, Timothy. (1983). The quality of long-term marriages. In Brubaker, Timothy (Ed.), Family relationships in later life, pp. 21-30. Beverly Hills: Sage Publications, 272p.

Barrell, Lorna. (1980). From wife to widow: the transitional process. Unpublished doctoral dissertation, University of Illinois at Chicago, 217p.

Barusch, Amanda, and Spaid, Wanda. (1989). Gender differences in caregiving: why do wives report greater burden? Gerontologist, 29(5), 667-676.

Bastida, Elena. (1978). Family structure and intergenerational exchange of the Hispanic American elderly. Gerontologist, 18(5), 48.

Bengston, Vern, and Robertson, Joan (Eds.). (1985). Grandparenthood. Beverly Hills: Sage Publications, 240p.

Bengston, Vern; Rosenthal, C.; and Burton, L. (1990). Families and aging: diversity and heterogeneity. In Binstock, Robert, and George, Linda (Eds.), Handbook of aging and the social sciences, pp. 263-287. New York: Academic Press, 489p.

Biggers, Trisha. (1981). The relationship between the grief reaction of older widows and their level of ego development. Unpublished doctoral dissertation, The University of Florida, 126p.

Block, Marilyn. (1979). Exiled Americans: the plight of the Indian aged in the United States. In Gelfand, Donald, and Kutzik, Alfred (Eds.), Ethnicity and aging, pp. 184-192. New York: Springer Publishing Company, 372p.

Bright, Carole. (1985). A study of the impact of normal and atypical grief patterns on the health and living environment of institutionalized and non-institutionalized elderly widows. Unpublished doctoral dissertation, University of San Francisco, 189p.

Brody, Elaine, and Leibowitz, Bernard. (1981). Some recent innovations in community living arrangements for older people. In Lawton, M. Powell, and Hoover, Sally (Eds.), Community housing choices for older Americans, pp. 245-258. New York: Springer Publishing Company, 326p.

Brody, Elaine; Johnsen, Pauline; and Fulcomer, Mark. (1984). What should adult children do for elderly parents? opinions and preferences of three generations of women. Journal of Gerontology, 39(6), 736-746.

Brody, Elaine; Johnsen, Pauline; Fulcomer, Mark; and Lang, Abigail. (1983). Women's changing roles and help to elderly parents: attitudes of three generations of women. Journal of Gerontology, 38(5), 597-607.

Browne, Colette, and Onzuka-Anderson, Roberta. (1985).
Reflections of three generations. In Browne, Colette, and
Onzuka-Anderson, Roberta (Eds.), Our aging parents: a
practical guide to eldercare, pp. 239-250. Honolulu:
University of Hawaii Press, 278p.

Brubaker, Timothy (Ed.) (1983). Family relationships in
later life. Beverly Hills: Sage Publications, 272p.

Brubaker, Timothy. (1985). Later life families. Beverly
Hills: Sage Publications, 144p.

Cherlin, Andrew, and Fustenberg, Frank, Jr. (1986). The new
American grandparent. New York: Basic Books, Inc.,
Publishers, 278p.

Cohler, Bertram, and Grunebaum, Henry (with the assistance of
Donna Robbins). (1981). Mothers, grandmothers, and
daughters: personality and childcare in three-generation
families. New York: John Wiley & Sons, 456p.

Cole, Charles. (1984). Marital quality in later life. In
Quinn, William, and Hughston, George (Eds.), Independent
aging: family and social systems perspectives, pp. 72-89.
Rockville, Maryland: Aspen Systems Corp., 300p.

Darnton, Frances. (1977). Aging with Grace and Harry.

Dobson, Cynthia. (1983). Sex-role and marital-role
expectations. In Brubaker, Timothy (Ed.), Family
relationships in later life, pp. 109-126. Beverly Hills:
Sage Publications, 272p.

Eisler, Terri. (1984). Career impact on independence. In
Quinn, William, and Hughston, George (Eds.), Independent
aging: family and social systems perspectives, pp. 256-
264. Rockville, Maryland: Aspen Systems Corp., 300p.

Ferraro, Kenneth, and Barresi, Charles. (1982). The impact
of widowhood on the social relations of older persons.
Research on Aging, 4(2), 227-247.

Fillenbaum, Gerda, and Wallman, Laurence. (1986). Changes
in household composition of the elderly: a preliminary
investigation. In Troll, Lillian (Ed.), Family issues in
current gerontology, pp. 284-300. New York: Springer
Publishing Company, 382p.

Finch, Janet, and Mason, Jennifer. (1990). Filial
obligations and kin support for elderly people. Aging and
Society, 10, 151-175.

Funder, K. (1989). Grandparents in children's post-divorce
families. Family Matters, 25, 47-49.

Furstenberg, Frank. (1981). Remarriage and
intergenerational relations. In Fogel, Robert; Hatfield,
Elaine; Kiesler, Sara; and Shanas, Ethel (Eds.), Aging,

stability and change in the family, pp. 115-142. New York: Academic Press, 341p.

Gibson, Rose. (1986). Outlook for the black family. In Pifer, Alan, and Bronte, D. Lydia (Eds.), Our aging society: paradox and promise, pp. 181-197. New York: W. W. Norton, 438p.

Gold, Deborah; Woodbury, Max; and George, Linda. (1990). Relationship classification using grade of membership analysis: A typology of sibling relationships in later life. Journal of Gerontology, 45(2), S43-S51.

Gwyther, Lisa; Gold, Deborah; and Hinman-Smith, Elizabeth. (No date given). Older people and their families: coping with stress and conflict. Durham, North Carolina: Duke University Medical Center, Center for the Study of Aging and Human Development, number of pages not given.

Hagestad, Gunhild. (1986). The family: women and grandparents as kin-keepers. In Pifer, Alan, and Bronte, D. Lydia (Eds.), Our aging society: paradox and promise, pp. 141-160. New York: W. W. Norton, 438p.

Hagestad, Gunhild. (1981). Problems and promises in the social psychology of intergenerational relations. In Fogel, Robert; Hatfield, Elaine; Kiesler, Sara; and Shanas, Ethel (Eds.), Aging, stability, and change in the family, pp. 11-46. New York: Academic Press, 341p.

Hatch, Laurie. (1986). A structural analysis of men and women in retirement. Unpublished doctoral dissertation, University of Washington, 327p.

Heinemann, Gloria. (1983). Family involvement and support for widowed persons. In Brubaker, Timothy (Ed.), Family relationships in later life, pp. 127-148. Beverly Hills: Sage Publications, 272p.

Hess, Beth, and Soldo, Beth. (1985). Husband and wife networks. In Sauer, William, and Coward, Ray (Eds.), Social support networks and the care of the elderly, pp. 67-92. New York: Springer Publishing Company, 284p.

Holahan, Carole. (1986). Marital attitudes over 40 years: a longitudinal and cohort analysis. In Troll, Lillian (Ed.), Family issues in current gerontology, pp. 15-31. New York: Springer Publishing Company, 382p.

Iris, Madelyn. (1988). Guardianship and the elderly: A multi-perspective view of the decision-making process. Gerontologist, 28, 39-45.

Jarvik, Lissy, and Small, Gary. (1988). Parentcare: a commonsense guide for adult children. New York: Crown Publishers, 309p.

Keith, Pat. (1986a). Isolation of the unmarried in later life. Family Relations, 35(3), 389-395.

Keith, Pat. (1986b). The social context and resources of the unmarried in old age. _International Journal of Aging and Human Development_, _23_(2), 81-96.

Kivnick, Helen. (1984). Grandparents and family relations. In Quinn, William, and Hughston, George (Eds.), _Independent aging: family and social systems perspectives_, pp. 35-57. Rockville, Maryland: Aspen Systems Corp., 300p.

Lein, Laura, and Sussman, Marvin (Eds.). (1983). _The ties that bind: men's and women's social networks_. New York: Haworth Press, 111p.

Mindel, Charles H. (1983). The elderly in minority families. In Brubaker, Timothy (Ed.), _Family relationships in later life_, pp. 193-208. Beverly Hills: Sage Publications, 272p.

Morgan, Leslie. (1984). Changes in family interaction following widowhood. _Journal of Marriage and the Family_, _46_(2), 323-331.

Mutran, Elizabeth. (1986). Intergenerational family support among blacks and whites: response to culture or to socioeconomic differences. In Troll, Lillian (Ed.), _Family issues in current gerontology_, pp. 189-203. New York: Springer Publishing Company, 382p.

O'Bryant, Shirley, and Morgan, Leslie. (1990). Recent widows' kin support and orientations to self-sufficiency. _Gerontologist_, _30_(3), 391-398

O'Rand, Angela, and Henretta, John. (1982). Women at middle age: Developmental transitions. _The Annals of The American Academy of Political and Social Science_, _464_, 57-64.

Palmore, Erdman. (1987). Cross-cultural perspectives on widowhood. _Journal of Cross-cultural Gerontology_, _2_, 93-105.

Rubinstein, Robert. (1989). The home environments of older people: A description of the psychosocial processes linking person to place. _Journal of Gerontology_, _44_(2), S45-S53.

Rubinstein, Robert. (1987). Never married elderly as a social type: Re-evaluating some images. _Gerontologist_, _27_(1), 108-113.

Snow, Robert. (1980). _Middle-aged persons' perceptions of their intergenerational relations_. Unpublished doctoral dissertation, The University of Chicago, number of pages not given.

Soldo, Beth, and Brotman, Herman. (1981). Housing whom? In Lawton, M. Powell, and Hoover, Sally (Eds.), _Community_ housing choices for older Americans, pp. 36-55. New York: Springer Publishing Company, 326p.

Stueve, Ann. (1983). The elderly as network members. In Lein, Laura, and Sussman, Marvin (Eds.), The ties that bind: Men's and women's social networks, pp. 59-87. New York: Haworth, 111p.

Tappen, Ruth. (1980). System characteristics of the middle-aged family and its activities on behalf of aging parents. Unpublished doctoral dissertation, Columbia University Teachers' College, 294p.

Troll, Lillian. (1983). Grandparents: The family watchdogs. In Brubaker, Timothy (Ed.), Family relationships in later life, pp. 63-76. Beverly Hills: Sage Publications, 272p.

Tuttle, Robert. (1987). Poverty over the family life cycle. Unpublished doctoral dissertation, University of Notre Dame, 153p.

U.S. Congress. House. (1980). Hearing before the Select Committee on Aging. Families: aging and change. Washington, D.C.: U.S. Government Printing Office, 118p.

Uhlenberg, Peter, and Myers, Mary. (1986). Divorce and the elderly. In Troll, Lillian (Ed.), Family issues in current gerontology, pp. 350-361. New York: Springer Publishing Company, 382p.

Wilson, Keren. (1983). Causes and consequences of divorce in late life. Unpublished doctoral dissertation, Portland State University, 196p.

Wright, Fay. (1986). Left to care alone. Brookfield, Vermont: Gower Publishing Company, 205p.

FAMILIES
AND
AGING

1

Middle-aged Families

Books

1   **Bailey, Caroline. (1982). <u>Beginning in the middle</u>. London and New York: Quartet Books, 271p.**

Explores changes during the middle years. Most women have more opportunity to make changes in their lives than is possible for most men. "It was not the changes as such which were of paramount interest but the way in which they came about, the motivation behind them and their effect on others. This became the real focus of attention: not so much the 'what changes' but the 'why' and 'how.'"

2   **Baruch, Grace, and Brooks-Gunn, Jeanne (Eds.). (1984). <u>Women in midlife</u>. New York: Plenum Press, 404p.**

The book is a collection of contributions on the middle years of American women. Presents interdisciplinary perspectives on present ideas about midlife and challenges existing myths and stereotypes about midlife changes. Examines roles and relationships for women in midlife. Explores diverse experiences within cultural, racial, and socioeconomic groups. Central themes are the impact of social change, the question of the extent, permanence, and the reality of improvement in the condition of midlife women, the heterogeneity of midlife women, and the need to reassess and improve therapy and research design and measurement.

3   **Cohen, Joan; Coburn, Karen; and Pearlman, Joan. (1980). <u>Hitting our stride</u>. New York: Delacorte Press, 280p.**

Includes interviews and mailed questionnaires from 842 women aged 29 to 72. Focuses primarily on women in the mid-thirties to the mid-sixties. Most subjects liked being the age they were and felt the benefits of being older outweighed the losses of no longer being young.

4   Derenski, Arlene. (1981). **Age taboo: older women-younger men relationships**. Boston: Little, Brown and Company, 262p.

Describes problems and satisfactions of relationships between older women and younger men. Looks at the psychological and cultural factors which affect taboos against such relationships and shows how successful emotional commitments can be developed in such older woman/younger man liaisons through role flexibilities. "The qualities that attract older women and younger men to one another are financial and emotional independence, role flexibility, the ability to discard inappropriate rules, and a willingness to share power. These qualities are the same ones that can create a solid, long-lasting relationship for a same-age couple in an ever-changing society."

5   Segalla, Rosemary. (1982). **Departure from traditional roles: mid-life women break the daisy chains**. Ann Arbor, Michigan: UMI Research Press, 151p.

Study of college-educated women aged 35 to 45 years and alternative lifestyles that traditional, married women choose. Examination of the ways in which these women are presently structuring their lives.

6   Seskin, Jane. (1979). **Older women/younger men**. Garden City, New York: Anchor Press/Doubleday, 143p.

Survey of older women and younger men involved in relationships with one another. Describes a type of relationship which may be a new, major, sociosexual trend.

Articles/chapters

7   Glass, J. Conrad, and Knott, Elizabeth. (1982). Effectiveness of a workshop on aging in changing middle-aged adults' attitudes toward the aged. **Educational Gerontology**, 8(4), 359-372.

Study of whether middle-aged adults' attitudes toward the aged could be changed through specially-designed educational experiences. "The adults' attitudes toward older persons changed significantly in a positive direction following the workshop experience, while those in the control group decreased." Authors conclude that the workshop had a significant impact.

8   Lopata, Helena and Barnewolt, Debra. (1984). The middle years: changes and variations in social-role commitments. In Baruch, Grace, and Brooks-Gunn, Jeanne (Eds.), **Women in midlife**, pp. 83-108. New York: Plenum Press, 404p.

One of the major differences found between 1956 and 1978 Chicago area women was the devaluation of the role of housewife. "Role conflict is alleviated through the process of assigning hierarchical placement to roles in which the women are actually involved and that demand most from them according to the value system: motherhood when the children are small, wifehood if the husband is in a demanding and rewarding occupation, and employment if those two roles are absent from the role cluster."

9   O'Rand, Angela, and Henretta, John. (1982). Women
        at middle age: developmental transitions. The
        Annals of The American Academy of Political and
        Social Science, 464, 57-64.

Diverse midlife role transitions exist for women. The transitions are dependent upon earlier life events connected with marriage, childbearing, and work. "The traditional family life cycle has been changed by trends such as the postponement of marriage and child bearing, divorce and separation, and early career entry. The trends lead to continuities and discontinuities in individual women's lives and in the experiences of different age cohorts of women over a period of time."

10   Spitze, Glenna, and Logan, John. (1990). More
        evidence on women (and men) in the middle. Research
        on Aging, 12(2), 182-198.

Four major roles are found for middle-aged persons--spouse, paid worker, adult child of aging parent, and parent--typical of those in their 40s and early 50s. However, each role falls off rapidly after that point. "Men are equally or more likely to experience each of these roles as are women, and marriage remains typical for men in older ages."

Dissertations

11   DeLago, Louise. (1986). Women at mid-life:
        mothers at home, mothers at work. Unpublished
        doctoral dissertation, University of Pennsylvania,
        180p.

Case study of differences and similarities, at mid-life, between mothers who stay at home and mothers who go to work.

12   Dobson, Cynthia. (1979). Marital role expectations
        for middle-aged and older men and women.
        Unpublished doctoral dissertation, Iowa State
        University, 187p.

Investigation of extent to which marital role expectations for women and men differ between middle age and old age, as seen as part of the definition of a distinct social role for older persons. Findings showed small, but significant, differences in marital role expectations between middle-aged and older men and women. There was less differentiation, by sex, in assigning household tasks and marital responsibilities for

older couples than for middle-aged couples. There also were
fewer sanctions for failure to meet responsibilities for older
spouses than for middle-aged spouses. The importance of
subroles and instrumental and expressive qualities was less for
older persons than for middle-aged persons. Findings suggest
that "a distinct social role for older persons may be defined
in terms of the expectations for marital role behaviors and
attributes."

13   **Friedman, Meredith.   (1987).   Successful men at
      midlife: changes in their relationships with women.**
      Unpublished   doctoral   dissertation,   Boston
      University, 189p.

Study of 10 professionally highly successful men and the
changes occurring at midlife in their relationships with women.
Major finding was that midlife men are becoming "more
relational, interested in and available for intimate
relationships with women in ways that seemed to be newly
emerging around midlife."

14   **Hoskins, George.   (1982).   The quality of
      relationships between young adults and their
      parents: an exploratory study.**   Unpublished
      doctoral dissertation, The Florida State University,
      218p.

Investigates the nature of relationships between young adults
and their parents. The exploratory study uses demographic data
and in-depth interviews. The author identifies a conceptual
theme as the redefinition of parent-offspring relationships and
four concepts--affectional bonds, parent-offspring involvement,
communication openness, and communication directiveness. Data
from this study suggest that "the redefinition process is
accentuated during two vital life cycle transitions: the
offspring's assumption of parenthood and the offspring's
leaving home. How the transition is dealt with is related to
a fit between the parent's 'letting go' and the offspring's
assumption of responsibility for decisions."

15   **Lewis, Constance.   (1985).   The empty nest
      revisited.**   Unpublished doctoral dissertation, The
      Fielding Institute, 245p.

Investigation of the impact of the return of adult children on
24 mothers in midlife. The major finding was that an adult
child who returns home makes it difficult for parents to
advance to the next stage of life.

16   **Massey, Veronica. (1983). Older women and younger
      men: the initiation narrative of the French
      eighteenth century.**   Unpublished doctoral
      dissertation, Columbia University, 224p.

Examines the relationship between the older woman and the
younger man in the initiation novel of the French eighteenth
century. Focus is on the older women as a seducer, as a
subject rather than as a passive object.

17   Robbins, Martha.   (1988).   **Midlife women and death of mother: a   study   of   psychohistorical   and spiritual   transformation.**   Unpublished   doctoral dissertation, Harvard University, 446p.

Exploration of "the psychohistorical and spiritual transformation of midlife women who experienced the death of their mothers during this period of their lives." Considers how the mother's death affects a woman's sense of self, her relationship to others, and her image of God.

18   Rohr, Karen.   (1984).   **Transition to the empty nest: changes in parental optimism and parental fatalism.** Unpublished doctoral dissertation, The Ohio State University, 136p.

Uses family developmental theory to explore whether middle-aged parents are satisfied with their parental role at this stage in the family life cycle. Also considers whether middle-aged parents are attending to the developmental task of "letting go." In this sample, parents were optimistic if the younger children were older, if they had launched their children, or if they felt "masterful" as persons. "Persons were more likely to 'let go'--i.e., be more fatalistic--if their youngest children were older or if they felt fatalistic about their lives in general."

19   Snow,   Robert.   (1980).   **Middle-aged   persons' perceptions of their intergenerational relations.** Unpublished doctoral dissertation, The University of Chicago, number of pages not given.

Perceptions of middle-aged husbands and wives of intergenerational interaction, obligation and emotional bonds in three-generation families. Findings include that the wives had the highest degree of emotional bondedness with their mothers and their daughters and husbands had the highest degree of emotional bondedness with their mothers and their fathers. For all relations, contact between the generations was frequent, the extent of a feeling of obligation to kin was high, and women across the generations saw relationships more similarly than did men.

20   Talan, Roberta.   (1983).   **A case study relating mid- life transition to level of differentiation from mother in re-entry women.**   Unpublished doctoral dissertation, University of Pittsburgh, 281p.

This study presents an in-depth investigation of the mid-life re-entry woman "to generate a better understanding of how differentiation from her mother relates to her expression of the major developmental themes of this period." It was determined that "a woman's family of origin, particularly her early relationship to her mother, has a far-reaching effect on her life." Subjects in this sample who originated in families that were highly cohesive, emotionally fused, and undifferentiated had difficulty attaining a separate sense of identity. Subjects who were in families with separated or disengaged relationships were still emotionally attached to their mothers in a negative manner, which hampered differentiation at mid-life. Subjects from families which exhibited balanced cohesion and which encouraged differentiation and independence developed members who differentiated themselves from their mothers and formed separate, independent identities. "Balanced cohesion in a family appeared to encourage emotional growth and differentiation."

21   Tappen, Ruth. (1980). **System characteristics of the middle-aged family and its activities on behalf of aging parents**. Unpublished doctoral dissertation, Columbia University Teachers' College, 294p.

Describes the middle-aged family as a support system for its aging parents and compares the characteristics of the middle-aged family as a system to the amount of help given, willingness to help, and planning regarding future living arrangements. Most families in this sample were involved in some type of exchange with their parents. "The highly functional or highly emerged family provided significantly more help to its aging parent(s) than did the low energized family." The amount of help given was most influenced by the distance between the family and its parent. "The middle-aged family's willingness to help was most influenced by the extent of the rest of the parent's support system and the quality of the relationship with the offspring." The conclusion of this study was that "the middle-aged family is a viable but limited source of support for the aged."

2

Singlehood

Books

22   Allen, Katherine.   (1989).   <u>Single women/family
ties. New perspectives on family</u>. Newbury Park,
California: Sage Publications, 149p.

"The exclusion of never-married, childless women from the
family life course emphasizes their deviance in relation to
married mothers, but a variant approach suggests that there are
other events that distinguish the family lives of life-long
single women."

23   Berger, Raymond.   (1982).   <u>Gay and gray: the older
homosexual man</u>. Urbana: University of Illinois
Press, 233p.

Although homosexuals are taxpayers, they are shortchanged when
it comes to publicly funded social services. There is
invisibility of older homosexuals within the gay community
itself. Older homosexuals are isolated from each other. The
older homosexual is despised and feared even within the gay
community. This study was intended to examine thoroughly the
situation of the older homosexual male in light of stereotypes
of gay aging. A sample of 112 men completed an extensive
questionnaire and ten, selected to reflect a wide diversity of
backgrounds and lifestyles, were interviewed. The
questionnaire is included.

24   Cauhape, Elizabeth. (1983). <u>Fresh starts: men and
women after divorce</u>. New York: Basic Books, Inc.,
Publishers, 338p.

A social psychologist examines the effects of divorce at midlife. The author's primary finding was that divorced men and
women can deal with their circumstances and take power over
their lives. Eight different and specific divorce aftermaths
that characterize these subjects are delineated--immediate
(planned) remarriers, graduates, comfortable courters,
steadies, enforced remarriers, hunters-and-sorters, runners in
place, and passionate searchers. It was determined that people

have to restructure their lives by themselves and that this may call for continual improvisation.

25   Commonwealth Fund Commission on Elderly People Living Alone. (1987). Old, alone and poor: a plan for reducing poverty among elderly people living alone. Baltimore, Maryland: The Commonwealth Fund Commission on Elderly People Living Alone, number of pages not given.

Report on current status and projected future of older persons who live alone. Describes existing and proposed programs and policies and probable impact of these programs on the elderly.

Articles/chapters

26   Adams, Rebecca. (1985-86). Emotional closeness and physical distance between friends: implications for elderly women living in age-segregated and age-integrated settings. International Journal of Aging and Human Development, 22(1), 55-76.

Reports on 70 in-depth interviews of senior, unmarried women. Positive relationships were found between emotional closeness and physical distance, duration and emotional closeness, and frequency of interaction and proximity. Age-segregated housing enhanced development of emotionally close, local friendships.

27   Adams, Rebecca. (1987). Patterns of network change: a longitudinal study of friendships of elderly women. Gerontologist, 27(2), 222-227.

White, non-married, elderly, middle-class women were interviewed and observed twice over a period of years. Middle-aged friendship patterns changed--subjects had more new friends than they had friends who had been eliminated or lost, but the average subject saw friends less frequently than she had in the past, felt emotionally distant from more friends, lived closer to more friends, and had a denser network of friends.

28   Adams, Rebecca. (1985). People would talk: normative barriers to cross-sex friendships for elderly women. (1985). The Gerontologist, 25(6), 605-611.

Interviews and observations of 70 non-married, white, elderly, middle-class women. Cross-sex friendship is defined as romance, and some norms inhibit romance during old age, while other norms encourage rejection of potential mates who cannot meet traditional sex role demands. Thus, elderly women may lack male friends.

29   Bengston, Vern; Rosenthal, C.; and Bunton, L. (1990). Families and aging: diversity and heterogeneity. In Binstock, Robert, and George, Linda (Eds.), Handbook of aging and the social sciences, pp. 263-287. New York: Academic Press, 489p.

Major finding was that data from many sources support the
thesis that married elderly, compared to unmarried older
persons, have: higher levels of morale, life satisfactions,
mental and physical health, economic resources, social
integration and social support, and lower rates of
institutionalization. Diversity in family structures, roles,
and relationships of elderly Americans is "a function of the
intersection of changing patterns of mortality, fertility, and
divorce with structural forms."

30   Braito, Rita, and Anderson, Donna.   (1983).   The
          Ever-single elderly woman.   In Markson, Elizabeth
          (Ed.), Older Women, Lexington, Massachusetts:
          Lexington Books, D. C. Heath & Co., 351p.

Ever-single older women represent a small, but increasing,
portion of the entire population. The group includes the
socially isolated and those who are socially connected
(maintain confidants). The ever-single elderly woman tends to
be better educated than her male counterpart. While ever-
single elderly women generally are healthy, they are
overrepresented in nursing homes or other health care
institutions.

31   Chiriboga, David.   (1982).   Adaptation to marital
          separation in later and earlier life.   Journal of
          Gerontology, 37(1), 109-114.

Examination of psychosocial functioning of recently separated
men and women aged from the twenties to the seventies. Older
subjects showed more psychological distress than did the
younger subjects. Women showed more psychological symptoms and
greater emotional tension than did men.

32   Hennon, Charles. (1983). Divorce and the elderly:
          a neglected area of research. In Brubaker, Timothy
          (Ed.), Family relationships in later life, pp. 149-
          172. Beverly Hills: Sage Publications, 272p.

Reports effects on individuals of becoming divorced in later
life or living as a divorced elderly person. Divorce is one of
the most neglected areas of gerontological research. Presents
data from an exploratory study of divorced women over the age
of 55, many of whom divorced during middle age. "The way of
becoming single again does not have major effects independent
of the fact of singlehood or aging. . . . Divorced elderly
women, as a group, are not worse off, except financially and
perhaps kin system-wise, than [are] widowed elderly women."

33   Keith, Pat. (1983). A comparison of the resources
          of parents and childless men and women in very old
          age. Family relations, 32(3), 403-409.

Compares the personal and social resources and psychological
well-being of 438 elderly parents and 103 childless people.
Findings showed both groups reported similar resources.
Children did not assure life satisfaction, less loneliness, or
greater acceptance of death.

34   Keith, Pat. (1988). Finances of unmarried elderly
          people over time. International Journal of Aging
          and Human Development, 26(3), 211-223.

Research on effects of widowhood, divorce, and lifelong
singlehood on income and evaluations of finances at two points
over the lifespan and on factors associated with satisfaction
with level of living in old age. The marital status of women,
more often than the marital status of men, affected the
economic circumstances and perceptions of finances.

35   Keith, Pat. (1986). Isolation of the unmarried in
          later life. Family relations, 35(3), 389-395.

Reports longitudinal research on isolation among the unmarried
aged and assesses personal characteristics associated with
isolation from family and friends. Men and women were more
isolated from neighbors and friends than from family, although
the never-married maintained more ties with friends.

36   Keith, Pat. (1986). The social context and
          resources of the unmarried in old age. (1986).
          International Journal of Aging and Human
          Development, 23(2), 81-96.

Develops a model of singleness in later life to show how the
social context may influence the personal and social resources
of older, unmarried persons. Role transitions of the unmarried
over the life course, finances, health, and social
relationships of older, single persons are presented, along
with implications for practice and for future research.

37   Keith, Pat, and Lorenz, Frederick. (1989).
          Financial strain and health of unmarried older
          people. Gerontologist, 29(5), 684-691.

Study of 1,782 older unmarried persons. Examines the effect of
financial strain on physical health over time and the degree
to which vulnerability to financial strain was linked to death.
No evidence that financial strain contributed to poor health.

38   Myers, Jane, and Navin, Sally. (1984). To have
          not: the childless older women. Journal of
          Humanistic Education and Development, 22(3), 91-100.

Discusses the special needs of older women who have no
children. Uses a developmental framework to discuss
physiological and social aging, adjustment to role losses, and
lack of coping resources. Authors suggest implications for
counselors.

39   Pratt, Clara; Jones, Laura; Shin, Hwa-Yong; and
          Walker, Alexis. (1989). Autonomy and decision
          making between single older women and their
          caregiving daughters. Gerontologist, 29(6), 792-
          797.

Examines perceptions of decisional autonomy and decision-making
processes among 64 elderly, single mothers and their caregiving

daughters.   The mothers were found to be highly involved in decisions affecting their lives, from daily care to major health decisions. The daughters were especially influential over major health, financial, and housing decisions. The mothers' level of personal care dependency was found to be negatively associated with both mothers' and daughters' confidence in the mothers' decision-making abilities.

40   Rubinstein, Robert.   (1987).   Never married elderly as a social type: re-evaluating some images. Gerontologist, 27(1), 108-113.

Data from two studies.   Re-evaluates some images that have appeared in the literature about never married elderly. Data suggest that never married elderly are not necessarily socially isolated, may experience some loneliness, do not have a uniform attitude concerning the possibility of marriage, and do suffer from the effects of loss in late life.

41   Uhlenberg, Peter, and Myers, Mary. (1986). Divorce and the elderly. In Troll, Lillian (Ed.), Family issues in current gerontology, pp. 350-361.   New York: Springer Publishing Company, 382p.

Examines the level of divorce among the elderly, suggests how it is likely to change in coming years, and discusses implications of these changes. The proportion of the elderly who will be divorced or formerly divorced is going to increase quite rapidly over the next several decades. This change may cause deterioration in the economic and social welfare of the elderly, but may also produce changes, such as ability to cope with widowhood, and more unattached men post-65 leading to increased non-marital sexual activity among the elderly.

42   Uhlenberg, Peter; Cooney, Teresa; and Boyd, Robert. (1990).   Divorce for women after midlife. Journal of Gerontology, 45(1), S3-S11.

Data from the U.S. Census, Vital Statistics, and Current Population Survey are used to determine current divorce patterns for women aged 40-plus, project marriage and divorce experiences of future cohorts of elderly women, and consider socioeconomic correlates of divorce for middle-aged and older women. The finding was that there was a marked decline in the proportion of future elderly women who will be married or widowed and dramatic increase in proportion who will be divorced. Data show socioeconomic well-being of divorcees is significantly below that of widowed or married women.

Films

43   Cavrell, Ira, and Cavrell, Otis. (Producers).   (No date). Mr. Arthur: his fear of growing old.

Middle-aged executive leaves his wife and marries his secretary, who is half his age. When the marriage becomes unhappy, he returns to his first family and tries to find out why he broke up his home and what drove him to enter a destructive second marriage.

44   **Cavrell, Ira and Cavrell, Otis. (Producers). (No date). <u>Mrs. Kay: her failing marriage</u>. Pictura Films.**

After a 26-year marriage, Mrs. Kay finds that her husband loves someone else. The story is of a middle-aged wife and mother whose children and husband have all left home, leaving her behind.

45   **Ideas and Images (Producer). (1980). <u>Lila</u>.**

Portrait of an 80-year-old woman who was one of the first five women admitted as a student in the Medical College of Virginia. She encourages people to proclaim their own values.

46   **Women in Communications (Producer). (1977). <u>Who remembers mama?</u>**

Problems of middle-aged women who are divorced are discussed. The focus is on the divorced woman who is suddenly faced with the emotional and economic plight of these older women.

Dissertations

47   **Allen, Katherine. (1984). <u>A life course study of never-married and ever-married elderly women from the 1910 birth cohort</u>. Unpublished doctoral dissertation, Syracuse University, 233p.**

Report on how women's lives unfold as they pursue different marital careers. Two patterns are compared--the atypical path of never-married, childless women and the more traditional path of marriage, motherhood, grandmotherhood, and widowhood. Common for all subjects was the importance of lifelong caretaking roles. "Widows extended their roles of wife and mother to descending generations. Never-married womens' extensions were multidimensional--as bearers of the family history, caretakers for aging parents, and second mothers to siblings' children."

48   **Enoch, Louise. (1987). <u>Never-married women: a study of adaptation</u>. Unpublished doctoral dissertation, Smith College School for Social Work, 174p.**

Investigated adaptation to the never-married experience in women with some interest in marrying. Findings showed correlation between developmental maturity and adaptation to the never-married experience. Not marrying, while disappointing for many, was seen as providing women with the opportunity to explore their potentials and strengthen their identities.

49   **Gander, Anita. (1988). <u>Older-divorced persons: intragroup comparisons and comparisons with younger-</u>**

divorced   persons.   Unpublished   doctoral
dissertation, The University of Utah, 192p.

Describes and compares the experiences of recently divorced,
long-married older persons with those of younger-divorced
persons on gender differences in experiences, and on
differences in the experiences of depressed and nondepressed
older-divorced persons.

50   Gordon-Jackson,   Patricia.   (1988).   Life
        satisfaction of retired married and single women.
        Unpublished   doctoral   dissertation,   U.S.
        International University, 110p.

Delineates factors involved in life satisfaction of retired
single and married women, basically comparing life satisfaction
of retired single and married women on social, economic, and
psychological levels.

51   Howard, Nelson. (1983). Grandfriends: a local
        church model for personal contact between senior
        high young people and single elderly persons.
        Unpublished   doctoral   dissertation,   School   of
        Theology at Claremont, 130p.

Tested two models for meaningful contact among young and
elderly in two suburban churches. Both models were based on
friendship and dialogue as theological concepts set in the life
of the church. One model involved pairing a youth with a
single, institutionalized, elderly person; the second model
involved pairing a youth with a single, independent, elderly
person. The thesis was that "cultivating contact between young
and elderly persons to share life and faith experiences meets
needs for both age groups."

52   Korthuis,   Kathleen.   (1982).   Functional
        characteristics   associated   with   feelings   of
        loneliness   in   older   persons   who   live   alone.
        Unpublished doctoral dissertation, The University of
        Toledo, 129p.

Investigation to determine whether a relationship existed
between feelings of loneliness and selected variables of human
functioning in older persons who live alone. Variables not
related significantly to loneliness included age, education,
income, satisfaction with housing, type of housing, frequency
of telephone use, number of visits, hearing, eyesight, self-
rated limitations of health on activities, use of checking
services, need for checking services, use of social and
recreational services, and need for social and recreational
services. Loneliness tended to be more frequent in men than
in women, in widowed than in single persons, in persons without
a confidant, in persons without a caretaker for help if needed,
and in persons needing transportation services. All five older
persons who participated were almost never lonely.

53   Rice, Susan. (1982). Single older childless women:
        a study of social support and life satisfaction.

Unpublished doctoral dissertation, University of California, Los Angeles, 153p.

Relationship between social support and life satisfaction for single, elderly, childless women was investigated. Presence of a confidant and numbers of contacts were associated with life satisfaction, as were background variables of age, self-reported health, education, and socioeconomic status. Never-married subjects were more able to create viable alternative lifestyles, while widowed subjects seemed to mourn for the longtime loss of their husbands and the traditional lifestyle that they had lived. The conclusion was that intervention needs to be in the area of encouraging skills in role creation and role substitution to facilitate flexibility in dealing with situational and emotional changes of later life.

54   **Wilson, Keren. (1983). Causes and consequences of divorce in late life. Unpublished doctoral dissertation, Portland State University, 196p.**

Persons divorced in late life generally were urban residing, low occupational status, few assets, weak religious and kinship ties. Generally, in this study, divorce resulted from a long-standing lack of emotional gratification aggravated by some type of precipitating event. Overall, females were found to have more negative divorce experiences and to suffer greater negative consequences than did males.

55   **Yeager, Garry. (1982). Developing a manual for ministering with a congregation having widowed, separated or divorced persons. Unpublished doctoral dissertation, Drew University, 137p.**

The focus of this research was to provide ideas for ministers and congregations in developing an inclusive ministry with widowed, separated, and divorced Christians.

3

Older Couples

Books

56   Brecher, Edward. (1984). <u>Love, sex and aging: a</u>
        <u>Consumer's Union Report</u>. Boston: Little, Brown,
        441p.

Reports a 1978-1979 study of 4,246 women and men aged 50 to 93
and describes their experiences through the decades--their
attitudes, opinions, hopes, and concerns. The report shows
that "older people, like younger people, differ from one
another in many ways and to a remarkable extent." Older people
were found to be sexually much freer than in their youth. The
"freeing-up" process was found to be a continuing one
throughout life. The subjects in this sample represented a
diverse assortment of individual women and men with very
different activities, opinions, goals, customs, and fantasies.
" 'What it's like to be 50,' or 'what it's like to be 60'
should be viewed . . . not as a single image but as a broad
panorama of alternatives. Both the general themes and the
individual life stories reveal the decades after 50 to be far
more exciting and far more fulfilling than is commonly
supposed."

57   Higgins, Loretta, and Hawkins, Joellen. (1984).
        <u>Human sexuality across the life span: implications</u>
        <u>for nursing practice</u>. Monterey, California:
        Wadsworth Health Sciences Division, 322p.

Presents a perspective of sexuality and sexual development from
conception to old age. Examines specific risks and issues for
sexuality related to developmental and situational life events.

Articles/chapters

58   Ade-Ridder, Linda, and Brubaker, Timothy. (1983).
        The quality of long-term marriages. In Brubaker,
        Timothy (Ed.), <u>Family relationships in later life</u>,
        pp. 21-30. Beverly Hills: Sage Publications, 272p.

Reviews research on marital quality across the life cycle and during retirement. The authors provide theoretical linkages of marital quality during the retirement years. Marital quality includes variables such as happiness, success, satisfaction, and adjustment.

59   Atchley, Robert, and Miller, Sheila. (1983). Types of elderly couples. In Brubaker, Timothy (Ed.), Family relationships in later life, pp. 77-90. Beverly Hills: Sage Publications, 272p.

Authors discuss the effects of various types of changes which occur in later life on middle-aged and older couples, and the mediating effect of the couple's own relationship type. Data from a longitudinal study of adaptation to aging are examined.

60   Cole, Charles. (1984). Marital quality in later life. In Quinn, William, and Hughston, George (Eds.), Independent aging: family and social systems perspectives, pp. 72-89. Rockville, Maryland: Aspen Systems Corp., 300p.

Author's central perspective is that marriage provides elderly couples with many life-sustaining resources which contribute to the quality of life during retirement. Research about the nature of marriage for husbands and for wives over the family life cycle as the nature of the marriage contributes to the retirement marriage is reviewed. Examined are the kind of contributions which marriage and marital satisfaction make to a variety of social psychological aspects of human development in later life and how retirement offers special opportunities for married couples to enhance their relationship and to develop support systems in order to achieve their full marital potential.

61   Dobson, Cynthia. (1983). Sex-role and marital-role expectations. In Brubaker, Timothy (Ed.), Family relationships in later life, pp. 109-126. Beverly Hills: Sage Publications, 272p.

Author reviews evidence for a redefinition of sex roles and marital roles with advancing age. Data are presented from a study of changes between middle age and old age in areas such as the importance of instrumental and expressive qualities for husbands and wives and the assignment of major marital-role responsibilities and household tasks. "As they enter their older years, husbands and wives may need to reexamine their own behavior and rebalance their relationships in light of the new definitions they encounter."

62   Garza, Joseph, and Dressel, Paula. (1983). Sexuality and later-life marriages. In Brubaker, Timothy (Ed.), Family relationships in later life, pp 91-108. Beverly Hills: Sage Publications, 272p.

Describes research on marital and nonmarital forms of sexual interaction in later-life marriages. Emphasis is on studies of noninstitutionalized populations and married-intact couples in which at least one member of the couple is 60 years of age or older.

63   Griffitt, William.   (1981).   Sexual intimacy in
          aging marital partners. In Fogel, Robert; Hatfield,
          Elaine; Kiesler, Sara; and Shanas, Ethel (Eds.),
          Aging, stability and change in the family, pp. 301-
          315. New York: Academic Press, 341p.

Discusses the stereotype that the importance of sex to people declines and ultimately disappears as they grow older and indicates that, generally, available data do not support such stereotypes. Although sexual activity for older persons may have less urgency and less focus on physical release than does that of younger people, for many persons sexual activity continues to serve as a source of sensual satisfaction, self-esteem, and tension reduction. The authors discusses aging and sexual response capabilities, aging and sexual activity, origins of declining sexual intimacy, and maintaining sexual intimacy. Whatever the ultimate solutions, "the potential benefits of freeing the elderly and the young from limited stereotypes of attractiveness and value would certainly include, but extend beyond, enhancing potentials for sexual intimacy in later life."

64   Hess, Beth, and Soldo, Beth. (1985). Husband and
          wife networks. In Sauer, William, and Coward, Ray
          (Eds.), Social support networks and the care of the
          elderly, pp. 67-92. New York: Springer Publishing
          Company, 284p.

Description of long-lived marriages, with indications of the implications for practice and for public policy. Critical examination of the limited research literature on espousal supports. Discussion of theoretical and methodological issues for the decades ahead. Conclusion that, typically, "it is better to be married than not be married in old age. The married have more income, primary group ties, sexual access, companionship, residential privacy, adequate nutrition, physical and mental health. The marital dyad is associated with a number of positive outcomes, particularly for husbands-- longer life, lower morbidity, higher standard of living, greater life satisfaction, and home-based care when disabled."

65   Holahan, Carole. (1986). Marital attitudes over 40
          years: a longitudinal and cohort analysis. In
          Troll, Lillian (Ed.), Family issues in current
          gerontology, pp. 15-31.   New York: Springer
          Publishing Company, 382p.

Study results suggest that "significant change in the direction of increased egalitarianism has occurred in marital attitudes for the [Terman study] subjects over the more than 40 years from 1940 to 1981. . . . These changes are in accord with the trend toward greater sex role equality in our society."

66   Katschke-Jennings, Bert, and Healy, David. (1987).
          Remarriage and the elderly. Journal of Religion and
          Aging, 3(3/4), 1-11.

Focus on how the church can counsel elderly persons who are considering remarriage.

67   Kelley, Harold. (1981). Marriage relationships and aging. In Fogel, Robert; Hatfield, Elaine; Kiesler, Sara; and Shanas, Ethel (Eds.), Aging, stability and change in the family, pp. 275-300. New York: Academic Press, 341p.

Outline of implications of a view of interpersonal relations for changes that might occur in marriage relationships as the marriage partners become more advanced in age. Emphasis is on the marital dyad. Suggestions on how aging and its effects on the marriage might be examined from the perspective of a social psychological analysis of interpersonal relations and identifies the most essential elements to be considered among the complexities of close relationships.

68   Margolin, Leslie, and White, Lynn. (1987). The continuing role of physical attractiveness in marriage. Journal of Marriage and the Family, 49, 21-27.

Examination of the role of physical attractiveness in marriage. Findings indicated that "the decreases in physical appearance normally associated with aging affected husbands' responses to their wives more than wives' to their husbands. Husband's sexual interest, happiness in the sexual relationship, and, to a lesser extent, unfaithfulness, were affected."

69   Markson, Elizabeth. (1987). Marital status. In Maddox, George (Ed.), The encyclopedia of aging, pp. 420-421. New York: Springer Publishing Company, 890p.

Discusses how patterns of marital status in later life vary dramatically by sex, by ethnicity, and by race. Also discusses divorce rate, remarriage rates, and living arrangements.

70   Montgomery, Rhonda. (1987). Marriage. In Maddox, George (Ed.), The encyclopedia of aging, pp. 421-423. New York: Springer Publishing Company, 890p.

Discusses differences in marriage patterns of older men and older women, characteristics of long-term marriages, marital relationships, and marital satisfaction.

71   Traupmann, Jane, and Hatfield, Elaine. (1983). How important is marital fairness over the lifespan? International Journal of Aging and Human Development, 17, 89-101.

Examination of equity in marriage in 400 middle-aged and older married women who described equity at eight points across their lifespan. Results show that women begin a marriage with a sense of overbenefit, move into a period of underbenefit during their middle years, and feel fairly treated in late middle age.

72   Traupmann, Jane, and Hatfield, Elaine. (1981).
        Love and its effect on mental and physical health.
        In Fogel, Robert; Hatfield, Elaine; Kiesler, Sara;
        and Shanas, Ethel (Eds.), Aging, stability and
        change in the family, pp. 253-274. New York:
        Academic Press, 341p.

Review of psychological, social psychological, sociological,
and gerontological evidence on love and intimacy among older
Americans. Conclusion is that although love may last a
lifetime for a few couples, for most couples "passionate and
companionate love continue to decline with the passage of
time." Presents evidence from a variety of sources which
suggests that intimacy may be critically important in promoting
mental and physical health.

73   Whitlach, Carol, and Zarit, Steven. (1988). Sexual
        dysfunction in an aged married couple a case study
        of   a   behavioral   intervention.   Clinical
        Gerontologist, 8(2), 43-62.

Presents a case study of a successful behavioral therapeutic
intervention used in the treatment of a sexual dysfunction in
an older married couple, aged 74 and 72. Argues that the
sexual problems of older people have treatable causes and that
these problems originate in misunderstandings, negative beliefs
and expectations, and behavioral patterns, rather than in age
alone.

Films

74   Bullfrog Films (Producer). (1976). Living the good
        life--with Helen and Scott Nearing.

Story of Scott Nearing, an economist, social critic, and
politician, and his wife, Helen, a concert violinist.   Both
left the "big city" for Vermont during the Depression.   Their
basic life philosophy is that "the good life is a pay-as-you-go
way," "whatever we do must be enjoyable to us." They believe
that all people are free, no one should be exploited, and each
person should, in even small ways, contribute to the good of
the whole.

75   Darnton, Frances (Producer). (1977). Aging with
        Grace and Harry, Hazel and Fred.

Presents 50 men and women who have celebrated 50 years of
marriage or more to the same partner. "The payoff of years of
companionship and mutual interests is the caring and nurturing
of each other in the later years of life. . . . Commitment,
companionship, care, and concern are found to be strengths in
the relationship."

76   Gilbert, Bruce, for ITC Films/IPC Films (Producer).
        (1985). On Golden Pond.

Presents the story of an 80-year-old man and his wife who come
to spend a "final" summer at Golden Pond. Ethel, the wife, is

seen as optimistic and supportive of her somewhat cantankerous husband, Norman.   Intergenerational relationships with their daughter, grandson, and the daughter's lover are considered, in addition to the marital dyad relationship, are shown.

77   Hoelcl, Gisela.   (Producer).   (1972).   The good life.

The story of a couple--he, 91; she, 71--who farm organically and are visited each year by many people interested in learning their farming methods.

78   INFORM   (1966).   Later years of the Woodleys.

Describes cause-effect interdependency of the biological process of aging and ill health.   Shows the effectiveness of appropriate social casework intervention as an indispensable adjunct to appropriate medical care.

79   Learning   Corporation   of   America   (Producer). (1974).   Does anybody need me anymore?

Story of the changing lives of a middle class, hardworking couple who love each other as their children grow up and leave home and as the wife begins to question her life's meaning and to wonder about the future.   One day, the wife decides to find a job, finds a job, and is reunited with her husband--as an equal.

80   Lutheran   Television   (Producer).   (1975).   The rainbow man.

Joe Kelly is an aging magician who is very skilled in bringing joy to others--except to his wife, Martha, who has been an unresponsive mental patient for the past 10 of their 40 years of married life.   Martha dies tragically, but eventually Joe will be able to bring joy to others, again.

81   National Film Board of Canada   (Producer).   (1976). The lady and the owl.

Story of a retired couple who have devoted their lives to the rehabilitation of injured owls.   This couple has achieved a satisfactory retirement through having continuing goals and the willingness to pursue them.

82   Paulist Productions (Producer).   (1975).   The last of the great male chauvinists.

Exploration of a modern marriage.   Once her children are in college, a woman who has always felt happy as a full-time wife and mother suddenly feels "stagnant."   Her husband cannot help her, since he has a very traditional and rigid idea of a woman's role.   There are tragic results when the woman takes steps toward personal growth and faces negative reaction from her husband.

83   Pinsker, Seth (Producer).   (1975).   See no evil.

Story of Bertha and Ralph, an unmarried couple in their seventies who live together in a senior citizen hotel. Bertha, who is almost blind, has become very resentful of her loss of independence because of her failing vision.

84   Productions Bella (Producer). (1976). One more winter.

Describes an older couple's romance, which generates jealousy in a blase young man who has not achieved romance.

85   Stanford University, John Else, Kristine Samuelson, and Steven Kovacs (Producers). (1976). Arthur and Lillie.

Story of the Hollywood film industry and about one older couple's adaptation to a new career late in life. The couple lives in the present. Lillie says, "We've never held the other person back."

Dissertations

86   Fuhrmann, Max. (1988). Androgyny in later life: its relation to marital satisfaction and life satisfaction in older couples. Unpublished doctoral dissertation, University of Southern California, number of pages not given.

Investigation of relationship between an older spouse's sex role flexibility and his or her marital and life satisfaction. Subjects had high levels of marital and life satisfaction. "Having an androgynous sex role orientation and performing cross-sexed role behaviors were important contributors to marital happiness, but they were not directly associated with life satisfaction."

87   Hubbard, Richard. (1979). Sex role differences in middle-aged and older adult married couples. Unpublished doctoral dissertation, University of Notre Dame, 86p.

Found in this study were significant age differences in the direction of greater sex role diffusion (the presence of both masculine and feminine personality styles and behaviors within a given individual) and higher life satisfaction for the older adult couples compared to the levels obtained from the middle-aged couples. In the older adults, activities seen as single-sex in the middle-aged group were more likely to be shared. The middle-aged subjects showed sex stereotypic scores (i.e., males high on aggression and autonomy, females high on affiliation and deference), and the patterns were reversed for the older adult group. "Older adults saw much more change in themselves and their mates with regard to sex roles than [did] the middle-aged couples."

88   Jones, Lind. (1985). The psychological experience of bereavement: lesbian women's perceptions of the response of the social network to the death of a

partner. Unpublished doctoral dissertation, Boston
University, 306p.

A phenomenological perspective of the bereavement experience
for a group of lesbian women who had lost their partners
through death.   Friends helped these women in the same ways
that families generally help heterosexual widows. Interactions
with the surviving women's families and with their partners'
families ranged from quite supportive to extremely negative.

89   Levine, David.   (1981). **Marital adjustment among
        remarried elderly dyads**.   Unpublished   doctoral
        dissertation, The Ohio State University, 145p.

Identifies variables which are significantly correlated with
marital   adjustment   among   elderly,   remarried   persons.
Significantly correlated with marital adjustment were approval
of offspring for remarriage and a satisfactory prior marital
experience.   Significantly correlated, negatively, was the
degree   of   consensus   as   to   what   is   important   in   the
relationship.

90   Sanders, Gregory.   (1983).   **Life satisfaction of
        older couples: a family strengths perspective**.
        Unpublished doctoral dissertation, University of
        Georgia, 89p.

Explores relationship between family interaction quality and
life satisfaction of older persons.   Family strengths, health,
and job prestige were related to higher life satisfaction for
older persons.   These characteristics were seen as "resources
or rewards that influence the outcome in social exchanges as
measured by life satisfaction."

91   Schnittger, Maureen.   (1988).   **Role strain and
        coping among dual-career men and women across the
        family   life   cycle**.   Unpublished   doctoral
        dissertation, Virginia Polytechnic Institute and
        State University, 82p.

Assessment of differences in role strain and coping across five
family life cycle stages.   Responses from 329 dual-career women
and men.   "Coping strategy use differed significantly by gender
and   life   cycle   stage,   with   women   utilizing   the   coping
strategies   of   cognitive   restructuring,   delegating
responsibility,   limited   responsibility,   and   using   social
support significantly more than men."

92   Shabad, Peter.   (1983).   **The interpersonal needs of
        middle-aged and older married couples**.   Unpublished
        doctoral dissertation, Washington University, 175p.

Comparison of interpersonal needs of middle-aged, married
couples with those of older, married couples.   No statistically
significant differences were found between the interpersonal
needs of the two age groups.   There was no demonstration of age
differences in marital satisfaction.

93   **Watson, Mary. (1982). <u>Marital power and resources in retired working class marriages: a test of resource theory</u>. Unpublished doctoral dissertation, University of California, Irvine, 257p.**

Uses Blood and Wolfe's 1960 resource theory in looking at older marriages (the theory that the spouse with more resources will be more powerful). "Health and social integration did not support resource theory in their relationships to power. Generally, the well spouses saw the sick ones as powerful, but the sick spouses did not see themselves as powerful. Social integration was negatively related to power. Highly integrated people make more decisions based on others' needs than do poorly integrated people. Behavioral power and normative power were related to different resources. Health and alternatives were related to the normative power measure. Social integration was more related to behavioral power."

4

Widowhood

Books

94 Brown, Judith, and Baldwin, Christine. (1986). <u>A second start: a widow's guide to financial survival at a time of emotional crisis</u>. New York: Simon and Schuster, 223p.

Provides practical information to help widows make informed decisions about their lives. Combines practical advice and emotional counseling. Includes "action checklist" at end of each chapter, other lists and guidelines, and sample form letters to insurance companies.

95 Foehner, Charlotte, and Cozart, Carol. (1988). <u>The widow's handbook: a guide for living</u>. Golden, Colorado: Fulcrum, Inc., 301p.

Discussion of legal, financial, and personal issues of widowhood. Includes specific guidelines, checklists, and sample letters and forms.

96 Lopata, Helena. (1970). <u>Widowhood in an American city</u>. Cambridge, Massachusetts: Schenkman Publishing Company, 369p.

A classic study which examines lives of Chicago widows aged 50 and over in terms of their social roles and which looks at the women's relationships with their children, kin, friends, and the larger community. Uses a cross-cultural approach.

97 Lopata, Helena. (1979). <u>Women as widows: support systems</u>. New York: Elsevier, 485p.

Lopata focuses on Chicago widows, basing her conclusions on interviews done in 1970. Her perspective is the role of support systems in the lives of these widows.

98 Sheehan, Susan. (1984). <u>Kate Quinton's days</u>. Boston: Houghton Mifflin Co., 158p.

Account of an independent Irish woman who has the emotional and physical problems associated with illness and who finds she must depend on others in her later years. She talks about her use of a new, home-care program.

99   Silverman, Phyllis. (1986). Widow-to-widow. New York: Springer Publishing Company, 227p.

Presents a perspective on bereavement as a transition period, the development of the mutual-help, widow-to-widow project, and how the widow-to-widow program has helped women adjust to being widows and to being women alone.

100   Strugnell, Cecile. (1974). Adjustment to widowhood and some related problems: a selective and annotated bibliography. New York: Health Sciences Publishing Corporation, 201p.

A comprehensive literature review on mutual help programs for widows. Sections include bereavement, widowhood, loneliness, the role of women, and mutual help groups.

Articles/chapters

101   Arens, Diana. (1982-1983). Widowhood and well-being: an examination of sex differences within a causal model. International Journal of Aging and Human Development, 15(1), 27-40.

The main sources of a sense of well-being for men and women were good health, participation in recreational activities, and socialization with friends. "For women, employment roles were also a source of positive effect. Low socioeconomic status . . . was a source of reduced well-being. . . ."

102   Feinson, Marjorie. (1986). Aging widows and widowers: are there mental health differences? International Journal of Aging and Human Development, 23(4), 241-255.

From this literature review of behavioral and psychological studies, there is little evidence that supports the perception that aging widowers experience more emotional problems during bereavement than do aging widows.

103   Ferraro, Kenneth. (1985-1986). The effect of widowhood on the health status of older persons. International Journal of Aging and Human Development, 21(1), 9-25.

Data from the Bureau of the Census interviews within The Survey of Low-income Aged and Disabled. The result, in widowhood, was found to be an immediate decrease in perceived health among older people. Women and the old-old are "health optimistic" compared to men and the old.

104   Ferraro, Kenneth, and Barresi, Charles.   (1982).
        The impact of widowhood on the social relations of
        older persons. Research on Aging, 4(2), 227-247.

Report of panel data from a national survey of the low-income
aged. One of the most important findings was general stability
of the recently widowed in regard to family relations.   For
people widowed more than four years, there were lower levels of
social interaction in terms of family contact.

105   Gentry, Margaret, and Shulman, Arthur.   (1985).
        Survey of sampling techniques in widowhood research.
        Journal of Gerontology, 40(5), 641-643.

The focus in this article is on use and reporting of sampling
procedures found in research on widowhood.   Thirty-three
percent of the studies did not report the sampling procedures
used and most investigators who did identify their sampling
procedures did not indicate awareness of the limitations of
generalizations of their results because of their sampling
procedures.

106   Greene, Ritsuko, and Feld, Sheila. (1989). Social
        support coverage and the well-being of elderly
        widows and married women. Journal of Family Issues,
        10(1), 33-51.

Examines relationship between social support and well-being.
Based on interview data collected on a national sample of women
aged 50 and over, ever-married and widowed. Findings were that
relationships between social support and well-being were
positive in some groups and negative in others, and not
necessarily linked with marital status.   Discusses the
importance of considering the causal directions of links
between social support and well-being and the possible negative
consequences of receiving social support.

107   Heinemann, Gloria. (1983). Family involvement and
        support for widowed persons. In Brubaker, Timothy
        (Ed.), Family relationships in later life, pp. 127-
        148. Beverly Hills: Sage Publications, 272p.

Reviews family involvement and support among the widowed.
Looks at family involvement and support among widowed persons
during the period of becoming widowed and during the period of
being widowed and at findings about family supports among
urban, widowed women. Literature review shows that relatives
help during the early bereavement period and "provide much-
needed support, services, and advice." As the widowed person
"adapts to the loss, roles and relationships with relatives are
renegotiated from the perspective of a single person."
Usually, widowed persons are able to establish satisfactory
relationships with their kin.

108   Hill, Connie; Thompson, Larry; and Gallagher,
        Dolores.   (1988).   The role of anticipatory
        bereavement in older women's adjustment to
        widowhood. Gerontologist, 28(6), 792-796.

Evaluated older widows at two months, six months, and one year after death of spouse. Finding that expectancy of death was not related to adjustment to bereavement. Widows prepared for widowhood adjusted no better than widows who did not rehearse.

109   Homan, Sharon; Haddock, Cynthia; Winner, Carol; Coe, Rodney; and Wolinsky, Frederic. (1986). Widowhood, sex, labor force participation, and the use of physician services by elderly adults. Journal of Gerontology, 41(6), 793-796.

Study of relationships of widowhood, sex, and labor force participation with the use of ambulatory physician services by elderly adults. Authors suggest that the effects of widowhood and labor force participation are spurious. "Widows are simply more likely to live alone and are less likely to work than widowers; those who live alone and do not work are more likely to use health services (and more of them) than those who live with others and are gainfully employed."

110   Kohen, Janet. (1983). Old but not alone: informal social supports among the elderly by marital status and sex. Gerontologist, 23(1), 57-63.

Among subjects 55 and over, the widowed elderly generally had an advantage over the married. Sex differences were similar between married and widowed elderly persons. Women indicated more anchorage points for expanding their social roles than did men.

111   Lopata, Helena. (1988). Support systems of American urban widowhood. The Journal of Social Issues, 44(3), 113-128.

The support systems which U.S. women have developed in widowhood are examined, based on Social Security interview data on Chicago-area (Illinois) widows (n=82,078). Results show a great heterogeneity of lifestyles and support systems, due to the coexistence of many social changes and the perseverance of traditional life patterns.

112   Lopata, Helena. (1984). The widowed. In Palmore, Erdman (Ed.), Handbook of the aged in the United States, pp. 109-124. Westport, Connecticut: Greenwood Press, 458p.

Briefly summarizes the history of widowhood in America, problems and advantages of widowhood, support systems, support groups, and research issues.

113   Morgan, David. (1989). Adjusting to widowhood: do social networks really make it easier? Gerontologist, 29(1), 101-107.

Examines positive and negative aspects of relations with friends and family. "Family relations showed commitment involving both problematic obligations and an inability to avoid undesirable behavior. Non-family relations showed flexibility, with increases in positive relationships and decreases in negative ones."

114   Morgan, Leslie.   (1984).   Changes in family
        interaction following widowhood.   Journal of
        Marriage and the Family, 46(2), 323-331.

Examines family reactions to widowhood. Uses data from the Longitudinal Retirement History Study. Findings that average frequency of interaction with available kin increased for both married and widowed persons over time, with the greatest increase among women who became widowed.

115   Morgan, Leslie. (1984). Continuity and change in
        the labor force activity of recently widowed women.
        Gerontologist, 24(5), 530-535.

Reports findings from the 1975 Longitudinal Retirement History Study, using data on changes in working caused by widowhood.

116   Northcott, Herbert.   (1984).   Widowhood and
        remarriage trends in Canada, 1956-1981. Canadian
        Journal on Aging, 3(2), 63-77.

Examines prevalence of widowhood in Canada from 1956 to 1981. Presents data on probability of remarriage following widowhood and the length of time a person can expect to stay widowed until either remarriage or death.

117   O'Bryant, Shirley. (1985). Neighbors' support of
        older widows who live alone in their own homes.
        Gerontologist, 25(3), 305-310.

Comparison of widows with no children, with children living elsewhere, and with children living in the same city. Childless widows did not receive higher levels of support, although they had, apparently, greater need.

118   O'Bryant, Shirley.   (1988).   Self-differentiated
        assistance in older widows' support systems.   Sex
        Roles, 19(1/2), 91-106.

Today's older women, belonging to a low-fertility cohort, have deficiencies in their informal support systems because of having small families. Study reports interviews of 225 recent widows, 60 to 85, regarding 10 areas of support provided by adult children, other kin, or friends/neighbors. Findings show significant differences in the receipt of traditionally male types of support between widows with and without sons, but no differences in receipt of traditionally female types of support for widows with or without daughters.

119   O'Bryant, Shirley, and Morgan, Leslie.   (1989).
        Financial experience and well-being among mature
        widowed women. Gerontologist, 29(2), 245-251.

Analysis of data from 300 widowed women aged 60 and older regarding financial experience prior to widowhood, planning undertaken before death of a spouse, and their effects on well-

being in early widowhood. The finding was that "preparation
was associated with somewhat better well-being among widows,
but financial experience prior to widowhood had no effect."

120   O'Bryant, Shirley, and Morgan, Leslie. (1990).
         Recent widows' kin support and orientations to self-
         sufficiency. Gerontologist, 30(3), 391-398.

Examines the role of the adult child network in task support to
widows and whether widows' attitudes toward independence result
in lower levels of task support. Many recently widowed women
are quite self-sufficient; when they need help, they largely
rely on children. "Widows' past experiences and attitudes
toward independence influence the amount of overall help they
receive, whereas income, number of children, and perceived
willingness of children to help affect the proportion of help
that comes from children."

121   Palmore, Erdman.   (1987).   Cross-cultural
         perspectives on widowhood. Journal of Cross-
         Cultural Gerontology, 2, 93-105.

Widowhood causes the problems of replacing the functions of the
dead spouse and those of the dead parent, and determining who
should inherit the property of the dead spouse and where the
surviving family should live.   Various solutions to these
problems, based on demographic characteristics of developing
and developed countries, are presented.

122   Rubinstein, Robert. (1986). The construction of a
         day by elderly widowers. International Journal of
         Aging and Human Development, 23(3), 161-173.

Explains how some older widowers who live alone organize time,
using the concept of a "day" as a focus for organization.

123   Scott, Jean, and Kivett, Vira. (1985). Differences
         in the morale of older, rural widows and widowers.
         International Journal of Aging and Human
         Development, 21(2), 121-136.

Reports the effect of sex differences on the morale of older
widowed individuals.   Sex of subject didn't affect morale,
but perceived financial status and self-rated health had
significant direct effects. Neither sex was more disadvantaged
than the other by widowhood.

124   Thompson, Larry; Breckenridge, James; Gallagher,
         Dolores; and Peterson, James. (1986). Effects of
         bereavement on self-perceptions of physical health
         in elderly widows and widowers. In Troll, Lillian
         (Ed.), Family issues in current gerontology, pp. 53-
         63. New York: Springer Publishing Company, 382p.

Reports data on self-perceptions of physical health status of
subjects about two months after their spouse's death.   The
report is part of an ongoing longitudinal study of the impact
of bereavement on elderly men and women over a 30-month period.
Results are similar to prior research, indicating that

"conjugal bereavement is a significant stressor that may adversely affect the physical health status of survivors."

Films

125   **American Film Institute.** (1973). **Mysto the great.**

After his wife dies, Mysto the magician doesn't mourn the happy past--he prepares for a happy future, though his two sons disagree. One son wants his father to be taken care of, the other thinks his father should lead his own life. Not griefstricken but wanting independence and able to be on his own, Mysto drives off with plans for tomorrow--perhaps another marriage and a new home.

126   **Brigham Young University Productions.** (1977). **The mailbox.**

Main character of this film is Lethe, a widow who lives alone in a rural setting, spending much of her time waiting for the mail carrier to arrive. She never receives a letter, even from her children, who seem to have forgotten how much she thrives on written communications. "To Lethe, letters are visible signs of an emotional bond, particularly among family members. Her huge mailbox, of course, is a visual symbol of her vast warm heart, capable of giving love to all family members and friends." The film also looks at intergenerational relationships--Lethe spends some time with a neighbor woman, the age of her children, and the neighbor's daughter, who enjoys a grandparent-grandchild relationship with Lethe. The emphasis on intergenerational relationships reinforces the enduring meaning of family ties.

127   **Centron.** (1982). **Grieving: suddenly alone.**

Explores the complex set of responses of one person grieving after the death of a spouse. The film follows a widow through weeks of personal agony as she attempts to adjust to her new role.

128   **Frances Flaherty: hidden and seeking.** (1971).

Frances Flaherty, 87, widowed, is a strong-minded Yankee, very active physically, and artistic. She discusses films, art, poetry, her life, and "how her strength comes from the land and from the young people she knows around her."

129   **Health Sciences Consortium.** (1984). **Older adults: looking back.**

Shows how an older couple with health problems tried to plan for the eventuality of death. The wife survived her husband and describes what it is like for her, now that he is gone.

130   **Hello in there.** (1979).

Mary, a widow, lives in a "sterile" retirement home. Mary is sensitive to others, enjoys simple pleasures, and has a sense of humor. These characteristics contrast with her feelings of loneliness, being forgotten, and frustration at being old.

131   Lorimar Productions. (1982). The widow.

After the death of her husband, a woman learns to deal with her grief, her children's traumas, and monetary worries. Film is based on Lynn Caine's best-selling novel about widowhood.

132   Lutheran TV. (1972). Heirloom.

Recently widowed, Arthur Langley feels there is nothing to live for. He sits on the porch staring at his wife's photo. The film shows a young boy striking up a friendship with the 70-year-old widower.

133   Mason, Edward. (1972). Widows.

Women comprise about 85% of the 12 million widowed persons in the United States. This film looks at several recently widowed women who describe their experiences and feelings. The focus is on middle-aged widows with children.

134   Mass Media. (1970). A yellow leaf.

An older woman sits in her rocking chair musing on her life, which she feels was "ended" when her husband died in World War I.

135   Michigan Media. (1980). Widowhood.

This film is part of the "Transitions: Caught at Midlife" series.

136   NFBC. (1966). Where Mrs. Whalley lives.

Illustrates one day in the life of an elderly widow, who lives both within her son's family and within the world of her memories.

137   National Film Board of Canada. (1977). For gentlemen only.

Film describes the relationship between two retired men who live in an old hotel and who have to deal with women now being allowed to live in the hotel, too.

138   NETCHE. (1979). Widowhood.

Case study of widowhood. Provides an analysis and willingness to share experiences by widow Mary Gallagher.

139   Roberts, William, and Darnton, Frances. (1976). Conversation with a widow.

A recent widow describes her 67-year-old husband's illness, the support she received during the course of his illness, the anguish she felt, and how she coped with the loss of her spouse. The interview provides "insights into the power of relationships and the dignity of the human spirit."

140   **San Diego State University.** (1978). **Widowhood: three personal perspectives.**

Presents three in-depth interviews with elderly widows. Examines the widows' efforts and successes in coping with the death of spouses and with surviving afterward.

141   **Stuart, Martha, Communications.** (1978). **Widows.**

Discusses the experiences and feelings of widows.

142   **Sun Life Assurance Company of Canada.** (1971). **For tomorrow . . . and tomorrow.**

Describes the problems of and solutions for five widows in the United States, England, and Canada.

143   **Vinton, Will.** (1977). **Martin the cobbler.**

Martin, a widower and a lonely old man experiences an emotional and spiritual regeneration and progresses toward psychological wholeness.

Dissertations

144   **Arsenault, Anne.** (1984). **The effect of social support systems and anticipatory socialization on the life satisfaction of widows.** Unpublished doctoral dissertation, Boston University, 215p.

Examination of the effects of social support systems and anticipatory socialization on the life satisfaction of widows. "Two measures of social support were significant--intensity of support and congruence between support desired and support received. Ethnicity, especially a British-Scottish heritage, was found to have a negative effect on life satisfaction. Anticipatory socialization did not have an effect on life satisfaction, with few of the widows reporting any socialization."

145   **Barrell, Lorna.** (1980). **From wife to widow: the transitional process.** Unpublished doctoral dissertation, University of Illinois at Chicago Circle, 217p.

For most of the widows in this study, the transition from wife to widow was orderly and congruent with their previous lifestyles. "The women studied had experienced major, catastrophic losses throughout their lives. Those most successful in the transition were personally strong, self-confident women with necessary knowledge, skills, and abilities to continue satisfying lives alone when their husbands died."

146   **Bensel-Myers, Linda.** (1985). **A "figure cut in alabaster": the paradoxical widow of Renaissance**

drama.   Unpublished   doctoral   dissertation,
University of Oregon, 250p.

Tests two assumptions: that the widow was a realistic
imitation,   and   that   she   was   an   historically   isolated
phenomenon.   The finding was that "the widow's prominence on
the Jacobean stage was a particular manifestation of the
emergence of this antiheroic late Renaissance man.   The widows'
paradoxical position as a relic of her past who cannot
legitimately re-establish herself in the present, exploited by
earlier dramatists, made her a particularly apt figure for the
individual Jacobean, who became increasingly disillusioned with
political and social ideals."

147   Biggers, Trisha. (1981). **The relationship between
          the grief reaction of older widows and their level
          of development**. Unpublished doctoral dissertation,
          The University of Florida, 126p.

Examination of factors which are important of resolution of the
grief process in older widows. Findings were: "the widows'
perceived financial status was the most important factor in
resolution of the grief process; the grief process lasts longer
than previously indicated for older widows, with intensity of
grief reaction diminishing over time and lessening between the
third and fourth years of widowhood.   There is an inverse
relationship between the grief reaction of older widows and
their level of ego development; the length of widowhood, length
of the husband's illness prior to his death, the widow's
perceived financial status, and her level of ego development
were the combination of factors most important in resolution of
the grief process in older widows."

148   Bottar, Karen. (1981). **The economic well-being and
          social adjustment of mid-life widows**. Unpublished
          doctoral dissertation, Syracuse University, 216p.

Examination of the economic well-being and social adjustment
adjustment of mid-life widows, 35 to 59 years old.   Adult
children, education, and health were statistically significant
determinants of economic well-being for white widows; for black
widows,   adult   children   and   health   are   statistically
significant. Older children, higher education, and good health
are associated with a higher economic well-being ratio. Widows
had higher scores on a scale (poorer life functioning) than
non-widows in the aggregate. Income, education, and employment
are correlates of social adjustment.

149   Brewer, Mary. (1986). **Loneliness in widowhood: an
          exploratory   survey**.   Unpublished   doctoral
          dissertation, The University of Arizona, 269p.

Loneliness in widows was significantly related to: depression,
fear, anger expression, poor health, low social involvement,
low general contact, high neighbor disclosure, receiving income
from work, and to having a living parent.

150   Bright, Carole. (1985). **A study of the impact of
          normal and atypical grief patterns on the health and**

<u>living environment of institutionalized and non-</u>
<u>institutionalized elderly widows</u>.   Unpublished
doctoral dissertation, University of San Francisco,
189p.

Author uses comparative-survey design to gather data on the
impact of spousal loss on elderly females. Factors which were
significantly associated with the normal grief pattern were:
higher education, a close relationship to husband, an action-
oriented coping style, having received professional
intervention, high family inclusion, and an active relationship
with friends. Variables which impacted on atypical grief were:
increased age, a long work history, a pink-collar job, less
education, more than one marriage, not being close to husband,
a shared family decisionmaking process, a dependent coping
style, an early move after the husband's death, less family
communication, and fewer activities with friends.

151   Clary, Freddie Mae.   (1983).   <u>Life satisfaction</u>
        <u>among elderly widowed women</u>. Unpublished doctoral
        dissertation, University of Minnesota, 300p.

Proposes that "satisfaction after a stressful life event can be
viewed as a consequence of effective coping styles."   The
finding was a positive relationship between style of coping and
the percentage of respondents who say that they are "delighted"
with their "life-as-a-whole."   "Variables representing life
domain satisfaction and personality characteristics affect
overall satisfaction in the same direction as well:
respondents who are satisfied with individual life domains and
those who exhibit androgynous personality characteristics also
tend to have higher levels of life satisfaction."

152   Coon, Ann. (1986). <u>Widows, spinsters and lovers:</u>
        <u>the controlling female figure in the fiction of</u>
        <u>Henry James</u>.   Unpublished doctoral dissertation,
        State University of New York at Buffalo, 185p.

Examination of the role of the controlling female--often a
widow, spinster, or estranged wife--who seizes control of a
weaker figure and of the events of a novel.

153   DeBord, Beverly. (1983). <u>The widow in Restoration</u>
        <u>comedy</u>.   Unpublished doctoral dissertation, West
        Virginia University, 195p.

The widow appears frequently on the Restoration comedy stage
and almost always provokes laughter at her own expense. "The
widow's financial exploitation is a common factor and a key to
understanding why widowhood, essentially tragic, became comic
during the Restoration. Representing the power of death and
unleashed sexual passion, the widow menaced social order, but
through her unprecedented ability to divide estates through
bargaining for jointure and establishing trusts for her
separate use, she had the potential to frustrate society's
attempts at economic stabilization and thus perpetuate
disorder. As an unattached, financially independent woman, the
widow threatened not only England's society and economy but
also the very chain of being, which established women as those

to be controlled.   In the classic pattern of comedy through degradation. . . . Restoration society neutralized the widow's threat by treating her as a scapegoat, victimizing her through ridicule and abuse.   The Restoration comic widow did not amuse; she menaced.   When Restoration society faced her anticharacterization on stage, behind their smiles hid a sneer."

154   **DiGiulio, Robert.   (1984).   Identity loss and reformulation in young, middle-aged, and older widowed women.   Unpublished doctoral dissertation, The University of Connecticut, 266p.**

Investigation of effects of spouse death upon the identity and adaptation of widowed women.   There seemed to be a more turbulent adaptation for middle-aged widows in widowhood than in young or older widows.   Higher on measures of adaptation were widows who had a confidant than those who had no confidant.   Children being present, the type and length of a widow's present or past employment, religion, marital happiness, and the "preventability" of husband's death did not appear to be important to the widow's adaptation.   However, appearing to be related to adaptation were level of formal education and foreknowledge of and cause of spouse's death.   "A strong sense of relief--experienced by many widows--was an unexpected accomplice to positive change widows perceived in their lives."

155   **Estrin, Harriet.   (1985).   Life satisfaction and participation in learning activities among widows.   Unpublished   doctoral   dissertation,   Syracuse University, 271p.**

Explores   relationship   between   life   satisfaction   and participation in learning activity for widows.   Findings suggested that participation in learning activity is related to enhancing life satisfaction.

156   **Farra, Robert.   (1982).   The widow/bureaucratic linkage during the transition to widowhood: an exploratory   study.   Unpublished   doctoral dissertation, The Florida State University, 117p.**

This study involved investigation of widow satisfaction and dissatisfaction with key organizational linkages following the death of a spouse, to identify problems which widows encounter in dealing with organizations,   and   to identify those persons to whom widows turn when they experience unsatisfactory organizational   linkages.   "Widows   indicated   greatest satisfaction in their dealings with banks and mortuaries. Widows experienced greatest dissatisfaction in their dealings with   physicians   and   hospital   personnel.   Widows   often complained about the cost of services, but most paid their bills without stating their dissatisfactions with the cost of services.   Widows experienced the greatest number of problems in their dealings with hospitals and insurance companies.   It was   speculated   that   the   larger   bureaucracies   may   have overwhelmed   the   widow,   thus   impeding   the   problem-solving process."   While widows did experience many problems with service-providers, in over 50% of the cases, they did not discuss linkage problems with anyone.

157   Ferraro, Kenneth.   (1981).   **The social impact of widowhood on older persons: a longitudinal analysis**.   Unpublished doctoral dissertation, The University of Akron, 158p.

This study uses longitudinal data from a national sample of the low-income aged to examine how widowhood affects the health and social participation of older people. Widows and widowers may compensate for decreases in some interactions by increasing their participation in other interactions. "Participation in formal associations, such as church and voluntary associations, is, in the long run, reduced. Yet, the results indicate that there is an increase in the probability of having an intimate friend immediately after widowhood." Findings of the study indicate the "reintegration in friendship relations for those widowed between one and four years," and emphasize the need to conduct a longitudinal examination of widowhood and "seriously to question the decremental model of role loss and social functioning."

158   Friday, Patricia.   (1985).   **Coping with widowhood: a study of urban and rural widows**.   Unpublished doctoral dissertation, The University of Wisconsin-Madison, 277p.

The theoretical perspective of this study is one of family stress and coping. Examination of the coping process of widowhood. Coping behaviors such as belief in God, awareness of personal strengths, and acceptance of present lives were considered. Four coping patterns were found: "managing psychological tension, social support, maintaining family integrity, and self development and reliance. No major differences . . . between urban and rural widows. Some significant relationships . . . between background and attitudinal variables and coping patterns."

159   Gibbs, Jeanne.   (1979).   **The social world of the older widow in the non-metropolitan community**.   Unpublished doctoral dissertation, Kansas State University, 371p.

Explores the structure and content of social relationships and the perception of social life of 40 women, widowed one year or more, 50 years of age and older, and living in a non-metropolitan community. Looks at the processes and outcomes of the widow's efforts to reconstruct her social life and attempts to determine how community structure (especially formal and informal social support systems) helped or hindered the widow's efforts at reformulating her social relations and activities. Concludes that "the social world of the older widow is spent primarily with other females during daytime hours." Widowed subjects in both communities said they had more female friends than male friends, and that they felt closer emotionally to female friends.

160   Heinemann, Gloria. (1980). <u>Determinants of primary</u>
           <u>support system strength among urban, widowed women:</u>
           <u>does life stage make a difference?</u> Unpublished
           doctoral dissertation, University of Illinois at
           Chicago Circle, 260p.

Sociological investigation of the later widowhood period when
the grieving period is over for the majority of widows, the
husband's loss has been accepted, and "rebuilding and
repatterning one's life have become paramount. . . . Considers
social integration, i.<u>e</u>., social support system strength
measured by the number of active family and friendship roles,
of relatively long-time urban widows. . . . Self-initiating
behavior is essential to the development of strong social
support systems."

161   Hornung, Karen. (1980). <u>Loneliness among older</u>
           <u>urban widows</u>. Unpublished doctoral dissertation,
           The University of Nebraska-Lincoln, 155p.

Investigates extent of loneliness among older urban widows in
relation to 17 social and demographic variables: age, length
of marriage, length of widowhood, education, household
companion, frequency of telephoning, organizational activity,
sufficiency of contact with a confidant, satisfaction with
visiting patterns of relatives and friends, confinement, self-
rated health, occupation, income, transportation, satisfaction
with housing, feelings about the past year, and time spent
alone. "Four factors which significantly contributed to the
loneliness scores of older urban widows were length of
marriage, length of widowhood, satisfaction with amount of
organizational activity, and feelings about the past year. The
13 other variables were not found to be significantly related
for the population studied."

162   Hudson, Cathie. (1984). <u>The transition from wife</u>
           <u>to widow: short-term changes in economic well-being</u>
           <u>and labor force behavior</u>. Unpublished doctoral
           dissertation, Duke University, 262p.

Examination of how widowhood affects the economic well-being of
the family and the labor force behavior of the widow.
Description of the timing and types of economic and labor force
changes in the five-year period from two years before widowhood
through two years after widowhood. "Most widows are worse off
financially two years after widowhood than before, and the drop
in total family income occurs in the year before widowhood.
The most common labor force pattern is an increase in mean
hours worked in the year before widowhood followed by a
decrease in the year after widowhood."

163   Keith, Judith. (1982). <u>The relationships between</u>
           <u>the adjustment of the widowed and social support,</u>
           <u>self-esteem, grief experience, and selected</u>
           <u>demographic variables</u>. Unpublished doctoral
           dissertation, The University of Tennessee, 144p.

Determines relationship between adjustment of widowed persons
and self-esteem, social support, the grief experience, and

specific demographic variables. Concludes "that adjustment to widowhood is a lengthy process; that variables such as age, sex, income, etc., do not appear to be related to adjustment over a long period of time; that males appear to have less interpersonal support than females; that personal self-esteem appears to be more important to adjustment than general or social self-esteem."

164   Kofie, Vincent.   (1983).   **The effects of some conditions of destabilization on the widowhood mortality technique.**   Unpublished   doctoral dissertation, The Johns Hopkins University, 357p.

Reports a simulation approach to demonstrate the effects of declining mortality, changing (increasing) nuptiality, and polygyny on the widowhood method (i.e., Widowhood Mortality Technique). Concludes that "the application of the widowhood technique in destablilized populations is susceptible to various degrees of error which, without adjustment, yields distorted estimates of morality."

165   Leavitt, Priscilla.   (1981).   **Grief resolution in widowed persons according to type of funeral chosen and mode of death and demographic and life experience variables.**   Unpublished   doctoral dissertation, Ohio State University, 277p.

Investigation of the grief resolution of three groups of widowed persons five to 14 months after the deaths of their spouses--public viewing and at least two hours of visitation, visitation with closed casket, and no visitation at funeral home. "There was no significant difference in grief resolution based on type of funeral chosen. . . It [may be] the coping skills of individuals rather than differences in the circumstances of death that account for most of the differences in grief resolution. . . Some indication that men have more difficulty with long illnesses than with sudden deaths. Study implies that a variety of funeral rituals should be offered to people with different approaches to life."

166   Malkinson, Ruth. (1983). **Adaptation to bereavement of widows who experienced a sudden loss of spouse.** Unpublished doctoral dissertation, The University of Florida, 196p.

Widows with high self-esteem generate and receive more support from others than do widows with low self-esteem. Low self-esteem widows reported more health problems and more difficulties with new friends and finances, and were not always able to obtain support from others. Avoidance of widows' "grief work" (normal intense and emotional reactions following a traumatic event) is socially reinforced.

167   Maqashalala, Theophilus.   (1984).   **An analysis of support systems among African widows in the Tyhume Basin, Ciskei, South Africa.** Unpublished doctoral dissertation, The University of Alabama, 115p.

Assessment of material and emotional support resources to widows and determination of the roles which significant others play in helping to cope with various problems. "Widows interact most with neighbors and friends and daughters. They receive both emotional and material support from neighbors, friends, and daughters, but little emotional support from sons or other relatives. Sons and daughters provide material support about equally, on a par with neighbors and friends. Widows are extremely poor. Those nearer town produce less of their own food than those more distant. More widows who are old were found farther away from town. All are poorly educated."

168   McGloshen, Thomas. (1985). **Factors related to the psychological well-being of elderly recent widows**. Unpublished doctoral dissertation, The Ohio State University, 84p.

Assesses factors related to how well the widow adjusts to her loss. "Widows who were healthy and active, especially in religious activities, had not worked outside the home during the marriage, were not beset with previous encounters with grief, and had husbands who died close to home experienced higher psychological well-being than other widows."

169   Morgan, Leslie. (1979). **Widowhood and change: a longitudinal analysis of middle-aged women**. Unpublished doctoral dissertation, University of Southern California, number of pages not given.

Uses longitudinal data to examine change over time in the circumstances of middle-aged women who became widowed. Examines: economic status, labor force participation, residential mobility, and consumer behavior.

170   Moss, Willodean. (1981). **An assessment of self-esteem and perceived needs of widowed and divorced women**. Unpublished doctoral dissertation, University of Kentucky, 149p.

Profile of divorced and widowed women to determine if there was a relationship between their self-esteem and selected variables. The finding was that there were no differences in perceived happiness and self-esteem between widows and divorcees nor between women who had children in the home and those who did not. In addition, age was not related to self-esteem; education, job satisfaction, past income, present income, and perceived happiness were all positively related to self-esteem; self-esteem was higher for those who were working outside the home and those who had worked during the marriage than for those who had not worked during the marriage. It was found that self-esteem was the same for those who had received counseling and those who did not.

171   Mouser, Nancy. (1983). **Social networks of older widowers in small town and rural settings**. Unpublished doctoral dissertation, Iowa State University, 294p.

Examines social networks of older widowers in small town and rural settings. Compares men in three marital settings-- married, widowed, and formerly-widowed-but-now-remarried. They differed in ties to some social networks, but widowers related to married and remarried peers were not socially isolated. Marital status explained little variance in child interaction, friend interaction, or life satisfaction. Network characteristics were found to be crucial for explaining interaction. Network ties, especially personal resources, are important in predicting life satisfaction.

172   Nagy, Mary. (1982). **Attributional differences in health status and life satisfactions of older women: a comparison between widows and non-widows.** Unpublished doctoral dissertation, University of Oregon, 150p.

Investigation to determine if widows aged 55 and over differed from married women in the same age group on their attributes of life satisfaction and health status. Both widows and married women were found to be satisfied with their lives. The top three elements of women's life satisfaction, for both widows and married women, were family members, friendship with others, and hard work.

173   O'Neill, Mary. (1984). **The widow's peak: popular images of widowhood in America, 1920-1960.** Unpublished doctoral dissertation, Boston University, 202p.

Traces and analyzes popular images of the middle-class widow as she appeared in articles and advertisements in selected national periodicals between 1920 and 1960. Generally, widows are cast as stoic mourners, thrifty homemakers, reluctant breadwinners, or independent grandmothers. The author suggests that "the attitudes which a culture most cherishes for married women are revealed in the idealized roles assigned to widowed wives and mothers."

174   Ray, Robert. (1983). **Effects of teaching coping skills to widows in groups.** Unpublished doctoral dissertation, The University of Arizona, 126p.

Tests whether widows, during the bereavement period, are able to learn coping skills through a model for group interaction. The treatment process had three foci: separation from the deceased, resolution of personal loss, and renewed social interest and relationship. The group treatment approach was found to have overall significance.

175   Scott, Jean. (1979). **The effect of sex differences on the subjective well-being of older widows and widowers.** Unpublished doctoral dissertation, The University of North Carolina, 148p.

Examination of the relationship between sex and the subjective well-being of older widows and widowers. Concludes that sex is not a critical factor in determining the subjective well-being of the widowed. Perceived income adequacy was an important influence on the subjective well-being of the widowed, with lower well-being resulting from perceived inadequate income. The author found that "environmental constraints appear to be more influential determinants of the widowed older adults' subjective well-being than sex differences."

176   Stanley, Arthur.   (1982).   Mary Lavin's widow stories.   Unpublished   doctoral   dissertation, University of Georgia, 168p.

Analysis of the widow stories, which are based on Mary Lavin's own experience.   "The intense physical, emotional, and spiritual dilemmas wrought by widowhood have as their basis the life that the woman experienced as a wife."

177   Sternberg, Malka.   (1982).   The long-term adaptations of young and middle-aged widows to the loss of a spouse.   Unpublished doctoral dissertation, Columbia University Teachers' College, 153p.

Interviews with 16 widows with dependent children in the United States and Israel.   The focus was on changes and adjustment in the lives of these women as a result of the loss of a spouse. The commonalities were found to be greater than the differences, cutting across cultural, ethnic, and religious lives.   "The problems resulting from the loss of the spouse were seen as lasting many years beyond the initial period of crisis."

178   Taich, Arlene.   (1980).   Reference other associations and perceived stress among older widows.   Unpublished doctoral dissertation, Saint Louis University, 170p.

"The meaning to the individual of old age and widowhood depends upon the social context in which it occurs, a social context composed of reference other influences.   The goals an individual sets for herself as well as her efficacy in dealing with the exigencies of everyday life are associated with the overt and covert influences of reference others.   The reference other concept links the individuals and the social structure in the attempt to reduce or eliminate stressful barriers to adaptation."

179   Talbott, Marie.   (1986).   Grief and social support: a study of older widows.   Unpublished doctoral dissertation, University of California, Berkeley, 346p.

Investigation of the effects of social support on the grief of older widows.   Evidence found that there are three widespread patterns in the social arrangements of older widows--the unsatisfactory relationships of widows with their children, the tendency of widows to have friends who are also widows, and the absence of men in their lives.   "All [three patterns] are imposed on widows without their consent, and to their detriment."

180   Tannenbaum, Robert.   (1981).   **The influence of widowhood and divorce, self-esteem and locus of dependence on volunteering help.**   Unpublished doctoral dissertation, Northern Illinois University, 174p.

Investigation of the effects of the similarity of marital status between subject and recipient (i.e., widowhood versus divorce), subject's self-esteem, and recipient's locus of dependence. "The widows' willingness to help was influenced primarily by similarity of marital status between themselves and recipients, while the willingness of divorcees to help was influenced primarily by the recipients' locus of dependence. Widowed and divorced subjects with high self-esteem volunteered more help to recipients than did their low self-esteem counterparts."

181   Tanner, Mary.   (1984).   **The experience of loss: a comparison of widowhood and divorce.**   Unpublished doctoral dissertation, University of Georgia, 140p.

Analysis of the effect of type of loss and gender on feelings of stress, perception of self, economic situations, feelings of attachment to former mates, attitudes toward new relationships, and adequacy of social support. The findings were that "males, both widowed and divorced, are significantly better off than females. In all other areas, i.e., stress, self-perception, social support, attachment to former spouse and attitudes toward new relationships, widowhood and divorce do not appear to be significantly different experiences."

182   Tate, Nellie.   (1983).   **Social interactional patterns and life satisfaction of a group of elderly black widows.**   Unpublished doctoral dissertation, Brandeis University, 207p.

Examination of the relationship between the social interaction patterns and life satisfaction of a group of elderly widowed blacks. "While these widows had a network of family and friends, communication appeared to flow from the widow to other members of the network. Communication among the various members of the network was almost nonexistent." Despite numerous physical complaints, 84% of these subjects were satisfied with life. The best variables in predicting life satisfaction for these widows were income, attitude toward present living situation, perceived health status, and the presence of a confidante.

183   Vachon, Mary.   (1979).   **Identity changes over the first two years of bereavement: social relationships and social support in widowhood.**   Unpublished doctoral dissertation, York University (Canada), number of pages not given.

Results of a two-year, longitudinal study of 162 Toronto widows aged 22-69 to assess psychosocial adaptation to bereavement. Describes interaction between the widows' perceptions of their social relationships and social support and the identity changes which occur during the status passage into widowhood.

The social network was seen to interact with the widow in one of three ways in facilitating identity change during bereavement, and the role of friends was found to be crucial. "The network could provide support for transition into the traditional widow role, support and facilitate the development of a new identity, or reject the widow (which could lead to her either becoming locked into the past or reaching out to develop her own identity)."

184   Waciega, Lisa. (1986). **Widowhood and womanhood in early America: the experience of women in Philadelphia and Chester Counties, 1750-1850.** Unpublished doctoral dissertation, Temple University, 332p.

Examines the position and opportunities of women in late colonial and early national America through the experience of widows in southeastern Pennsylvania. "It was the cooperation of widow and children together which shaped how families responded to the loss of husband and father."

185   Walters, Judith. (1983). **Life satisfaction among urban and rural elderly widows.** Unpublished doctoral dissertation, Michigan State University, 171p.

Describes the interaction of urban and rural elderly widows with their environments. The sample was found to be highly competent, independent, and with high life satisfaction and morale scores and a high level of closeness with their children.

186   Wambach, Julie. (1983). **Widowhood as the interruption and reconstruction of temporal reality.** Unpublished doctoral dissertation, Arizona State University, 301p.

Description of the sociopsychological aspects of the widow experience from the perspectives of widows and analysis of the perspectives from a phenomenological framework. "The core process that emerged was the widow experience of an interruption and a reconstruction of everyday temporal reality. Recognizing the extent of their temporal disruption was an emotionally jarring experience for widows. They developed a series of temporal maneuvers to once again integrate their past with their present and future, and to bridge the temporal realms."

187   Warner, Sandra. (1985). **A comparative study of widows and widowers based upon measurements of grief and social support.** Unpublished doctoral dissertation, University of Texas at Austin, 182p.

This study investigated support of widows and widowers during their first year of bereavement, differences on grief and social support, and relationships between the expressions of grief and perceived social support. The finding was that there was "no difference between groups in a multivariate sense, but widowers scored significantly higher than widows on the guilt scale."

188   **Whitted, Mabel.   (1983).   <u>An exploratory study:
       life satisfaction of elderly widows</u>.   Unpublished
       doctoral dissertation, The University of Michigan,
       199p.**

Study of differences between high and low satisfaction groups among widows.   The finding was that "the high satisfaction widow is one who is optimistic, has good self-esteem, has formed and continues to form good social relationships, and has at least one activity which is important to her.   The low satisfaction widow is often depressed, does not have any one activity she enjoys, and has very little self-esteem."

5

Grandparents

Books

189   Bengston, Vern, and Robertson, Joan (Eds.). <u>Grandparenthood</u>. Beverly Hills: Sage Publications, 1985, 240p.

Edited book of chapters exploring the nature and importance of the grandparent role. Includes discussion of diversity in grandparenting roles, continuity and connectedness, styles of grandparenting, black grandmothers, grandparenting options in divorcing families, parent-adult child relations as affected by the grandparent status, Judaic perspectives on grandparenthood, a Christian perspective on the role of grandparents, and policy considerations.

190   Cherlin, Andrew, and Furstenberg, Frank, Jr. (1986). <u>The new American grandparent</u>. New York: Basic Books, Inc., Publishers, 278p.

Based on first, representative, nationwide study of American grandparents. Found strong sentimental ties and loose bonds of obligation. Grandparents are companions to grandchildren, but are careful not to "interfere." More substantial roles are played during family crises, such as divorce. While modern grandparents may not be physically close, they can keep in touch through modern communication. The authors discuss the modernization of grandparenthood, styles of grandparenting, grandparental careers, variations, grandparents and divorce, the influence of grandparents on grandchildren, and the future of grandparenthood.

Articles/chapters

191   Aldous, Joan. (1985). Parent-adult child relations as affected by the grandparent status. In Bengston, Vern, and Robertson, Joan (Eds.), <u>Grandparenthood</u>, pp. 117-132. Beverly Hills: Sage Publications, Inc., 240p.

Author looks at changing structures, expectations, and functions in grandparenthood. Tests hypothesis that the aging parents will have closer ties with their adult children (who have children) when the adult children are divorced, and that, otherwise, grandparent status will not make a difference in intergenerational contacts--the author's findings support this. The author concludes that "grandparenting becomes a major activity, an important status, only when there are problems in the younger generation."

192   Bengston, Vern. (1985). Diversity and symbolism in grandparental roles. In Bengston, Vern, and Robertson, Joan (Eds.), Grandparenthood, pp. 11-25. Beverly Hills: Sage Publications, Inc., 240p.

Suggests two principal themes that characterize the scholarly research to date on grandparental roles: diversity in styles, characteristics, behaviors, and satisfactions of grandparents; and the symbolism that grandparenthood represents in quickly changing societies.

193   Burton, Linda, and Bengston, Vern. (1985). Black grandmothers: issues of timing and continuity of roles. In Bengston, Vern, and Robertson, Joan (Eds.), Grandparenthood, pp. 61-77. Beverly Hills: Sage Publications, Inc., 240p.

Authors link the symbolism of grandparent role to the age of becoming a grandparent and the consequences of social clocks that measure "on-time" and "off-time" grandparenthood.

194   Cherlin, Andrew, and Furstenberg, Frank. (1985). Styles and strategies of grandparenting. In Bengston, Vern, and Robertson, Joan (Eds.), Grandparenthood, pp. 97-116. Beverly Hills: Sage Publications, Inc., 240p.

Study using a nationally representative sample of families in which a divorce had occurred, relates the variety of styles in grandparental involvement. Identified five styles of grandparenting: detached, passive, supportive, authoritative, influential. No single or dominant style of grandparent behavior was found.

195   Conroy, Donald, and Fahey, Charles. (1985). Christian perspective on the role of grandparents. In Bengston, Vern, and Robertson, Joan (Eds.), Grandparenthood, pp. 195-207. Beverly Hills: Sage Publications, Inc., 240p.

Discussion of the role of grandparents in the transmission of religious heritage. "This is a key function of grandparents, from earliest Christian times; they may be more effective transmitters than the parents because of their longer memories of the traditions and their distance from primary disciplinary functions."

196   Funder, K. (1989). Grandparents in children's post-divorce families. Family Matters (Australia), 25, 47-49.

Considered relationship of grandparents to their grandchildren some years after divorce. "Grandparent roles are flexible and negotiable within the nuclear family: there are few rules."

197   Gladstone, J. (1989). Grandmother-grandchild contact: the mediating influence of the middle generation following marriage breakdown and remarriage. Canadian Journal on Aging/Revue Canadienne du vieillissement, 8(4), 355-365.

Focus on ways that adult children and children-in-law (their spouses) mediate contact between grandmothers and grandchildren, following marriage breakdown and remarriage in the middle generation. Qualitative analysis of face-to-face contact between 110 grandmother-grandchild pairs. Finding was that children have a more direct influence on visiting, by arranging or obstructing visits between grandmothers and grandchildren. Also discusses ways that grandparents can negotiate relationships with adult children and children-in-law, especially in areas of monitoring communication exchanges, maintaining friendly relationships with children-in-law and step-grandchildren, and acting as resources for the family.

198   Gutmann, David. (1985). Deculturation and the American grandparent. In Bengston, Vern, and Robertson, Joan (Eds.), Grandparenthood, pp. 173-181. Beverly Hills: Sage Publications, Inc., 240p.

Discusses grandparents as "conveyors of culture to aid in reversing malaise and deculturation." He posits that "elders, the living repositories of change, can be actively engaged to provide younger groups with the knowledge, skills, and experiences that will foster age-integrated society, as well as to be a contributing force in ensuring social equilibrium."

199   Hagestad, Gunhild. (1985). Continuity and connectedness. In Bengston, Vern, and Robertson, Joan (Eds.), Grandparenthood, pp. 31-48. Beverly Hills: Sage Publications, Inc., 240p.

Discusses recent historical changes affecting grandparenthood. Uses content analysis of popular magazines and work of family demographers. Looks at gender differences, the lack of grandparent roles, and grandparenthood and family continuity.

200   Janelli, Linda. (1988). Descriptions of grandparents in children's literature. Educational Gerontology, 14(3): 193-202.

Reviews 73 children's storybooks to analyze depictions of grandparents. Both grandmothers and grandfathers were portrayed in stereotyped roles.

201   Johnson, Colleen. (1983). A cultural analysis of the grandmother. Research on Aging, 5(4), 547-567.

Analysis of the role of the contemporary American grandmother. Subjects in this study kept uniform conceptions of the traditional grandmother, although the ideas have been adapted to the subjects' own middle-age norms.

202   Johnson, Colleen. (1985). Grandparenting options in   divorcing   families: an   anthropological perspective. In Bengston, Vern, and Robertson, Joan (Eds.), Grandparenthood, pp. 81-96. Beverly Hills: Sage Publications, Inc., 240p.

Anthropological view of situational and cultural factors affecting   the   voluntaristic   nature   of   grandparental relationships   with   their   children   and   grandchildren. Especially looks at how current patterns of divorce may mold and shape expected and real functions and meanings of grandparenthood.

203   Kennedy, George.   (1990).   College students' expectations of grandparent and grandchild role behaviors. Gerontologist, 30(1), 43-48.

Presents survey responses from 704 college students--the majority with at least one grandparent and some with eight or more. Perceptions of grandparent and grandchild roles were generally   positive,   showing   affection   and   respect   for grandparents. Compares this study with Robertson's study of student attitudes from 12 years ago. "Analyses of variance with gender, race, and family form as independent variables reveal differences on role attitudes among students from various backgrounds."

204   Kivnick, Helen. (1985). Grandparenthood and mental health: meaning, behavior, and satisfaction.   In Bengston,   Vern,   and   Robertson,   Joan   (Eds.), Grandparenthood, pp. 151-158. Beverly Hills: Sage Publications, Inc., 240p.

Author argues that meaning, behavior, and satisfaction are interrelated, but "it is necessary to focus on each separately in order to adequately understand grandparenting behavior." She says that the meaning of grandparenthood in her clinical sample can be seen in terms of five dimensions: role centrality, valued eldership, immortality through clan, reinvolvement   with   personal   past,   and   indulgence.   "The dimensions are of differential importance to each individual, and these relative levels of dimensional importance are likely to shift as the individual ages and life circumstances change."

205   Kivnick, Helen. (1984). Grandparents and family relations. In Quinn, William, and Hughston, George (Eds)., Independent aging: family and social systems   perspectives, pp.   35-57.   Rockville, Maryland: Aspen Systems Corporation, 300p.

Discussion   of   family   contact   patterns,   parent-child relationship, family structure, and grandparenthood--conceptual complexities, methodological complexities, role components, autonomy, and control. Grandparenthood represents a series of ongoing, longstanding bonds. As a role, it involves a unique range of behaviors and meanings. From the perspective of the intergenerational family, grandparenthood behavior, meaning, and satisfaction must be "negotiated to achieve optimal levels of overall needs satisfaction for all family members." Like other family relationships, grandparenthood is mutual. With decreasing internal control over their physical, social, and internal worlds, older family members must be able to take advantage of the special qualities inherent in grandparenthood in order to maximize their actual and perceived internal control. These controls may be crucial to the grandparents' well-being and to the long-term well-being of the entire intergenerational family.

206   Kornhaber, Arthur. (1985). Grandparenthood and the "new social contract." In Bengston, Vern, and Robertson, Joan (Eds.), Grandparenthood, pp. 159-171. Beverly Hills: Sage Publications, Inc., 240p.

Relates grandparenting to the psychiatric and social well-being of family members and of society. He suggests that grandparenthood "provides an avenue for vital emotional and social connections to occur between and within generations, lest pathology prevail." Among other topics, the author discusses grandparental role abdication and grandparental rejection of grandchildren.

207   McCready, William. (1985). Styles of grandparenting among white ethnics. In Bengston, Vern, and Robertson, Joan (Eds.), Grandparenthood, pp. 49-60. Beverly Hills: Sage Publications, Inc., 240p.

Uses national survey data on Irish, English, Poles, Scandinavians, Italians, and Germans to discuss issues related to grandparents' socialization and transmission. Author says that white ethnic grandparents "reflect somewhat different values of what is desirable in the socialization of children than other ethnics."

208   Robertson, Joan; Tice, Carol; and Loeb, Leonard. (1985). Grandparenthood: from knowledge to programs and policy. In Bengston, Vern, and Robertson, Joan (Eds.), Grandparenthood, pp. 211-224. Beverly Hills: Sage Publications, Inc., 240p.

Authors identify examples of policy and programs directed at grandparenting. Discussion of generational interdependence.

209   Roebuck, Janet. (1983). Grandma as revolutionary: elderly women and some modern patterns of social change. International Journal of Aging and Human Development, 17(4), 249-266.

Reviews the ways in which women in Western nations have coped with the problems of aging during the past century and have responded positively to great social and personal changes. "Studies of female aging may provide insights necessary to clarify our vision of the past and the future."

210   Thomas, Jeanne. (1986). **Age and sex differences in perceptions of grandparenting.** <u>Journal of Gerontology</u>, <u>41</u>(3), 417-423.

Fairly young grandparents indicated the greatest willingness to provide childrearing advice. Regardless of their grandchildren's ages, grandmothers indicated relatively high levels of satisfaction with grandparenting.

211   Troll, Lillian. (1985). **The contingencies of grandparenting.** In Bengston, Vern, and Robertson, Joan (Eds.), <u>Grandparenting</u>, pp. 135-149. Beverly Hills: Sage Publications, Inc., 240p.

Troll discusses how grandparenting is "a process that is shaped by the synchronicity of its timing with previous expectations and other life processes. . . . Its meaning and behavior are determined by complementary issues in psychological and social development, as well as by marital, filial, work, or parental status."

212   Troll, Lillian. (1983). **Grandparents: the family watchdogs.** In Brubaker, Timothy (Ed.), <u>Family relationships in later life</u>, pp. 63-76. Beverly Hills: Sage Publications, 272p.

Reviews research on recent conclusions on: "1) grandparents are not absent from central family dynamics, but often play an important part in them, even though they usually play a secondary role to parents, 2) grandparental interactions and roles are much more diverse than parental ones and vary with social class, ethnicity, and sex, as well as with individual feelings and preferences and life circumstances, 3) developmental status of grandchild and grandparent influences their interactions and their reciprocal feelings, and 4) the most important role of the grandparents may be that of maintaining the family system as a whole."

213   Wechsler, Harlan. (1985). **Judaic perspectives on grandparenthood.** In Bengston, Vern, and Robertson, Joan (Eds.), <u>Grandparenthood</u>, pp. 185-194. Beverly Hills: Sage Publications, Inc., 240p.

Considers the Judaic tradition of grandparenthood. Examines the tension between the Talmudic precept that "what is good is old" and the physical challenges of old age.

214   Wentowski, Gloria. (1985). **Older women's perceptions of great-grandmotherhood: a research note.** <u>Gerontologist</u>, <u>25</u>(6), 593-596.

Exploratory anthropological study of 19 older women's perceptions of great-grandmotherhood. Great-grandmotherhood was significant for symbolic and emotional reasons.

Films

215   **Atlantis Films. (1985). <u>Caroline</u>.**

Caroline's grandfather, a Native American, grudgingly comes to love Caroline, even though her father is white.

216   **Baker, Diane. (Producer).   (1977).   <u>Portrait of Grandpa Doc</u>.**

An artist, Greg, prepares a painting exhibit emphasizing memories of his grandfather. When the artist's mother views the exhibit, she and the artist share memories about their grief.   Grandpa Doc was able to see his grandchild's development as unique and open to limitless possibilities and not restricted to the roles to which society expects the young to conform.

217   **Blum, Michael, and Learning Corporation of America (Producers). (1977). <u>Death of a gandy dancer</u>.**

Tells of the special relationship between Ben Matthews, a former railroader, and his grandson, Josh. As Ben is dying of cancer, the significant, intergenerational relationship is tested.

218   **Center for Southern Folklore.   (1973).   <u>Greene Valley grandparents</u>.**

Documentary about the Foster Grandparents program initiated by the Greene Valley Developmental Center, where retired citizens give their days and their hearts to severely retarded children.

219   **Consiglio, Jeff (Producer).   (1985).   <u>From a shadowbox</u>.**

Describes the special relationship between an 11-year-old girl and her grandfather. The grandfather's "shadowbox" is a closet where he displays objects which have a sentimental and personal meaning in his life. Some of the objects are associated with the granddaughter's "growing up" and help her remember more vividly her childhood lessons.

220   **Daughters of St. Paul.   (1985).   <u>Grandpa O'Shea tells a story</u>.**

A grandfather tells his grandchildren an important story about judging a person's true worth.

221   **Forman, Stephen, and Desaulniers, Paul. (Producers). (1977). <u>Grandpa</u>.**

Story of Ben Forman, a Jewish immigrant who built a successful family business through hard work, tenacity, and charm. It tells the story of a man who has lived deeply and, as he is dying, reveals himself to his grandson.

222   Fruchtman, Milton. (Producer). (1974). <u>Yonder come</u>
         <u>day.</u>

At 72, Bessie Jones had extensive knowledge of folklore and
traditions associated with slavery in the South.   On St.
Simon's Island, Georgia, she participated in all aspects of
community life, enjoyed being with her grandchildren and great-
grandchildren, worshipped in her church (where her son is the
minister), and passed on to young people on the island some of
her knowledge of oral history.

223   Greenhouse Films (Producer). (1975). <u>Annie and the</u>
         <u>old one</u>.

Describes the importance of what very young family members can
learn from older family members.

224   Illumination Films (Producer).   (1978).   <u>Mandy's</u>
         <u>grandmother</u>.

Mandy receives a visit from her grandmother, who is from
England.   Both grandchild and grandmother have stereotypes.
Film depicts a growing friendship and dispelling of
stereotypes.

225   Independent Film Laboratory   (1978).   <u>The</u>
         <u>grandfather</u>.

Ralph Vandewart reminisces and reveals the way life is now that
he is old and living alone.

226   JOYCE Motion Picture Co.   (no date). <u>Supergranda</u>.

Tells the story (in American sign language and verbal
narration) about an 1,100-mile bicycle race that was won by a
man who was 66 years old and who finished 24 <u>hours</u> before the
next-closest contestant.

227   King Screen Productions (Producer).   (1970).   <u>The</u>
         <u>day grandpa died</u>.

A young boy cannot accept death within his family.   However,
during burial rites, he remembers happy times with his
grandfather, and gradually comes to accept death as a part of
his life.

228   Knapp, Daniel, and Berman, Leonard. (Producers).
         (1973). <u>Peege</u>.

Shows a family's Christmas visit to grandmother Peege's nursing
home room.   The oldest grandson reminisces and reclaims the
memories he has of growing up with Peege; his caring gestures
touch Peege.   The film provides a celebration of life and
illustrates the beauty of human relationships.

229   Learning Corporation of America and Columbia.
         (1973). <u>Granny lives in Galway</u>.

Illustrates a journey filled with adventure and suspense as two orphans find the welcoming arms of their grandmother. They then feel that their future will be secure and happy.

230   Lucerne Media. (1980). Grandma and me.

Jeffrey has to decide whether to help his grandmother or participate in basketball practice. He decides to keep his promise to his grandmother. Reactions by both grandson and grandmother show their understanding of each other's needs.

231   McDonald, Donald. (1976). My grandson Lew.

Memories of a grandson are depicted. The film is about life, death, and the joy of memories.

232   MCGH. (1963). Three grandmothers.

Lives of three grandmothers are described--one in an African village, one in Brazil, and one in rural Manitoba. Each grandmother finds, in her later years, purpose, usefulness, and wisdom.

233   National Film Board of Canada (Producer). (1977). David and Bert.

A portrait of two memorable Canadians. Bert, an 87-year-old prospector, lives alone in the remote forests of British Columbia, and still hikes through the mountains, digging and drilling for gold. David, a North Coast Indian lives surrounded by many of his 60 grandchildren, to whom he teaches the songs and dances of his traditional culture. The two men share more than 40 years of friendship, seeming agelessness, love of nature, and a rich philosophy of life.

234   National Film Board of Canada (Producer). (1976). The street.

The life of an aging grandmother, dying in the back room, becomes the focal point of family tensions, squabbles, and guilt. Her young grandson is an important part of all this. The story is told through his eyes--his recollections of fear, disgust, and childlike wonderment.

235   Paulist Productions, Media Guild. (1982). Grandpa's day.

A young girl must learn how to care for her grandfather.

236   Pennsylvania State University Audiovisual Services (Producer). (1973). Make a wish.

Features a family birthday party for a grandmother, 75, and granddaughter, 5. Audio and visual simulation enable viewers to experience the restricted sensory feedback received by an elderly person with sight and hearing loss.

237   Suburban Cablevision/Educational Consortium for Cable. (1987). Grandparents.

This educational film explores the unique relationship between a grandparent and a grandchild.

238   **Susskind, David. (Producer). (1979). Home to stay.**

Story of an adolescent girl's special relationship with her grandfather, who is becoming senile.   Sarah is sensitive, caring, nonjudgmental, and committed to helping Grandpa live his life to his fullest potential.

239   **TeleKET ICS Films (Producer).   (1975).   With just a little trust.**

An elderly, black woman marches, with pride and determination, through an urban ghetto on her way to help her daughter, a widow with three children, with "after work" chores.

240   **WGBH-TV.   (1968).   The grandfather.**

Portrays the life of a 93-year-old grandfather who has lived all of his life in Friesland, the northernmost province of the Netherlands. The grandfather, oldest person in the village, is the only one who remembers the older people.

241   **WTTW.   (no date).   Grandmother and Leslie.**

Describes a day's activities between a grandmother and her grandchild, and shows the interrelationship between the two.

Dissertations

242   **Barranti,   Chrystal.   The   maternal grandmother/grandchild relationship: relationship quality as perceived by the young-adult grandchild. Unpublished doctoral dissertation, University of Georgia, 131p.**

Exploration of relationship quality between grandmother and grandchild was based on selected dimensions of attachment feelings—present emotional closeness to maternal grandmothers, compatibility with grandmothers, perceived traits of the grandmothers, and personal significance of the relationship with the grandmothers—and attachment behaviors—overt and symbolic proximity behaviors.   The finding was that "women expressed   closer   feelings   of   attachment   to   maternal grandmothers than did men, young adult women engaged in more attachment behaviors with their maternal grandmothers than did young adult men, individuals' childhood relationship with maternal grandmothers was found to have an effect on the young adults' present attachment feelings toward their grandmothers." There was support for the concept that parents act as mediators for the grandparent/grandchild relationship.

243   **Gladstone, James. (1986). A study of grandparents whose child was separated or divorced. Unpublished doctoral dissertation, University of Toronto, number of pages not given.**

Explores relationships between grandmothers and grandchildren
following marriage breakdown in the middle generation. Several
factors, especially geographic proximity and custodial status
of the adult child, influence contact and support.

244   Guillory, Ann. (1983). **The relationship of contact
        with grandparents and ethnic background to
        adolescents' attitudes toward older persons.**
        Unpublished doctoral dissertation, Columbia
        University Teachers' College, 144p.

Examination of the relationship between adolescents' attitudes
toward older persons and adolescents' contact with older
persons, particularly the grandparent known best. Attitudes
toward older persons and attitudes toward the grandparent known
best were not similar, although they were related. Social
contact with older persons was a factor in adolescents'
attitudes toward older people. Ethnic background and
grandparent contact were important in adolescents' attitudes
toward their grandparent known best.

245   Joyce, Rosemary. (1980). **A woman's place: the
        life history of a rural Ohio grandmother.**
        Unpublished doctoral dissertation, The Ohio State
        University, 273p.

Combines anthropological, historical, and folkloristic
techniques to depict the life history of one woman. The
"common-woman biography focuses on the generational and
residential continuity of her life: five generations of her
and her husband's family in the same three-mile radius, with
focus on the traditional overlay of their ongoing life
patterns."

246   Lang, Martha. (1980). **An exploratory study of
        children's perceptions of grandparent-grandchild
        relationships.** Unpublished doctoral dissertation,
        Columbia University Teachers' College, 201p.

This study determined that "children's attitudes toward their
grandparents were favorable, that the majority of the children
stated that they needed their grandparents, and that the
parents' perceptions of the grandparent-grandchild relationship
agreed with the child's."

247   McCord, William. (1981). **"Giving them love": a
        study of foster grandparents at institutions and
        community schools.** Unpublished doctoral
        dissertation, Syracuse University, 158p.

This qualitative study of the Foster Grandparents program
examines grandparents' own perceptions of their duties and work
situations. Foster grandparent duties and perspectives vary
from place to place. Foster grandparent duties and attitudes
are shaped by the setting in which they work and the work
priorities of direct service staff. Foster grandparents in
institutions were found to be more likely to experience
conflict with staff, carry out meaningless, boring duties, and
experience dissatisfaction with their work situation than were

their counterparts in smaller community schools.   Conclusion
that "solutions" such as the Foster Grandparents Program "often
camouflage the underlying issues of prejudice and stereotypes
which confront both elderly people and disabled children in our
society."

248   Shea, Loretta.   (1987).   <u>Grandparent-adolescent
         relationships as mediated by lineage and gender</u>.
         Unpublished   doctoral   dissertation,   Virginia
         Polytechnic Institute and State University, 131p.

Exploration of the eight dyadic grandparent-grandchild
relationships.   Investigation of the relationship between
lineage and gender and the frequency and quality of
grandparent-adolescent contact.   The broad picture was of
frequent, dynamic, intergenerational involvement.

249   Sonnek, Ida. (1983). <u>The maternal grandmother role
         in families with young handicapped children</u>.
         Unpublished   doctoral   dissertation,   Indiana
         University, 160p.

The role of grandparents may take on additional significance,
when a family is faced with crises.   Emphasized in this
study is the maternal grandmother role in families with a
handicapped child between 0 and three years of age.   Grounded
theory methodology was used.   "Four categories describe the
maternal grandmother role as a set of activities defined by a
set of circumstances that create a need for grandmothering
activities; a set of parameters which determine the when, why,
and how for grandmothering activities; and a set of factors
which influenced the continual involvement of grandmothers in
grandmothering activities in their daughters' families."

250   Swihart, Judson.   (1985).   <u>Older grandparents'
         perception of generativity in the grandparent-
         grandchildren relationship</u>.   Unpublished doctoral
         dissertation, Kansas State University, 154p.

Study to determine if the developmental task of generativity,
defined by Erikson as a mid-life task, is expressed in the
grandparent-grandchild relationship.   Explores whether or not
grandparents indicated a plan for generativity, whether they
have a quality of relationship that would allow generativity to
occur, and whether they felt successful in fulfilling
generativity.

6

Adult Children

Books

251   Baruch, Grace; Barnett, Rosalind; and Rivers, Caryl.
         (1983). **Life prints: new patterns of love and work**
         for today's women. New York: New American Library,
         291p.

Features a chapter on mothers and daughters. Women often see
their older mothers as role models for their own aging process.
The ways mothers age seem to have a strong impact on the
daughters.

252   Gross, Zenith. (1985). **And you thought it was all**
         over!: mothers and their adult children. New York:
         St. Martin's/Marek, 308p.

Description of the mothering period _after_ children have left
home for school, work, or marriage. Report of a study of
almost 500 women (mothers of over 1,000 children). Discusses
money matters, adult sibling relationships, guilt feelings,
family gatherings, crisis mothering, "the crowded empty nest,"
and the father's role in parenting with the mother.

253   Wright, Fay.   (1986).   **Left to care alone**.
         Brookfield, Vermont: Gower Publishing Company,
         205p.

Family members often are the principal sources of support for
infirm, elderly people living in the community. Reported
herein is that most parents were so disabled that without
carers' support they would find it virtually impossible to
continue living alone at home. Findings were that single
caregivers found a caring role difficult to sustain, caring had
more effect on the employment of the daughter than on the
employment of the son, neither friends nor volunteers gave
significant support, there is sparse participation by the wider
community in the caring process, social workers were the least
evident of caring professionals, meals on wheels and home help
service were the most widely used services, there was absence
of appropriate support for individuals who had given up outside

employment because of their parents' need for attention, there was a loss of personal freedom, and day care was not very evident.

Articles/chapters

254   Aldous, Joan, and others.   (1985).   The understanding heart: aging parents and their favorite children. Child Development, 56(2), 303-316.

In this article, the authors compare the characteristics of adult children who provide comfort and sympathy and serve as confidants with those whom parents perceive as disappointing. Analysis of interview information from 117 couples whose children had left home.

255   Bankoff, Elizabeth. (1986). Aged parents and their widowed daughters: a support relationship.   In Troll, Lillian (Ed.), Family issues in current gerontology, pp. 64-74.   New York: Springer Publishing Company, 382p.

Investigates the role of social support from parents, as well as from other family members, friends, and neighbors in improving the psychological well-being of recent and still grieving widows. Findings indicated that the source of support makes a significant difference with regard to how effective the help is for these widows. Elderly parents appear to play an important supportive role for their widowed daughters. Parents were the single most important source of support gained from the informal social network. The help of no other network associates seemed to be sufficient. Demonstrates the useful support role which aged parents can play for their adult children.

256   Borgatta, Edgar. (1987). Filial responsibility. In Maddox, George (Ed.), The encyclopedia of aging, p. 256. New York: Springer Publishing Company, 890p.

Discussion of who should take care of older persons as they become disabled and unable to care for themselves.

257   Cicirelli, Victor. (1983). A comparison of helping behavior to elderly parents of adult children with intact and disrupted marriages. Gerontologist, 23(6), 619-625.

Compares the help of 141 adult children with disrupted marriages with that of 164 adult children with intact marriages. Little difference was found in the amount of help given by divorced, widowed, and remarried subgroups. Children with disrupted marriages gave significantly less total help than children with intact marriages.

258   Cicirelli, Victor. (1983). Adult children and their elderly parents. In Brubaker, Timothy (Ed.),

Family relationships in later life, pp. 31-46.
Beverly Hills: Sage Publications, 272p.

Consideration of the interpersonal relationship between adult
children and their elderly parents and the helping relationship
between them.   Looks, also, at some of the problem areas in
helping older parents, such as communication, absence of adult
children, and the stresses of caregiving.

259   Climo, Jacob.   (1988).   Visits of distant-living
         adult children and elderly parents.   Journal of
         Aging Studies, 2(1), 57-69.

Describes the visiting patterns of 40 adult children and their
elderly parents who live 200 miles or more from one another.
Factors influencing the visiting patterns and satisfaction with
visits include sociodemographic variables, extent of distance,
parents' health status, and situational factors.

260   Cooney, Teresa.   (1989).   Co-residence with adult
         children: a comparison of divorced and widowed
         women. Gerontologist, 29(6), 779-784.

Compares patterns of co-residence with adult offspring for
divorcees and widows, aged 40 and over, using 1985 Current
Population Survey data.   "Co-residence with offspring is most
likely for recent widows in midlife and recent divorcees in
later life. Older recent divorcees are less likely than recent
widows to be household heads   in these living situations.
Finally, daughters appear especially important in the co-
resident situation of divorcees."

261   Coward, Ray, and Dwyer, Jeffrey.   (1990).   The
         association of gender, sibling network composition,
         and patterns of parent care by adult children.
         Research on Aging, 12(2), 158-181.

Explores the degree to which separating adult children by the
composition of their sibling network provides insight into the
association between gender and patterns of parent-care.
"Within all sibling network categories, daughters were more
likely than sons to be providing care to an impaired parent."

262   Dean, Alfred; Kolody, Bohdan; Wood, Patricia; and
         Ensel, Walter. (1989). Measuring the communication
         of social support from adult children.   Journal of
         Gerontology, 44(2), S71-S79.

Applies social support scales tapping the quality and content
of interactions of elderly persons with their adult children.
Factor analyses show one instrumental and three expressive
dimensions of support: caring and concern, social integration,
and love and affection.   "Where potential sources of support
exist, expectations for support exist."

263   Dobson, Judith, and Dobson, Russell.   (1985).   The
         sandwich generation: dealing with aging parents.
         Journal of Counseling and Development, 63(9), 572-
         574.

Discusses a workshop emphasizing providing middle-aged adults "with information and opportunities to process their attitudes, emotions, and the realities of exchanging roles with aging parents."

264   Finley, Nancy; Roberts, M. Diane; and Banahan, Benjamin. (1988). Motivators and inhibitors of attitudes of filial obligation toward aging parents. Gerontologist, 28(1), 73-78.

Presents interviews with 667 adult children with elderly parents to investigate motivators and inhibitors of attitudes of filial obligation. Degree of obligation was explained by structural and demographic factors such as distance and role conflict. "Associations of predictor variables with filial obligation varied by parent type and gender of adult child."

265   Gold, Deborah. (1989). Sibling relationships in old age: a typology. International Journal of Aging and Human Development, 28(1), 37-51.

Examination of the different kinds of relationships that exist between siblings in old age and the ways in which each type meets or ignores the social and psychological needs of older people. Five types of sibling relationships were found in the data collected in open-ended, exploratory interviews with 30 men and 30 women aged 65 and over who had at least one living sibling each. Each of the types indicates a discrete pattern of instrumental support, emotional support, and contact, and different degrees of closeness, envy, resentment, approval, and involvement. There is a suggestion of gender differences in sibling interactions based on the gender composition of the sibling dyad, rather than on the gender of the respondent.

266   Hagestad, Gunhild. Parenting. (1987). In Maddox, George (Ed.), The encyclopedia of aging, pp. 511-512. New York: Springer Publishing Company, 890p.

Discusses the meaning of parenthood in later life for the parent and the child. There are conflicting findings on the degree and type of involvement most promoting of the well-being of older persons. Some research indicates that rates of contact with children are related to morale and well-being, while other studies show that the variables are negatively related. Parenting seems to have different meanings for men and for women, and little is known about parenting over time.

267   Hanson, Sandra, and Sauer, William. (1985). Children and their elderly parents. In Sauer, William, and Coward, Ray (Eds.), Social support networks and the care of the elderly, pp. 41-66. New York: Springer Publishing Company, 284p.

Examination of the kinship network of children and their elderly parents. For most families, this relationship is the "critical core" of the extended kinship network; however, these kinship ties may vary considerably across groups.

268   Hanson, Sandra; Sauer, William; and Seelbach, Wayne.
          (1983).   Racial and cohort variations in filial
          responsibility norms.   Gerontologist, 23(6), 626-
          631.

Examines whether racial differences exist in the endorsement of
five filial responsibility norms and the extent to which age
and cohort effects influence these patterns. Finding was that
there was stronger support for filial norms among the white
respondents than for blacks. There was an inverse association
between age and endorsement of the norms.

269   Hatch, Ruth, and Franken, Mary.   (1984).   Concerns
          of children with parents in nursing homes. Journal
          of Gerontological Social Work, 7(3), 19-30.

One hundred and six children were questioned about their
perception of factors related to the placement of their parents
in nursing homes.

270   Houser, Betsy, and Berkman, Sherry.   (1984). Aging
          parent/mature child relationships.   Journal of
          Marriage and the Family, 46(2), 295-299.

Describes interviews with 400 elderly women to identify factors
contributing to the mother's satisfaction with filial
relationships.   Finding was that satisfaction with filial
relationships was related primarily to satisfaction with
quality of contact with children and secondarily to children's
potential filial behavior and mother's satisfaction with
quantity of contact with children.

271   Kivett, Vira, and Atkinson, Maxine. (1986). Filial
          expectations, association, and helping as a function
          of number of children among older rural-transitional
          parents.   In Troll, Lillian (Ed.), Family issues in
          current gerontology, pp.   204-213.   New York:
          Springer Publishing Company, 382p.

Comparison of older parents about filial expectations and
frequency of parent-child association and assistance according
to the number of children. Considers the differential effects
of factors which affect expectations and interaction.   The
results indicated that the number of children is related to how
recently which older parents living in a rural-transitional
area have seen a child, how much assistance the parents
receive, and factors influencing their interaction with
children. However, the amount of assistance expected by older
parents appears not to be related to the number of offspring.
In spite of the rural-transitional nature of the area studied,
older adults and children with most contact had remained
residentially stable.

272   Mercier, Joyce; Paulson, Lon; and Morris, Earl.
          (1989). Proximity as a medidating influence on the
          perceived aging parent-adult child relationship.
          Gerontologist, 29(6), 785-791.

Examines whether proximity has a mediating influence on the quality of the relationship between aging parents and adult children. Findings indicate no difference in quality of relationships between groups of parents whose children live near them and those whose children live more than 60 miles away. "Significant predictors of the relationships for the proximate group were personal sense of control and education, and, for the distant group, sex of the child and number of living children. The findings support the contention that the modified extended family can maintain psychological closeness, regardless of physical distance."

273   Miller, Sheila. (1982). Aging parents and their middle-aged children. Educational Horizons, 60(4), 179-183.

Reports that current research does not support the negative stereotypes reinforced by the media which encourage the belief that Americans abuse and neglect their aging parents. Author suggests that public education about aging and the relationships among older adults and their children is needed.

274   Myers, Jane. (1988). The mid/late life generation gap: adult children with aging parents. Journal of Counseling and Development, 66(7), 331-335.

Discussion of psychosocial and personal needs and concerns of adult children and aging parents which may create conflicts. Author presents intervention strategies and considerations for counselors.

275   Remnet, Valerie. (1987). How adult children respond to role transitions in the lives of their aging parents. Educational Gerontology, 13(4), 341-355.

Describes ways in which adult children responded to role transitions in the lives of their aging parents and the preferences of the adult children for educational activities that would enhance their abilities to respond to future parental transitions. "Adult children identified the need for information in communication skills, normal and abnormal aging, and available community resources."

276   Scott, Jean, and Roberto, Karen. (1984). Older rural parents and their children. In Quinn, William, and Hughston, George (Eds.), Independent aging: family and social systems perspectives, pp. 182-193. Rockville, Maryland: Aspen Systems Corporation, 300p.

Presents an empirical investigation of support and contact patterns in rural aging families. The study indicates extensive mutual aid in two generations--adult children and their parents. Describes and compares the variability in aging rural families and the type of intergenerational involvement which they have.

277   Seelbach, Wayne. (1984). Filial responsibility and
           the care of aging family members.   In Quinn,
           William, and Hughston, George (Eds.), Independent
           aging: family and social systems perspectives, pp.
           92-105.   Rockville, Maryland: Aspen Systems
           Corporation, 300p.

Author predicts that the "concept of filial responsibility will
become even more crucial in family involvement of the aged as
governmental and other formal support mechanisms for the
elderly are reduced to accommodate more pressing economic
burdens."   Author says children define this relationship
structure by coordinating the family network--managing
resources, using the human support network, and connecting with
interventionists.

278   Stoller, Eleanor.   (1990).   Males as helpers: the
           role   of   sons,   relatives,   and   friends.
           Gerontologist, 30(2), 228-235.

Describes the contributions of men other than husbands who
provide assistance to a sample of community-based elderly
persons living in northeastern New York.   Data from personal
interviews with elders and their primary helpers at two points
in time.   Men drop out of the helper role when caregiving
demands increase. Except for husbands, over time the stability
in helpers is greater for sons than for other categories of
male helpers.

Films

279   Aster   Productions.   (1984).   Decisions   of   a
           lifetime.

In this film, adult children discuss the problems and benefits
of caring for their aged parents who are unable to live on
their own because of physical and/or mental conditions.
Different caregivers' perspectives are provided on care at home
and in nursing facilities.

280   Brooks, Hildy (Producer).   (1980).   Bloomers.

A daughter confronts an unresolved relationship with her mother
and acknowledges how important it is to sustain her
relationship with her husband.

281   Churches TV and Radio Centre in Great Britain
           (Producer).   (1971).   Robert (handle with care
           series).

Robert is an employed, 29-year-old male with an invalid mother
and an anxious fiancee.   Robert feels very obligated to care
for his mother, and has not told her of his romance. However,
his fiancee's ultimatum and the offer of a job promotion are
forcing him to make a painful decision.

282   Columbia (Producer).   (1970).   When parents grow
           old.

Considers the adult children's responsibility to aging parents and society's treatment of the elderly. Questions addressed include: What is it like to grow old in a youth-oriented society? How can we understand and accept aging as a part of the human condition? What are the limits of obligation and even compassion of middle-aged children for their aging parents?

283   Media. (1980). Aging parents.

Describes how parents, as they age, end up needing their children's help.

284   Quality Productions (Producer). (no date). Divided horsecloth (this is Charles Laughton).

Presents a thirteenth-century tale of a father who gives all his wealth to his son as part of a marriage contract with a young lady. The father expects, therefore, to live with his son and daughter-in-law in comfort for the rest of his life. However, the father is not welcomed and, finally, is ordered to leave, with only an old horse blanket to keep himself warm. The grandson gives his grandfather the blanket, tearing it in half, and explains to his father, "I'm saving the other half for you when you are old." When the child has made that point, the father(son) reconsiders his actions, and welcomes the grandfather back into the home.

Documents

285   Schorr, Alvin. (1980). "...thy father and thy mother...": a second look at filial responsibility and family policy. Washington, D.C.: U.S. Department of Health and Human Services, Social Security Administration, 62p.

Focus on filial responsibility--the responsibility for parents by children. Includes discussion of duties required by law, by custom, or by personal attitude.

Dissertations

286   Anderson, Roxanne. (1982). Mothers and daughters: their adult relationship. Unpublished doctoral dissertation, University of Minnesota, 141p.

Focus on emotional differences between mothers and daughters, ego development comparisons, and types of relationships. There is evidence of continued importance for the mother-daughter relationship into adulthood, for women at all ego levels.

287   Ferrante-Wallace, Joan. (1984). A structural analysis of contact patterns among adult siblings. Unpublished doctoral dissertation, University of Cincinnati, 140p.

Study of sibling relations from a structural frame of reference. Considers the role of the family and larger societal factors in influencing the structure of adult sibling contact. Presents a model explaining the structure of such contact. Evaluates the model's predictive usefulness.

288   Hawkins, Barbara. (1984). **Older people and their children: interaction and emotional well-being.** Unpublished doctoral dissertation, Washington State University, 81p.

Uses exchange theory perspective to consider the correlation between morale of the elderly and the frequency with which they have contact with their adult children. Hypothesizes that "elderly with few resources and no alternative reward sources would be more dependent on their children for rewards than those elderly with relatively more resources and alternatives, and that they would be more likely to experience inequity in their relationships with their children, thereby producing low morale. Conversely, high morale would be associated with elderly who have more resources and alternatives and who would be less likely to perceive inequity in their relationships with their children."

289   Jache, Ann. (1986). **The adult children of elderly widows: the consequences of being part of a support network for adult children's socialization for their own old age.** Unpublished doctoral dissertation, University of Notre Dame, 186p.

Examination of the consequences of various types of involvement with their widowed mothers for adult children's socialization for old age. The most significantly related variable to thinking about old and actual preparation for old age is the confidant relationship between parent and child.

290   Krach, Margaret. (1985). **Rural adults' perceptions of filial responsibility for and affectional bonds with their aged parents.** Unpublished doctoral dissertation, The Ohio State University, 148p.

Investigates whether perceived levels of filial responsibility of rural, adult children for their aged parents is significantly related to their perceived levels of affection and the extent to which gender and financial strain of adult children, as well as other demographic variables, influenced these relationships. Finding was that perceived levels of filial responsibility of rural, adult children for their aged parents are significantly related to perceived levels of affection for their parents. "Both perceived levels of filial responsibility and perceived levels of affection for aged parents were related to the gender of the adult children, although both responsibility and affection were lower for females than for males."

291   Learner, Richard. (1984). **Sex linkages and older parent-adult child interactions: effects on social activities, mutual assistance, and expectations for filial support.** Unpublished doctoral dissertation,

The University of North Carolina at Greensboro, 156p.

Investigation of the patterns of social interaction between older parents and their adult children. Examination of the effects of sex of parent, type of sex linkage (e.g., mother-daughter), and other variables on measures of social activity, help received from children, help given to children, and parental expectations for filial responsibility. The finding was that "there was no difference between fathers and mothers on measures of social activity, help given, and expectations for filial support; mothers received help more often; the mother-daughter linkage scores were not significantly higher than all other linkages on the dependent measures; mothers who had both sons and daughters were more likely to report a daughter to be most often in contact, while fathers were equally likely to report on sons and daughters; sons and daughters were comparable in proximity to parents and contact them with similar frequency; geographic proximity and marital status of the parent were significant contextual variables."

292   Nkongho, Ngozi. (1983). **The relationship between content, completeness of self-disclosure to an adult child, a friend, and well-being in the elderly.** Unpublished   doctoral   dissertation,   New   York University, 111p.

Investigation of relationship between content and completeness of disclosure to an adult child, a friend, and well-being in the elderly. Hypothesizes that people grow and become human only in relationship with other people and that the need for contact with other people is continuous throughout life. Hypothesizes that elderly persons who disclose more completely to an adult child and a friend will have a greater sense of well-being than those who disclose less completely.

293   Scharlach, Andrew. (1985). **Filial relationships among women and their elderly mothers**. Unpublished doctoral dissertation, Stanford University, 137p.

Examines the idea that the strain experienced by an adult daughter may interfere with her relationship with her aging mother and have a potentially harmful impact on the mother. Findings   support   the   hypothesis   that   "mother-daughter relationships in later life can be improved when daughters are helped to resolve potentially conflictual personal expectations regarding their responsibilities to their aging mothers."

294   Stueve, Charlotte. (1985). **What's to be done about mom and dad?** Unpublished doctoral dissertation, University of California, Berkeley, 239p.

Investigates adult daughters' interactions with elderly parents and how the daughters respond when their parents need help. Also   considers   the   daughters'   conceptions   of   filial responsibilities and the types of problems they encounter when their parents grow old. "Daughters were more attentive when they lived near their parents and when their parents were in poor health."

295   Tortorici, Joseph.   (1983).   **The adult brother role
         in the family, its nature and meaning: a case study
         approach**.   Unpublished   doctoral   dissertation,
         Michigan State University, 341p.

Examination of the nature, meaning, function, and expectations
of the brother role through a case study of five families.
Identifies the effects of the brother role on extra-familial
relationships with men and women during adulthood.   Explores
individual perspectives on the extra-familial social meaning of
the term "brother."   Concludes that the "fundamental nature of
the adult brother role [is] that 'he be there when needed' in
whatever way he is needed, physical or emotional."   The primary
expectation in terms of behavior is related to family survival.
The   qualities   most   often   ascribed   to   brothers   were
"availability, dependability, and trustworthiness."

7

Intergenerational Relationships

Books

296   Cohler, Bertram, and Grunebaum, Henry (with the assistance of Donna Robbins) (1981). <u>Mothers, grandmothers, and daughters: personality and childcare in three-generation families</u>. New York: John Wiley & Sons, 456p.

Uses interviews, observations of families, and personality measures to consider relationships between young adults and their middle-aged or older mothers. A quantitative study of the modified, extended family focusing on the psychological significance of contact and support of family members across generations for the continued adult development of these family members.

297   Kingson, Eric; Hirshorn, Barbara; and Cornman, John. (1986). <u>Ties that bind: the interdependence of generations</u>. Cabin John, Maryland: Seven Locks Press, 195p.

How society should approach the challenges posed by an aging population. Includes a chapter on "The Common Stake in Family Care-Giving," pp. 51-68.

Articles/chapters

298   Back, Kurt. (1987). Generation. In Maddox, George (Editor in Chief), <u>The encyclopedia of aging</u>, pp. 272-273. New York: Springer Publishing Company, 890p.

Defines generation. Discusses biological generations, lineage, stepwise sequences, relation of familial model to the general macrosocial model.

299   Bartz, Karen. (1984). Reach out to . . . senior citizens and grandparents. <u>PTA Today</u>, <u>10</u>(1), 18-19.

Describes a Camp Fire, Inc., program offering "friendship across the ages" that brings adults and children together. The adults share knowledge and skills, and the young people benefit from having an adult listen to them.

300   Browne, Colette, and Onzuka-Anderson, Roberta. (1985). Reflections of three generations. In Browne, Colette, and Onzuka-Anderson, Roberta (Eds.), Aging parents: a practical guide to eldercare, pp. 239-250. Honolulu: University of Hawaii Press, 278p.

Presents perspectives of three generations of a caregiving family about their new interdependence. Discusses helping a loved one who is lonely and in need, along with mutual exchange. The decision to care for a frail, aging relative is a decision involving the entire family--elder, spouse, children, other siblings. Interdependence is more often a characteristic of caring families than is dependence.

301   Butler, Robert. (1981). Overview on aging: some biomedical, social, and behavioral perspectives. In Fogel, Robert; Hatfield, Elaine; Kiesler, Sara; and Shanas, Ethel (Eds.), Aging, stability, and change in the family, pp. 1-8. New York: Academic Press, 341p.

"The extended multigenerational family of this century offers a new kind of opportunity for care and support." Given the changing age structure of the United States population, "we must look to the implications [of this changing age structure] on problems in the areas of labor, housing, and health care. . . . In order to enhance the quality of life of older people, we must also develop the knowledge to treat and prevent the diseases that currently interfere with normal, healthy aging." Butler advises solving the problems of old age by applying the latest information available from the biological sciences, clinical medicine, and studies of personal and social behavior.

302   Cheal, David. (1983). Intergenerational family transfers. (1983). Journal of Marriage and the Family, 45(4), 805-813.

Discusses the nature of family resource redistribution throughout the life cycle. Presents a linear redistribution principle and the availability of transaction capacities as a modifying principle.

303   Fogler, Janet. (1989). An intergenerational women's group. Gerontologist, 29(2), 268-271.

Describes a model for an intergenerational women's group to provide social support and interchange of ideas between women of different generations.

304   Furstenberg, Jr., Frank. (1981). Remarriage. In Fogel, Robert; Hatfield, Elaine; Kiesler, Sara; and Shanas, Ethel (Eds.), Aging, stability and change in

the family, pp. 115-142. New York: Academic Press, 341p.

Explores "implications of emerging changes in the kinship system that have resulted from an unprecedented increase in the incidence of divorce and remarriage." Looks at "whether and how patterns of divorce and remarriage are likely to restructure our notions of kinship and the functioning of the kinship system in American society." The author stresses the possibility for adaptation within the American kinship system, saying that "remarriage presents possibilities as well as merely posing problems for family members."

305   Gelfand, Donald. (1989). Immigration, aging, and intergenerational relationships. Gerontologist, 29(3), 366-372.

Examines intergenerational relationships and roles of older Salvadorans who have come to the U.S. in their later years. There were many similarities between these parents' roles in El Salvador and in the U.S., but fewer were employed and more had taken on childcare responsibilities. "Although their children had a strong sense of filial obligation, the parents asked for little concrete assistance from the children."

306   Hagestad, Gunhild. (1981). Problems and promises in the social psychology of intergenerational relations. In Fogel, Robert; Hatfield, Elaine; Kiesler, Sara; and Shanas, Ethel (Eds.), Aging, stability, and change in the family, pp. 11-46. New York: Academic Press, 341p.

Considers some of the recent demographic and cultural changes which have created a new context for intergenerational ties. Author argues that intergenerational relations must be approached "on a social-psychological level in order to pursue questions that cannot be answered on an aggregate level, through the analysis of life-course patterns of birth cohorts or through census information on households." Families are cultural units which bring together members of different cohorts and which create life patterns, crises, and resources. The author predicts that a social psychology of intergenerational bonds promises new insights into how individual lives are shaped, mediation of social change, and the maintaining of long-term primary ties.

307   Kauffman, Janice, and Ames, Barbara. (1983). Care of aging family members. Journal of Home Economics, 75(1), 45-46.

Describes aspects of a home economics curriculum for the care of aging family members, including one focus for junior and senior high school students and another for adult students.

308   Koh, James, and Bell, William. (1987). Korean elders in the United States: intergenerational relations and living arrangements. Gerontologist, 27(1), 66-71.

Presents results of interviews with 151 Korean elders living in the New York City area regarding their living arrangements, service needs, and orientation to filial and formal support systems. Compares these data with available data on elders in South Korea. Findings were that changes have occurred in intergenerational relations and living arrangements for older Koreans in the United States.

309   Korbin, Jill; Anetzberger, Georgia; and Eckert, J. (1989). Elder abuse and child abuse: a consideration of similarities and differences in intergenerational family violence. Journal of Elder Abuse and Neglect, 1(4), 1-14.

Describes similarities between elder abuse and child abuse, but authors suggest that differences argue against linking these two problems. The authors suggest dimensions relevant to comparing intergenerational physical abuse of elder parents and young children.

310   Lambert, Donna; Dellmann-Jenkins, Mary; and Fruit, Dorothy. (1990). Planning for contact between the generations: an effective approach. Gerontologist, 30(4), 553-556.

Describes a program for preschoolers and elders designed to promote three types of prosocial behavior in the children: sharing, cooperating, and helping. Used five types of contact: with natural grandparents in the preschool, regular elderly volunteers in the preschool, competent elderly visitors who shared their expertise, contact with less able elders through regular visits to a nursing home, and classroom activities providing positive and realistic information about older people and aging. The program resulted in increased prosocial behaviors in the children.

311   Lee, Gary. (1987). Aging and intergenerational relations. Journal of Family Issues, 8(4), 448-451.

Discusses the rapid aging of the American population and the changing age structure of society, as well as the needs of older adults, the role of the family in providing support to older members, and issues of intergenerational relations.

312   Markides, Kyriakos; Costley, Delia; and Rodriguez, Linda. (1981). Perceptions of intergenerational relations and psychological well-being among elderly Mexican-Americans: a causal model. International Journal of Aging and Human Development, 13(1), 43-52.

Sample of 98 Mexican-Americans aged 60 or over. Adding intergenerational solidarity to health, socioeconomic status, and activity contributed significantly in explaining life satisfaction, but did not play a significant intervening role, except between health and life satisfaction.

313   **Mindel, Charles. (1986). Multigenerational family households: recent trends and implications for the future. In Troll, Lillian (Ed.), Family issues in current gerontology, pp. 269-283. New York: Springer Publishing Company, 382p.**

Discusses living arrangements of elderly individuals, in particular those elderly who share households with kin other than their spouse. Examines and challenges some current beliefs regarding relationships of elderly and their families. Uses data from U.S. Bureau of the Census to examine trends in the living arrangements of elderly in the twentieth century. Suggests policy recommendations.

314   **Morgan, Leslie. (1983). Intergenerational financial support: retirement-age males, 1971-1975. Gerontologist, 23(2), 160-166.**

Examines intergenerational financial support for married males at retirement age. Uses data from the Longitudinal Retirement History Study. Findings show a substantial number of these men remain in the middle generation. Many provide financial aid to children, fewer to aged parents, and still fewer to both.

315   **Qureshi, Hazel. (1986). Responses to dependency: reciprocity, affect and power in family relationships. In Phillipson, Chris; Bernard, Miriam; and Strang, Patricia (Eds.), Dependency and interdependency in old age: theoretical perspectives and policy alternatives, pp. 167-179. London: Croom Helm, 371p.**

Reports carers' views of responses to dependency by the elderly people to whom they gave assistance and factors which influenced the carers to provide the help. "When carers became convinced that their parents' demands were not based on physical disability, such experiences could be damaging to the relationships. No matter what the past relationship or carer's current feelings, other possible helpers (formal or informal sources) all made prima facie assumptions that the relatives were the first choice of people to help them."

316   **Rasinski, Timothy. (1988). Bridging the gap: intergenerational collaboration. (1988). Educational Forum, 53(1), 77-88.**

Describes intergenerational learning programs that allow young students to interact with senior citizens for mutual benefits. Discusses a six-week program in Ohio in which 30 eighth-grade students spent time with residents of an area retirement home and worked with them on a one-to-one basis.

317   **Schmall, Vicki, and Stiehl, Ruth. (1988). Teaching about family relationships and decision making in later life. Illinois Teacher of Home Economics, 31(3), 110-112.**

Discussion of the need for teaching about how families deal with the problems of aging as part of the home economics curriculum. Describes a series of slide-tape programs and a game that are potential classroom resources on this topic.

318   **Sundstrom, Gerdt.   (1986).   Intergenerational mobility and the relationship between adults and their aging parents in Sweden.   Gerontologist, 26(4), 367-371.**

In this study of adults and their aging parents in Sweden, geographic distance and contacts between adults and their aging parents vary by social class and by social mobility of the offspring. Middle class adults live further from their parents and have less contact with them. For those who live near their parents, degree of contact is quite similar between social classes.

319   **Wattenberg, Esther.   (1986).   The fate of baby boomers and their children. Social Work, 31(1), 20-28.**

As the "baby boomer" generation ages, family compositions and living arrangements are being reshaped.   Social workers are needing to rethink their practice framework for families and children.   Crucial issues and mandates for social work are identified.

Films

320   **AIA. (1973). To be growing older.**

Interviews with young and old persons. Older people speak of loneliness, solitude, financial worries, housing, physical and mental health, boredom, activities, and hobbies.

321   **Callner Film Productions (Producer).   (1980).   The antique collector.**

Film focuses on Grandma, owner of an antique shop; a young boy, Tom, who is "learning the trade"; and a mysterious stranger who sees Grandma as an object to collect.   The antique collector believes that old people are of such great value that they are worth collecting--even more than the rare and precious objects most collectors prize.   He treats old people as if they were the most precious commodities in the world, takes care of all their physical needs, and his "antiques" have a large, comfortable home to live in, a center for social interaction among their peers.

322   **Churchill Films (Distributor). (1979). The hundred penny box.**

Centers on the relationship between a 100-year-old black woman and a young boy. The box represents the promise of her youth and her ties to the past. Michael's mother wants to dispose of Aunt Dew's box. Emphasizes the beauty and timelessness of relationships.

323   **Corinth. (1980). The female line.**

Documents three generations of women in one family--Mary Parkman Peabody, activist; Marietta Tree, businesswoman and former United Nations ambassador; and Frances Fitzgerald, Pulitzer Prize-winning author. Story of the "passing of the torch" from generation to generation.

324   **Grana, Saverio, and Fortier, Robert. (Producers). (1984). The last right.**

Shows the devastating effects of senility on a family. A young couple have chosen to care for his grandfather, who has an advanced stage of arteriosclerosis. The film documents how a family struggles to respect an old person's right to decide his own fate.

325   **Kino Productions (Producer). (1980). Clare's wish.**

Shows attempts to resolve grief over the drowning death of a younger son two years earlier.

326   **Luther Metke at 94. (1978).**

At 94, Luther Metke is a man of action who wants to learn, to grow, and to change. He is still helping others--e.g., a young couple who want to build a cabin.

327   **Mareth, Paul (Producer). (1974). Two daughters.**

After the death of her young daughter, a woman returns to their former apartment in Stockholm. It is now deserted, and she is overwhelmed by memories of her daughter's life, illness, and death and by memories of her own mother.

328   **Michigan State University. (1983). The aging family.**

Interview with three generations of one family.

329   **Moctesuma Esparza Productions. (1977). Agueda Martinez: our people, our country.**

Explores the history and values of Agueda Martinez, a 77-year-old woman of Navajo Mexican descent. Her roots are in the traditions of her ancestors and in the land that supports her life as a farmer and weaver. Her life reflects the rhythms of nature, and a special harmony with herself and her surroundings.

330   **A modern Egyptian family.**

The film shows a family party on grandfather Mahmoud Allam's 78th birthday. Through the eyes of the children and grandchildren, the viewer sees some of the changes that have taken place in Egypt during his lifetime.

331   **Rothschild, Amalie (Producer). (1974). Nana, mom, and me.**

Provocative portrait of three generations of women and the different motivating influences, philosophies, and rivalries that shape their interactions with one another.

332   Soto, Richard. (Producer). (1977). La familia: a celebration.

The film shows Juan and Delores Venegas celebrating their sixtieth wedding anniversary with 10 children, 55 grandchildren, 15 great-grandchildren, and over 200 in-laws and friends. Captured are the warmth and love of an extended family. Examines changing roles within the Hispanic social structure.

333   WETZ-TV (Producer). (1975). Tres mujeres.

In this film, three generations of Puerto Rican women in New York speak about their conflicts, the characteristics in one another which they value, and how they view themselves and each other as mothers, daughters, and women. The focus is on the mother-daughter relationship and how it touches all women deeply.

334   WGBH-TV (Producer). (1976). Dying.

An intensely religious man who lives according to his individual values is featured in this film. His family patiently and with love takes care of him in his home. He is able to express his philosophy of life as he is dying. He demonstrates that his ministry to others is completed by his acceptance of his death and his inspiration of others to live more fully. Other vignettes feature a 44-year-old with brain cancer, cared for by her mother, who exhibits courage and acceptance; and a middle-aged couple who deny the melanoma of the husband and display stoicism and avoidance of the illness. In the latter story, the wife feels angry and cheated by the disease, as well as feeling trapped and cut off from her future.

335   Wombat Productions (Producer). (1972). Family.

Shows various aspects of the family in a changing American society. During an outdoor supper, family members speak about feelings and concerns regarding their particular role in the family and in today's society. The closing thoughts are from the aging grandmother, who feels something has been lost in the family life of today--she hopes that the "family of yesteryear" will return.

336   Zagreb Films (Producer). (1973). Weekend.

A three-generation family leaves for a picnic in the country, leaving the grandfather "out to pasture" with many other old persons at the end of the film. Film leaves viewer with the perspective that the expected thing to do is to discard the oldest members of a family when they have outlived their usefulness.

Documents

337   **Roche, B. (1985). <u>Celebration of growing older: a</u>**
      <u>community-wide program on elder issues</u>.
      Massachusetts: Greenfield Community College, 19p.

Addresses some of the social, health, economic, and cultural
issues of growing older in America, including intergenerational
programming.

338   **U.S. Congress. House. Hearing before the Select**
      Committee on Aging. (1980). <u>Families: aging and</u>
      <u>change</u>, 118p.

Hearing report presents the views of a number of
multigenerational families on the positive aspects of living
together and apart. Discussion of how older family members can
help strengthen family bonds, establish pride in heritage, care
for younger family members, and contribute to the productive
force of the family unit, as well as of services which could
help those who are caregivers in the family. Discussion of
innovative approaches designed to strengthen the extended
family where it is functioning effectively and to support
alternatives where it is not.

Dissertations

339   **Atkinson, Lynn. (1986). <u>The generation gap: an</u>**
      <u>analysis of similar age-cohorts and their parents at</u>
      <u>two time periods</u>. Unpublished doctoral
      dissertation, Oklahoma State University, 189p.

Examines differences in generational continuity between two
similar age-cohorts and their parents at two different periods
of time using life-span developmental theory as a framework.
A major factor which influences generational continuity was
found to be historical time period.

340   **Floyd, James. (1987). <u>Black family in transition:</u>**
      <u>a multigenerational study of crisis resolution</u>.
      Unpublished doctoral dissertation, Boston College,
      384p.

Examines growth and development of a selected black family.
Author argues that the disorganization view of black families
does not mesh with the New World experiences of all black
families. The author's premise is that the real indicator of
a kinship unit's resilience is its ability to adjust to crisis
situations over a period of several generations.

341   **Howard, Judith. (1981). <u>Four generation families:</u>**
      <u>intergenerational relationships and public policy</u>.
      Unpublished doctoral dissertation, University of
      California, Los Angeles, 183p.

Study of middle-aged adult children and their interaction with
their aging parents. It was found that the second generation
provided much support for their parents. There was greater

frequency of interaction among working class subjects than among middle class subjects. The greater the amount of assistance given to aging parents, the less the harmony in other family relationships. Found was a significant correlation in sibling and child relationships, but not in the spousal relationship, although the trend was in the same direction. There was found a perception of being "caught" between generations in trying to provide support both to aging parents and to young adult children; this perception was more prevalent among the working class subjects than among middle class subjects. Among these subjects, there was overwhelming support for public provision for the elderly and their families--"many saying even if it means higher taxes." There was found no correlation between whether people agreed with the public policy proposals and the amount of assistance they provided to their parents.

342   James, Jean. (1980). **Children's association with an older affiliated family, reading achievement, and attitudes toward the elderly**. Unpublished doctoral dissertation, University of South Carolina, 122p.

Examines relationship between second grade children's association with an older affiliated family, reading achievement, and attitudes toward the elderly. Children with older affiliated families scored higher in word reading than did children without older affiliated families. There was a similar relationship between the two variables for boys and girls. A statistically significant relationship was found between association with an older affiliated family member and children's attitudes toward the elderly in these areas: "1) a greater number of children with older affiliated families had affective knowledge of the elderly, 2) children with older affiliated families described the elderly less often in physical terms and were less negative when they did so, 3) there was a positive relationship between association with an older affiliated family member and children's ability to order a series of pictures of adult males into appropriate age sequences, from youngest to oldest."

343   Leigh, Geoffrey. (1980). **Kinship interaction over the family life span**. Unpublished doctoral dissertation, Brigham Young University, 38p.

Concludes that family life span has no effect on the amount of interaction. Other variables were found to have substantial effect. A great deal of difference in the kinship interaction is made by the degree of kinship propinquity. Study found that adults have considerable interaction with close relatives, such as parents, married children, and siblings, and less interaction with more distant relatives, such as cousins. Geographical distance has a negative effect on amount of interaction, but there is still substantial interaction occurring between relatives despite distances. Especially for more extended kin, affectional closeness and enjoyment affect the amount of kinship interaction.

344   Martin, Mary. (1988). **Filial responsibility in three generation families: the influence of gender**

and generation. Unpublished doctoral dissertation, University of Southern California, number of pages not given.

Examines the sense of filial responsibility expressed by adult members of three generation families and the importance of gender and family generational position on responses about filial responsibility. From oldest to youngest generation, attitudes about filial responsibility become stronger, with women reporting stronger norms than men. The most consistent explainer of an adult child's feelings of filial responsibility is generated by the quality of the parent-child relationship. Other findings include that "norms of filial responsibility are not unique within families across generations, there were no significant differences between caregiver and non-caregiver families regarding attitudes about filial responsibility, and, within caregiver families, attitudes about filial responsibility are most similar between the women in the oldest and middle family generations."

345   Riley, Robert.   (1980).   **Kinship patterns in Londonderry, Vermont, 1771-1900: an intergenerational perspective of changing family relationships**. Unpublished doctoral dissertation, University of Massachusetts, 355p.

Analysis of nineteenth-century Londonderry, a predominantly agricultural community located in southern Vermont. "Demographic and economic processes affecting family and kinship relations occur as an intergenerational phenomenon. Despite increasing national social and economic integration, social and family stability was maintained in the community throughout the century by a farming tradition, extensive family and kinship ties and residential continuity, and a balance between population, available resources and employment opportunities."

346   Rosen, Rheta.   (1987).   **Filial responsibility, ethnicity, and social exchange: a study of helping behavior in the older family**. Unpublished doctoral dissertation, York University, number of pages not given.

Uses the social exchange perspective to examine helping behavior in the older family. Findings show "generational and cultural variations in intergenerational interaction in older families."

347   Seagle, Audra. (1988). **Intergenerational dynamics of adult offspring living in the parental home**. Unpublished doctoral dissertation, Virginia Polytechnic Institute and State University, 97p.

Investigates adult offspring living in the parental home. Looks at variables, such as intimacy with parents, individuation from family of origin, triangulation, intimidation, and personal authority. In this population, moving home after a separation or a divorce is not prevalent. Few subjects paid regularly for rent and household expenses.

"Adult children reported significant degrees of intimacy and personal authority under conditions of satisfaction with living arrangements and significant levels of fusion in conjunction with both satisfaction and age being over 40."

8

Family Caregiving

Books

348   Browne, Colette, and Onzuka-Anderson, Roberta.
        (1985). <u>Our aging parents: a practical guide to
        eldercare</u>. Honolulu: University of Hawaii Press,
        278p.

Provides practical suggestions for families faced with caring
for a dependent elder at home. Overview of eldercare. "When
you care for an elder and watch the person grow old, you will
see someone manage feelings of joy and sorrow and develop a
stronger sense of self because of these experiences. . . .
Aging relatives can also help you find what is really important
in your own life by readjusting your priorities."

349   Daniels, Norman. (1988). <u>Am I my parents' keeper?:
        an essay on justice between the young and the old</u>.
        New York: Oxford University Press, 194p.

Discussion of the distribution, by generation, of public funds
for human services, and of filial obligations.

350   Eyde, Donna, and Rich, Jay. (1983). <u>Psychological
        distress in aging: a family management model</u>.
        Rockville, Maryland: Aspen Systems Corp, 254p.

Provides a "systematic approach to the identification,
management, and treatment of psychological stresses and psycho-
pathologies of older persons within a family system." The
authors indicate that, "It is necessary to consider
simultaneously the evolution of the family system itself and
the stages of development attained by the individual members
who complement the family system." The authors discuss an
integrated model for family management, the family as a case
manager and environmental counselor in the continuum of care,
home-based habilitation and maintenance strategies, scope of
concerns, community-based services, promises and pitfalls of
the family management model, and wellness and maintenance of
mental health.

351   Hooyman, Nancy.   (1986).   **Taking care: supporting
           older people and their families**.   New York: Free
           Press; London: Collier Macmillan, 322p.

Responses to families' needs for information, social support,
respite, and financial assistance in providing care to older
relatives.   Includes reasons for caring for aging parents,
spouses as caregivers, sharing the care among family members,
natural helping networks, care for the caregivers, coping with
physical and mental changes, depression in homebound older
people, money, bringing services into the home, using services
outside the home, alternative   living situations, living
together in the   caregiver's home, and extending family
caregiving into the nursing home.   In this book, "professionals
and families are . . . viewed as collaborators, each supporting
the other's efforts to enable the older person to remain in the
community."

352   Jarvik,   Lissy,   and   Small,   Gary.   (1988).
           Parentcare: a commonsense guide for adult children.
           New York: Crown Publishers, 309p.

Pragmatic responses are provided for major problems associated
with caring for aging parents.   Topics include dealing with the
anger and stress of caregiving, managing financial resources,
facing dying and death.   Useful resources in appendices.

353   Litwak, Eugene. (1985).   **Helping the elderly: the
           complementary roles of informal networks and formal
           systems**. New York: Guilford Press, 306p.

Describes essential services of formal organizations and
informal networks and contrasts relationships between the
formal and informal systems.   Litwak describes the "modified
extended family structure, where members legitimate geographic
mobility while at the same time exchanges by kin are maintained
over   distances."   Chapters   include   discussion   of   the
theoretical   bases   for   primary-group   networks   and   formal
organizations in modern industrial society, differential
structures and tasks of primary groups, formal organizations,
dynamics   of   network   change   from   community   to
institutionalization, ideal and nonideal forms of kinship
structure and exchange, ideal and nonideal forms of marital
ties and exchange, ideal and nonideal forms of neighborhood
structure and exchange, ideal and nonideal forms of friendship
groups,   networks,   subsocialization   groups,   volunteers,
exchange, social theory, and social policy.

354   Moroney, Robert.   (1986).   **Shared responsibility:
           families and social policy**.   New York: Aldine
           Publishing Company, 218p.

Explores questions about the relationship between families and
the state, especially the appropriateness of state intervention
in family life.   Questions include: Under what conditions is
intervention appropriate? For what purposes?   In which areas
of family life?   What is appropriate for the family to carry
out?   What should families be required to do?   What should be
shared by both families and the state?   The author concludes

that, "If families are to be strengthened, if family members are to be more capable caregivers, the state, through its social welfare system, should not consider retrenchment. It needs to enter into a partnership with families, a relationship characterized by reciprocity. Otherwise, more and more families will become dependent."

355   Pelham, Anabel, and Clark, William (Eds.). (1986). Managing home care for the elderly: lessons from community-based agencies. New York: Springer Publishing Company, 196p.

A collection of essays about research and demonstration projects in home care for the frail elderly. Some of the projects are seen as societal attempts to create hybrid symbiotic kinship and institutional relationships, or "kinstitutions." Community-based long-term care agencies are viewed as kinstitutions in every sense of the word. "Their experience of struggling to become both family and formal organizations to frail elders promises to change the terrain of long-term care in the foreseeable future."

356   Phillipson, Chris; Bernard, Miriam; and Strang, Patricia (Eds.). (1986). Dependency and interdependency in old age: theoretical perspectives and policy alternatives. London and Wolfeboro, New Hampshire: Croom Helm in association with the British Society of Gerontology, 371p.

Theoretical and policy evaluation of the idea of dependency of older people. A collection of essays, including discussion of family care, family relationships, and living independently.

357   Powers, James; Morgan, Susan; and Brawner, Debbie. (1988). The second midlife crisis: relating to aging parents: visions of our future. New York: Vantage Press, 84p.

Health professionals describe how to deal with the elderly in a humane fashion. Family dynamics, difficult choices, and sources of help are among the topics covered.

358   Shulman, Bernard, and Berman, Raeann. (1988). How to survive your aging parents: so you and they can enjoy life. Chicago, Illinois: Surrey Books, 192p.

Guidelines on handling daily problems and major issues of caring for older parents. Focus on restructuring relationships so that both middle-aged children and their parents can enjoy one another.

359   Sloan, Bernard. (1980). The best friend you'll ever have. New York: Crown Publishers, Inc., 218p.

The author's personal account of bringing his widowed mother to live with his family.

360   Springer, Dianne, and Brubaker, Timothy. (1984). Family caregivers and dependent elderly: minimizing

stress and maximizing independence.   Beverly Hills:
Sage Publications, 159p.

This book was "written to bridge the gaps among research,
practice, and older people and their families." The emphasis
is on caregiving responsibilities of family members. Primary
objectives of this book are: "to maximize the independence of
the dependent older person, to minimize the stressful
situations experienced by the caregiver, and to strengthen the
family relationships of the caregivers and dependent older
persons." Topics include an overview of the aging process,
stressful structural situations within the family, stressful
emotional situations within the family, general communication
skills, potential communication experiences for the caregiver,
informal support systems, and formal support systems.

361   **Stephens, Susan, and Christianson, Jon.   (1986).
         Informal   care   of   the   elderly**.   Lexington,
         Massachusetts: Lexington Books, 174p.

Describes the characteristics and experiences of individuals
who regularly provide assistance to their elderly relatives and
friends.   Includes study of 2,000 subjects who are primary
caregivers to older persons at risk of institutionalization.
Covers public policy and informal support for the elderly, the
channeling study of informal caregivers, the elderly and their
primary caregivers, care by primary informal caregivers,
informal caregiving networks, informal financial assistance,
and well-being of caregivers.   Includes coded survey
instrument.

Articles/chapters

362   **Abel, E.   (1989).   The ambiguities of social
         support: adult daughters caring for frail elderly
         parents. Journal of Aging Studies, 3, 211-230.**

Describes types of support adult daughters caring for frail
elderly parents receive from various sources and the barriers
they face in requesting additional help.   In-depth interviews
provide data.   The finding is that family and friends helped
exacerbate stress as well as alleviating it.

363   **Arling, Greg, and McAuley, William.   (1984).   The
         family, public policy and long-term care.   In Quinn,
         William, and Hughston, George (Eds.), Independent
         aging: family and social systems perspectives, pp.
         133-148. Rockville, Maryland: Aspen Systems Corp.,
         300p.**

Describes the role of the family in long-term care of the
impaired elderly. Discusses the extent of family care given
and factors that influence it.   The authors suggest that
nonfamily sources of care do not displace, but rather
supplement, family caregiving, and specify the conditions of
support system functioning.

364   Arling, Greg, and McAuley, William.   (1986).   The
        feasibility   of   public   payments   for   family
        caregiving.   In Troll, Lillian (Ed.), Family issues
        in current gerontology, pp. 162-177.   New York:
        Springer Publishing Company, 382p.

Examines feasibility of public financial payment as a method of
encouraging or maintaining family support in long-term care of
the impaired elderly.   In this study, families provided
assistance voluntarily, and only a minority relied upon
agencies or other paid sources for in-home care.   The authors
indicate that efforts to sort out families in greatest need of
financial assistance should be based on criteria which take
into account many different family circumstances, although such
efforts may increase administrative costs.

365   Bain, Patrice; Greene, Victoria; and Ledesma,
        Bernadette.   (1985).   Visiting your relative in an
        institution.   In Browne, Colette, and Onzuka-
        Anderson, Roberta (Eds.), Our aging parents: a
        practical   guide   to   eldercare,   pp.   213-227.
        Honolulu: University of Hawaii Press, 278p.

Coming to terms with feelings about the institutionalization of
a family member is "often an involved, painful, and difficult
process" for the entire family.   For older nursing home
residents, high-quality care increases with the involvement of
the family and the family's willingness to understand and
accept   the   parent's   disabilities.   Involving   the
institutionalized elder in all components of family and
community life can help to make visits to an institution more
meaningful and more enjoyable.   Families are a part of
institutional life, just as are staff.   Family members are
vital in the survival and livelihood of the relative.   The
authors contend that the family's participation and welfare
should be considered an essential part of the care plan of the
institution.

366   Barusch, Amanda, and Spaid, Wanda.   (1989).   Gender
        differences in caregiving: why do wives report
        greater burden? Gerontologist, 29(5), 667-676.

Used data from interviews with 131 older spouse caregivers to
explore potential explanations for a difference between men and
women in reporting caregiving burden.   The most important
predictor of burden was the patient's cognitive and behavioral
difficulties, followed by caregiver age, unpleasant social
contacts, caregiver sex, and overall coping effectiveness.   The
finding was that "age differences in male and female caregivers
contribute to the observed differences in burden."

367   Beh, Hazel; Murayama, Diane; and Ramsey, Mildred.
        (1985).   Community services: help does exist!   In
        Browne, Colette, and Onzuka-Anderson, Roberta
        (Eds.), Our aging parents: a practical guide to
        eldercare, pp. 186-198.   Honolulu: University of
        Hawaii Press, 278p.

An assessment of an individual case is the most thorough way of determining what services are needed. Community programs may offer a variety of services to help supplement a family's care of dependent, elderly relatives.

368   Breneman, Mary, and Browne, Colette.   (1985). Keeping your relative mobile and independent. In Browne, Colette, and Onzuka-Anderson, Roberta (Eds.), Our aging parents: a practical guide to eldercare, pp. 149-158. Honolulu: University of Hawaii Press, 278p.

Family members can learn many of the techniques needed to care for a disabled person at home, when instructed by a trained professional, and can use them successfully with the disabled relative within the home environment.

369   Brody, Elaine.   (1985).   Parent care as a normative family stress. Gerontologist, 25(1), 19-29.

Explores complex factors which interact to determine filial behavior, and notes ways in which social policy responds to knowledge about filial behavior. Author suggests a hypothesis to explain persistence of myth that adult children today do not take care of elderly parents.

370   Brody, Elaine; Dempsey, Norah; and Pruchno, Rachel. (1990). Mental health of sons and daughters of the institutionalized aged. Gerontologist, 30(2), 212-219.

Compares predictors of depression and emotional effects between sons and daughters. "Predictors of depression in a study of 331 adult children whose parents resided in nursing homes were respondent's poor health, time pressures, viewing the parent as demanding, and lack of involvement with activities of daily living tasks. Emotional effects specific to parent's situation were predicted by poor health, negative perceptions of nursing home staff, upsetting visits, time pressures, and being female and young."

371   Brody, Elaine; Hoffman, Christine; Kleban, Morton; and Schoonover, Claire.   (1989).   Caregiving daughters and their local siblings: perceptions, strains, and interactions. Gerontologist, 29(4), 529-538.

Study compares daughters who are principal caregivers to disabled elderly mothers with their geographically proximate sisters and brothers as to the amount of help each group provides, the effects of care they experience, and the problems and benefits of the siblings' interactions about the caregiving situations.

372   Brody, Elaine; Johnsen, Pauline; and Fulcomer, Mark. (1984). What should adult children do for elderly parents?   opinions and preferences of three generations of women. Journal of Gerontology, 39(6), 736-746.

Three generations of women were surveyed on their opinions of appropriate filial behavior toward elderly parents and on their preferences for providers of services which they might need in old age. Women preferred adult children as providers of emotional support and financial management but not of income. The middle generation was least in favor of receiving financial support or instrumental help from children, preferring to have formal sources of assistance.

373   Brody, Elaine; Johnsen, Pauline; Fulcomer, Mark; and Lang, Abigail. (1983). Women's changing roles and help to elderly parents: attitudes of three generations of women. Journal of Gerontology, 38(5), 597-607.

Data from three generations of women on effects of women's changing roles on attitudes toward responsibility for care of elderly adults. "The oldest generation was most receptive (and the youngest the least receptive) to formal services for elderly persons, but all three generations agreed that old people should be able to depend on adult children for help. Values about family care of elderly adults have not eroded despite demographic and socioeconomic changes."

374   Browne, Colette, and Onzuka-Anderson, Roberta. (1985). The family's role in eldercare. In Browne, Colette, and Onzuka-Anderson, Roberta (Eds.), Our aging parents: a practical guide to eldercare, pp. 15-29. Honolulu: University of Hawaii Press, 278p.

Most older adults keep in fairly close communication with their children. "Families benefit themselves when there is a reciprocal arrangement with their aging relative. . . . By viewing aging as a continuous process we all go through, we preserve a sense of our roots and the true meaning of 'family.' . . . By separating the aging individual from society, we lost touch with aging as a process we will all experience--and thus we lost touch with ourselves."

375   Brubaker, Ellie. (1983). Providing services to older persons and their families. In Brubaker, Timothy (Ed.), Family relationships in later life, pp. 229-242. Beverly Hills, California: Sage Publications, 272p.

Discusses the service-delivery process for older clients. Includes discussion of initiation of relationship with older persons and families, information collection, development of priorities, service provision, and evaluation and continuation or termination of relationship. "Service-providers . . . increase the effectiveness of service delivery by involving appropriate family members in the client-practitioner relationship."

376   Brubaker, Timothy, and Brubaker, Ellie. (1984). Family support of older persons in the long-term care setting: recommendations for practice. In Quinn, William, and Hughston, George (Eds.), Independent aging: family and social systems

perspectives, pp. 106-114.   Rockville, Maryland:
Aspen Systems Corporation, 300p.

The authors encourage long-term care practitioners to
understand and integrate family involvement to reinforce family
ties for the elderly and to solicit their cooperation.   The
authors illustrate that "the family is the client."   The
authors provide recommendations with guidelines to help
practitioners form a link with aging families.

377   Campbell, Ruth, and Brody, Elaine. (1985). Women's
         changing roles and help to the elderly: attitudes
         of women in the U.S. and Japan. Gerontologist,
         25(6), 584-592.

Three-generation study of women's attitudes toward gender-
appropriate roles and filial responsibility. U.S. gender-role
attitudes were found to more egalitarian than those of the
Japanese.   In both the U.S. and Japan, all three generations
said care of the elderly is a family responsibility, but
attitudes toward filial responsibility were more positive among
Americans than among Japanese.

378   Cantor, Marjorie. (1983). Strain among caregivers:
         a study of experience in the United States.
         Gerontologist, 23(6), 597-604.

The finding suggests the extent of stress and dislocation
involved in the role of primary caregiver for the frail elderly
is very different for different groups of caregivers.   "The
closer the bond, the more stressful the caregiving role, and
spouse and child would appear to be priority targets for
interventions to strengthen the capacity of informal supports
to assist the frail elderly."

379   Cavanaugh, John; Dunn, Nancy; Mowery, Doug; Feller,
         Cathy; Niederehe, George; Fruge, Ernest; and
         Volpendesta, Darci.   (1989).   Problem-solving
         strategies in dementia patient-caregiver dyads.
         Gerontologist, 29(2), 156-158.

Comparison of caregiver-patient dyads to normal elderly dyads
in the instructional strategies they used to complete the Block
Design subtest of the WAIS-R.   Finding was that caregiver-
patient dyads can be observed to learn how cognitively
supportive environments work. "Successful sharing of the load
in a cognitive task may have positive effects on the patient-
caregiver relationship, e.g., caregivers who are used to
observing patients fail on cognitive tasks may adopt a more
positive attitude if successes begin to accrue through their
assistance.   Initial successes could lead to more and better
cognitive support, which could further enhance the
relationship.   However, perhaps the cognitive decline of
patients is actually speeded up as a result of increasingly
negative relationships with unsupportive caregivers."

380   Chapleski, Elizabeth.   (1989).   Determinants of
         knowledge of services to the elderly: are strong

ties enabling or inhibiting? Gerontologist, 29(4), 539-545.

Examination of older persons' social network ties and awareness of services available to them. For this sample, "having nonkin advisers, membership in clubs, or contacts with other community agencies and availability of transportation, education, and moderate-size kin networks predicted service awareness."

381   Chiriboga, David. (1987). Social supports. In Maddox, George (Ed.), The encyclopedia of aging, pp. 635-638. New York: Springer Publishing Co., 890p.

Discusses informal and formal support systems, theories of support, practical implications of social support.

382   Cicirelli, Victor. (1986). A comparison of helping behavior to elderly parents of adult children with intact and disrupted marriages. In Troll, Lillian (Ed.), Family issues in current gerontology, pp. 123-144. New York: Springer Publishing Co., 382p.

Explores how divorce, widowhood, and remarriage affect adult children's behavior toward elderly parents. Compares the amount of help provided to elderly parents by divorced, widowed, and remarried adult children and by comparing help provided by children with marital disruption with help provided by children with intact marriages. Adult children with disrupted marriages provided less help to elderly parents than did adult children with intact marriages (although the mean amounts of help were relatively low for both groups). Marital disruption affects help to elderly parents. From a practitioner's viewpoint, the author recommends that there be more emphasis on encouraging communication between adult children with marital disruption and elderly parents who are frail and dependent, so that both groups can better understand critical events in their lives and develop a better idea of what to expect of each other.

383   Cicirelli, Victor. (1985). The role of siblings as family caregivers. In Sauer, William, and Coward, Ray (Eds.), Social support networks and the care of the elderly, pp. 93-107. New York: Springer Publishing Company, 284p.

Explores the nature of the sibling relationship by examining three questions: Do most elderly have living siblings? What is the proximity of the elderly to their siblings? What is the quantity and quality of contact among elderly and their siblings? "If factors leading to sibling help are understood, ways of promoting and maintaining sibling help can be devised. Sibling help may be limited in amount, but siblings do appear to fulfill important and valuable functions in old age."

384   Clark, Noreen, and Rakowski, William. (1983). Family caregivers of older adults: improving helping skills. Gerontologist, 23(6), 637-642.

Summarizes and categorizes caregiving tasks reported by family members. Analyzes reports of education and support programs for family caregivers.

385   Clipp, Elizabeth, and George, Linda.   (1990).
        Caregiver needs and patterns of social support.
        Journal of Gerontology, 45(3), S102-S111.

Used levels of caregiver need to predict four patterns of continuity and change in social support over a one-year interval among 376 adults caring for a family member with Alzheimer's disease. The finding was that "caregiver need does not necessarily elicit support. Needs do, however, predict several patterns of social support, the most common of which is characterized by stability (high or low support). . . . The neediest caregivers are those who receive the least tangible assistance. This suggests that something other than need operates to elicit social support from family and friends."

386   Collado, Cathy, and Rogers, Jane.   (1985).
        Encouraging self-care.   In Browne, Colette, and
        Onzuka-Anderson, Roberta (Eds.), Our aging parents:
        a practical guide to eldercare, pp. 159-175.
        Honolulu: University of Hawaii Press, 278p.

Self-care, here, refers to eating, dressing, bathing, and caring for one's own bathroom needs independently. Sometimes, family members ignore the self-care skills of the frail elderly and do things for them, not with them. Helping frail elders maintain a level of independence may be accomplished by encouraging their taking part in household chores and encouraging independence by reducing unnecessary help from family members.

387   Daatland, Svein.   (1983).   Use of public services
        for the aged and the role of the family.
        Gerontologist, 23(6), 650-656.

Public services for the aged in a Norwegian small town are used by more than one-third of the population above the age of 70. Both need and demand factors affect use of services.

388   Dilworth-Anderson, Peggye.   (1987).   Effectiveness
        of family support group involvement in adult day
        care.   Family Relations, 36(1), 78-81.

Group meetings were held at two adult day care centers in the Chicago area with adult children caring for older relatives. The discussions focused on problems common to caregivers, information on aging, and resources to help caregivers. Caregivers benefitted more from the sessions when the administrator and staff were involved and where there was high and consistent attendance.

389   Dura, Jason; Haywood-Niler, Elizabeth; and Kiecolt-
        Glaser, Janice.   (1990).   Spousal caregivers of
        persons with Alzheimer's and Parkinson's disease
        dementia: a preliminary comparison. Gerontologist,
        30(3), 332-336.

Compares caregiver stress to the unique features of Alzheimer's type senile dementia and Parkinson's disease. Compares spousal caregivers for two types of patients and a control group on self-and other-rated depression. "The two caregiving groups were similar in the length of time they had been providing assistance and in caregiver distress, and both caregiver groups were more depressed than comparison subjects."

390   Engelhardt, Jean; Brubaker, Timothy; Lutzer, Victoria. (1988). Older caregivers of adults with mental retardation: service utilization. Mental Retardation, 26(4), 191-195.

Examination of the relationship between service utilization and characteristics of older parents and other caregivers, their dependents with mental retardation, and their ability to provide care. "Caregivers' assessment of current ability to provide care was significantly related to amount of service use, but caregiver and dependent characteristics were not."

391   Evandrous, Maria; Arber, Sara; Dale, Angela; and Gilbert, G. Nigel. (1986). Who cares for the elderly? family care provision and receipt of statutory services. In Phillipson, Chris; Bernard, Miriam; and Strang, Patricia (Eds.), Old age: theoretical perspectives and policy alternatives, 150-166. London: Croom Helm, 371p.

Uses nationally representative data to examine the roles of formal and informal care networks in providing care for elderly people living at home. This study found that "community care was primarily for elderly people living alone; for elderly in other household units, kin are the main care providers. . . . Support by formal agencies was influenced by the household structure in which the elderly person lived rather than whether they were able to carry out various activities of daily living without help." Authors found that social policies were based on assuming that the "family network" (especially female family members) will be available to provide such care in the future.

392   Farley, Joanne, and Fay, Patricia. (1983). Promoting positive attitudes among the caregivers of the elderly. Nurse Educator, 8(1), 43-45.

Describes educational strategies that can help the nursing staff reduce the frustrations and stress often related to caring for the elderly. Explains how to help staff members recognize their own feelings about the elderly, become aware of misconceptions, and develop positive attitudes.

393   Finch, Janet, and Mason, Jennifer. (1990). Filial obligations and kin support for elderly people. Aging and Society, 10, 151-175.

Looks at the nature of obligation and responsibility within kin groups. Focus is especially on how these underscore the assistance which may be offered by children to their elderly parents. Authors contend that "relationships between parents and children are founded on a sense of obligation up to a point, but assent for this is not universal and such obligations are seen as having definite limits." The authors suggest looking at "ways in which support for elderly parents is a matter for negotiation in families," and "to examine the principles which are incorporated into such suggestions."

394   **Friss, Lynn. (1990). A model state-level approach to family survival for caregivers of brain-impaired adults. Gerontologist, 30(1), 121-125.**

Profile of a statewide program to support family caregivers of brain-impaired adults identifies the major needs and problems of these family caregivers and delineates service interventions to meet those needs. Reports demographic data on the major characteristics of over 3,000 family caregivers and their cognitively impaired patients.

395   **Gallagher, Dolores. (1987). Caregivers of chronically ill elders. In Maddox, George (Ed.), The encyclopedia of aging, pp. 89-91. New York: Springer Publishing Co., 890p.**

Provides overview of caring for the caregivers of chronically ill elders, intervention efforts (to decrease caregiver burden), educational and supportive programs, respite programs, and psychotherapeutic interventions.

396   **Gallagher, Dolores; Rose, Jonathon; Rivera, Patricia; Lovett, Steven; and Thompson, Larry. (1989). Prevalence of depression in family caregivers. Gerontologist, 29(4), 449-456.**

Describes the results of a screening for depression of family caregivers who sought help to increase coping skills and caregivers who volunteered for a longitudinal study of Alzheimer's disease. Among help-seekers, 46% had depression; among non-help-seekers, 18% had depression. Women were found to be more depressed than men, but there were no major differences in the extent of depression found in those who cared for more impaired persons.

397   **Goodman, Jane, and Waters, Elinor. (1985). Conflict or support: work and family in middle and old age. Journal of Career Development, 12(1), 92-98.**

Describes career and family issues which may arise for adults. Suggests possible counseling interventions. Makes several assumptions about the work/family connection: renegotiation of work/family balance continues throughout work life; a variety of demographic variables affect work/family roles; and some issues relate more to roles and others more to affective variables.

398   **Greene, Vernon; and Monahan, Deborah. (1989). The effect of a support and education program on stress and burden among family caregivers to frail elderly persons. Gerontologist, 29(4), 472-477.**

Reports the results of an eight-week, professionally-led caregiver support group program. The program produced statistically significant reductions in anxiety, depression, and sense of burden among family caregivers to frail elderly persons living in the community.

399   Haley, William. (1989). Group intervention for dementia family caregivers: a longitudinal perspective. Gerontologist, 29(4), 478-480.

Reports data from caregivers who participated in an experimental study of group intervention for dementia caregivers. This long-term follow-up "shows differential attrition from treatment, issues in selection of participants, and need for measures appropriate to long-term outcome."

400   Halpert, Burton, and Sharp, Tessa. (1989). A model to nationally replicate a locally successful rural family caregiver program: the volunteer information provider program. Gerontologist, 29(4), 561-563.

Discusses transplanting a local caregiver program beyond state lines. Identifies the strategy, steps taken, and key elements of piloting and dissemination of the Volunteer Information Provider Program.

401   Harmelink, Ruth. (1987). Who nurtures the nurturer? special needs of farm women. Journal of Extension, 25, 18-20.

Interviews with 11 Iowa farm women about the various demands they face from children, aging parents, husbands, and their many duties. Author lists possible programs that Extension professionals can provide to address this population's needs.

402   Henton, June; Cate, Rodney; and Emery, Beth. (1984). The dependent elderly: targets for abuse. In Quinn, William, and Hughston, George (Eds.), Independent aging: family and social systems perspectives, pp. 149-162. Rockville, Maryland: Aspen Systems Corp., 300p.

Addresses the frequency and definition of abuse and the lack of protective mechanisms for the elderly. Authors recommend intervention and support provisions to aid the practitioners or persons providing support to the abused elderly.

403   Hooyman, Nancy; Gonyea, Judith; and Montgomery, Rhonda. (1986). The impact of in-home services termination on family caregivers. In Troll, Lillian (Ed.), Family issues in current gerontology, pp. 214-225. New York: Springer Publishing Company, 382p.

The focus is on whether chore service reductions were related to changes in family members' caregiving behaviors and perceptions of burden and stress. Finding was that presence or absence of chore services did not affect the extent of family caregiving involvement. The family still remains very involved, even when formal services are used. The lack of difference in the amount of assistance by family caregivers of terminated and continued clients indicates that these families may already be providing all the support of which they are capable or willing. The authors suggest that the greatest policy significance may be the relationship they found among performing personal care tasks, perceptions of the burden by caregivers, and the detrimental effects of stress as a long-run consequence of providing personal care.

404   Horowitz, Amy. (1985). Sons and daughters as caregivers to older parents: differences in role performance and consequences. Gerontologist, 25(6), 612-617.

Looks at gender differences within 131 adult children primary caregivers to older frail parents. The finding is that sons become caregivers only when an available female sibling is absent; they are more likely to rely on support of their own spouses, provide less overall assistance to their parents (especially "hands-on" services), and tend to have less stressful caregiving experiences independent of their involvement.

405   Howell, Mary. (1984). Caretakers' views on responsibilities for the care of the demented elderly. Journal of the American Geriatrics Society, 32(9), 657-660.

Provides a perspective on the day-to-day care of demented elderly persons.

406   Jarrett, William. (1985). Caregiving within kinship systems: is affection really necessary? Gerontologist, 25(1), 5-10.

Discussion of filial affection for aged dependents as insufficient to enable caregivers to cope with caregiving strains. Author suggests relabeling strategy (cognitive therapy) to help caregivers redefine situations "so that caregiving is done from motives of kinship obligations which historically have formed the basis for family aid."

407   Johnson, Colleen, and Catalano, Donald. (1981). Childless elderly and their family supports. (1981). Gerontologist, 21(6), 610-618.

Compares the social supports of a small subsample of childless elderly to a larger group of older parents. Marital status was found to be the major determinant of the quality of the support received and the patterns of adaptation to childlessness in later life. Childless, married persons were more isolated and relied primarily upon each other. Unmarried individuals were more resourceful in using a long-term accumulation of social resources to meet their needs. The potential social isolation of childless elderly "places them at the greatest risk of slipping through the net of community resources."

408   Johnson, Colleen, and Catalano, Donald. (1983). A longitudinal study of family supports to impaired elderly. Gerontologist, 23(6), 612-618.

Study of the family supports of 115 individuals 65 years and older after discharge from the hospital and an average of eight months later. For the group as a whole at Time 2, the mean functional level had stabilized. Family supports declined, and more patients reported problems with morale and loneliness. Describes adaptive mechanisms to the burdens of care.

409   Kendig, Hal, and Rowland, Don. (1983). Family support of the Australian aged: a comparison with the United States. Gerontologist, 23(6), 643-649.

Presents findings on the involvement of older Australians with members of their modified-extended families, especially their adult children. Uses a 1981 survey of 1,050 persons aged 60 or over living in private households in Sydney. Relationships show close emotional bonds, regular interaction, and a two-way flow of instrumental support. More frequently than Americans, Australians were found frequently to live in joint households and to make greater use of community and institutional services.

410   Kinney, Jennifer, and Stephens, Mary. (1989). Caregiving hassles scale: assessing the daily hassles of caring for a family member with dementia. Gerontologist, 29(3), 328-332.

Examines a scale designed to assess the daily hassles of caring for a family member with Alzheimer's Disease. "The 42-item scale provides a reliable and psychometrically sound instrument for assessing hassles associated with assistance in basic Activities of Daily Living (ADL), assistance in instrumental ADL, care-recipients' cognitive status, care-recipients' behavior, and caregivers' social network."

411   Kovar, Mary, and Harris, Tamara. (1988). "Who will care for the old?" American Demography, 10(5), 34-37.

Estimates of need for homebased services to prevent institutionalization of those who have no family to provide help are based on the 1984 Health Interview Survey Supplement on Aging.

412   Krauss, Marty, and Erickson, Marji. (1988). Informal support networks among aging persons with mental retardation: a pilot study. Mental Retardation, 26(4), 197-201.

Reports data collected on the informal support networks of 49 aging persons with mental retardation. Findings indicated that persons living with family had significantly smaller support networks (composed primarily of family members), and those mentally retarded aging persons living in community residences or institutions had informal support networks composed equally of family, friends, and professionals.

413   Longino, Charles, and Lipman, Aaron.   (1985).   The
         support systems of women.   In Sauer, William, and
         Coward, Ray (Eds.), Social support networks and the
         care of the elderly, pp. 219-233.   New York:
         Springer Publishing Company, 284p.

The support available to older women will become more important
as women increasingly dominate the over age 70 population in
the United States during this decade, the authors indicate.
They discuss married women, spouseless women (including the
never married), the principle of family substitutions,
antecedent and causal factors, and current research priorities.

414   Masciocchi, Carla; Thomas, Adria; and Moeller,
         Tamerra.   (1984).   Support for the impaired elderly:
         a challenge for family caregivers.   In Quinn,
         William, and Hughston, George (Eds.), Independent
         aging: family and social systems perspectives, pp.
         115-132. Rockville, Maryland: Aspen Systems Corp.,
         300p.

Authors begin with idea that family provides the majority of
services to impaired elderly. They consider the assessment of
the consequences to families of their acceptance of provider
roles. Discussion of types and sources of aid which family and
friends provide, the effects of this role on the families
providing care, and possible intervention strategies for formal
helping networks that aid family caregivers.

415   McMahon, Betty, and Ames, Barbara.   (1983).
         Educational programming for midlife adults with
         parent-caring responsibilities.   Educational
         Gerontology, 9(5-6), 377-387.

Describes the use of adult education programming to address the
needs of 50 midlife caregivers.   Findings indicated that
younger respondents had more requests for information, with
information related to the aging process being of greatest
concern.

416   Miller, Baila, and Montgomery, Andrew.   (1990).
         Family caregivers and limitations in social
         activities. Research on Aging, 12(1), 72-93.

Analyzes correlates of perceived limitations in social
activities using data from a national sample of the frail
elderly and their caregivers. Two issues were presented: What
differences in demographic, family, and caregiving attributes
are associated with variation in perceived restricted social
activities? How does the process influencing restriction of
social activities vary by family relationship of the caregiver?
Those who reported social limitations showed higher levels of
elder dependency and task demands. Daughters and wives were
more likely to report such limitations than were sons and
husbands. More important influences than objective caregiving
activities, for all family caregivers, were subjective
assessment of time and task demands.

417   **Miller, Dulcy, and Goldman, Lorraine.   (1989). Perceptions of caregivers about special respite services for the elderly.** Gerontologist, 29(3), 408-410.

Study of 48 family members who had arranged for respite care for ill elderly relatives.   "Caregiver families used their respite for vacations, personal business, freedom from caregiving, and surgery. Eighteen (78%) wished to participate in respite again because they thought it the best possible arrangement to maintain their mental health during caregiving."

418   **Miller, Dulcy; Gulle, Natividad; and McCue, Fern. (1986).   The realities of respite for families, clients, and sponsors.** Gerontologist, 26(5), 467-470.

Evaluated two respite programs for families caring for aged relatives--an institutional program for elderly persons needing constant nursing attention and a residential plan for housekeeping and companion services.   Based on a year's experience, "benefits of respite services to the client, family, and community appear to be indisputable."

419   **Montgomery, Rhonda, and Borgatta, Edgar.   (1989). The effects of alternative support strategies on family caregiving.** Gerontologist, 29(4), 457-464.

Authors randomly assigned family units of impaired elderly persons and caregivers to a control group or to one of five treatment groups eligible for a variety of respite or educational services.   After one year of eligibility, caregivers of elderly in the community reported lower levels of subjective burden.   "Services appeared to delay nursing home placement among families with adult child caregivers, but encouraged placement by spouse caregivers."

420   **Motenko, Aluma.   (1989).   The frustrations, gratifications, and well-being of dementia caregivers.** Gerontologist, 29(2), 166-172.

Results of face-to-face interviews with 50 older women caring at home for a husband with dementia. Gratification was found to be associated with greater well-being and frustration with more distress.   "Wives who perceived continuity in marital closeness since the illness had greater gratification than those who perceived change. Frustrations, in disrupting life plans, are apparently greatest at the onset of symptoms and as routines are developed, diminish despite the need to provide more care.   Still, the meanings of caregiving are more important to caregiver well-being than the amount of care provided."

421   **Norris, Virginia; Stephens, Mary; and Kinney, Jennifer.   (1990).   The impact of family interactions on recovery from stroke: help or hindrance.** Gerontologist, 30(4), 535-542.

Examination of family networks of 47 geriatric stroke patients
for social supports and social problems as they related to
well-being after hospital discharge.   Through structured
interviews, the authors assessed positive and negative family
interactions and patients' independence in activities of daily
living, time use, personal adjustment, and cognitive
functioning. After controlling for patients' medical status at
hospital discharge, social supports were found not to be
associated with any of the outcomes examined. Social problems
explained additional variance in personal adjustment and
Activities of Daily Living independence.

422   **Novak, Mark, and Guest, Carol. (1989). Caregiver
         response to Alzheimer's disease.   International
         Journal of Aging and Human Development, 28(1), 67-
         69.**

Questionnaire data from 30 caregivers of Alzheimer's disease
patients in Manitoba.   There was found no significant
correlation between length of time a caregiver has given care
to a particular patient and the caregiver's subjective feelings
of burden.   There was found a significant, moderate
correlation between length of time a caregiver has given care
to a particular patient and the patient's functional ability.
Authors conclude that "caregivers' subjective feelings and
needs best predict their feelings of burden." Authors offer
suggestions on how to improve support for caregivers in light
of these findings.

423   **Pearson, M., and Deitrick, E. (1989). Support for
         family caregivers: a volunteer program for in-home
         respite care. Caring, 8(12), 18-201.**

Describes Respite Care Corps, a community-based, in-home,
volunteer respite program, and discusses issues involved in
developing and implementing such a program.   The volunteer
program is one component of a nurse-managed range of services
identified as important by caregivers.

424   **Poulshock, S. Walter, and Deimling, Gary. (1986).
         Families caring for elders in residence: issues in
         the measurement of burden. In Troll, Lillian (Ed.),
         Family issues in current gerontology, pp. 226-245.
         New York: Springer Publishing Company, 382p.**

Uses data from a study of family members living with and caring
for impaired elders. Uses a model in which burden plays a
central role between the elder's impairment and the impact that
caregiving has on the life of the caregiver and the family.
The meaning of burden and the measurement of burden are
connected to the care recipient's impairment. The exact nature
of the relationships among elder impairment, caregiver
perception of burden, and the report of impact depends on the
specific types of impairment and impact that are considered.

425   **Pratt, Clara; Nay, Tim; Ladd, Linda; and Heagerty,
         Bobby. (1989). A model legal-financial education
         workshop for families caring for neurologically
         impaired elders. Gerontologist, 29(2), 258-262.**

Describes a program through which families become familiar with issues, legal terminology, and resources for planning to provide andfinance care to neurologically impaired elderly. In a survey of 68 participating families, over 90% had taken one or more planning actions following the workshop, including developing a specific plan for providing and financing services and developing a power-of-attorney for decision making.

426   Premo, Terri. (1984-1985). A blessing to our declining years: feminine response to filial duty in the New Republic. International Journal of Aging and Human Development, 20(1), 69-74.

Examination of the ties that bound adult daughters to their aged parents in the late 18th and early 19th centuries. The contemporary dilemma of filial duty has a long history.

427   Pruchno, Rachel. (1990). The effects of help patterns on the mental health of spouse caregivers. Research on Aging, 12(1), 57-71.

Investigates patterns of task assistance and social support received by 315 people who were the primary caregivers to spouses suffering from Alzheimer's disease. Although spousal caregivers were old and frail, they continued to provide the bulk of care. There was minimal help provided for any other source. There was no relationship found between existence of task support or social support and mental health.

428   Pruchno, Rachel, and Resch, Nancy. (1989). Husbands and wives as caregivers: antecedents of depression and burden. Gerontologist, 29(2), 159-165.

The sole predictor of depression for caregiving spouses of persons suffering from Alzheimer's disease was ill health. For wives, less emotional involvement also was predictive. There were found no significant predictors for burden among husbands. For wives, burden was associated with poorer health, less emotional investment, greater spouse impairment, and provision of more assistance with tasks. Authors suggest that demands of the caregiver role are experienced differently by men and by women. "Greater attention to the ways in which men and women attach meaning to the role of caregiver and incorporate this role into the rest of their lives is important."

429   Quayhagen, Mary, and Quayhagen, Margaret. (1989). Differential effects of family-based strategies on Alzheimer's disease. Gerontologist, 29(2), 150.

Assessment of home-based program of cognitive stimulation for the functional status of patients with Alzheimer's disease as well as the well-being of caregivers. Patients in this home-based program maintained their levels of cognitive and behavioral functioning while improving emotionally. The comparison group of patients deteriorated. Caregivers who participated in this program maintained their well-being and improved their resources for coping.

430   Quinn, Joan. (1987). Family therapy. In Maddox,
         George (Ed.), The encyclopedia of aging, pp. 250-
         251. New York: Springer Publishing Company, 890p.

Explains the history and theoretical foundation of family
therapy. Discusses problems associated with aging and the
family, as well as group therapy for caregivers.

431   Quinn, William; Hughston, George; and Hubler, David.
         (1984).   Preservation of independence through
         nonformal support systems: implications and
         promise. In Quinn, William, and Hughston, George
         (Eds.), Independent aging: family and social
         systems perspectives, pp. 214-242.   Rockville,
         Maryland: Aspen Systems Corp., 300p.

Consideration of social networks of family, friends, and
neighbors as valuable support systems. "The presence of energy
and strength in these networks, the shortages of professionals
trained to work with the elderly, the financial limitations of
providing formal support, and the qualitative aspects of these
network contribute to the justification for considering the
importance of nonformal support."

432   Rakowski, William, and Clark, Noreen.   (1985).
         Future outlook, caregiving, and care-receiving in
         the family context. Gerontologist, 25(6), 618-623.

Investigated future outlook as an aspect of family caregiving
and care-receiving. Restricted future outlook for both groups
was found to be associated with situations of greater
impairment, more extensive assistance, and greater stress. The
finding was the central role played by family communication and
the importance of maintaining a future orientation.

433   Reed, Bruce; Stone, Arthur; and Neale, John.
         (1990). Effects of caring for a demented relative
         on elders' life events and appraisals.
         Gerontologist, 30(2), 200-205.

Analyzed weekly ratings of events and appraisals from 19
caregivers of dementia patients and 19 control subjects over
four weeks. Caregivers reported more negative events overall
than did control subjects, but significant differences were
found in events of only two of the 11 life areas that were
measured. "Caregivers' negative appraisals were more frequent
and more intense than those of control subjects in virtually
every life area."

434   Roberto, Karen, and Scott, Jean.   (1984-1985).
         Friendship patterns among older women.
         International Journal of Aging and Human
         Development, 19(1), 1-10.

Friendship patterns among white, middle class, urban women, 65
or older, were studied. Older widows received more help from
their friends than did married older women. Older women, in
general, were found to be making use of the natural support
systems around them.

435   Rubin, Allen, and Shuttlesworth, Guy.   (1983).
         Engaging families as support resources in nursing
         home care: ambiguity in the subdivision of tasks.
         Gerontologist, 23(6), 632-636.

Partially corroborates a previous study which found that
substantial ambiguity in the subdivision of tasks between
families and staff may hinder efforts to engage families as
support resources in nursing home care. Combines this study
with the previous one to identify tasks in the care process
that appear to contain the greatest amount of role ambiguity
and that require improved communication and clarification among
relatives and staff.

436   Rubinstein, Robert. (1984). Old men living alone:
         social networks and informal supports. In Quinn,
         William, and Hughston, George (Eds.), Independent
         aging: family and social systems perspectives, pp.
         194-211. Rockville, Maryland: Aspen Systems Corp.,
         300p.

Reports a study of elderly men using a participant-observation
method. Uses exchange framework to examine network functioning
and emphasizes the "contextualized" idea of support systems.
Significant differences were found in late life between ever-
married and never-married men, between men with children and
men without children, and between men whose children are sons
and men with at least one daughter. "For men, the
contextualization and segregation of areas of social networks
(paid work, volunteer work, senior center) was common; other
contacts were enduring."

437   Scogin, Forrest; Beall, Colleen; Bynum, Jerry;
         Stephens, Gretchen; Grote, Nicholas; Baumhover,
         Lorin; and Bolland, John.   (1989).   Training
         for abusive caregivers: an unconventional approach
         to an intervention dilemma. Journal of Elder Abuse
         and Neglect, 1(4), 73-86.

Proposes a model of elder abuse intervention based on a
recently implemented caregiver training program. "Caregivers
at-risk for abuse were offered training through mental health
centers on biopsychosocial issues in aging, problem-solving,
stress and anger management, and utilization of community
resources. . . . Participants experienced some reduction in
symptoms of psychological distress and caregiving burden over
time while symptoms worsened or remained unchanged for nonparticipants."

438   Shanas, Ethel.   (1986).   The family as a social
         support system in old age. In Troll, Lillian (Ed.),
         Family issues in social gerontology, 85-96. New
         York: Springer Publishing Company, 382p.

Reports research findings on two aspects of the family as a
social support system--family care for the elderly in time of
illness, and family visiting patterns as these are reported by
old people in the U.S. Data from a national survey of
noninstitutionalized persons 65 and over. It was found that

the immediate family of the older person--husbands, wives, and children--is the major social support of elderly persons in time of illness. The major tie of the elderly to the community is the extended family of the old person--children, siblings, and other relatives. Patterns of family help to the elderly in time of illness and family visiting indicate need on the part of the elderly and the mutual expectations of each generation of the other. Old people seek help, first, from their families, then neighbors, and, finally, from bureaucratic replacements for families (social workers, ministers, community agencies, and others). Family members help the elderly as best they can, either directly or by linking older family members with bureaucratic institutions.

439   Shanas, Ethel, and Sussman, Marvin. (1981). The family in later life: social structure and social policy. In Fogel, Robert; Hatfield, Elaine; Kiesler, Sara; and Shanas, Ethel (Eds.), Aging, stability and change in the family, pp. 211-231. New York: Academic Press, 341p.

Focuses on the need for care of the frail and other vulnerable persons among the elderly. Families are changing, but traditional concepts of the family still seem to be important in the thinking of decisionmakers. The authors discuss family structure and living arrangements for the elderly, linkages between older people and their families, the use of the family as a link with bureaucracy on behalf of elderly family members, and policy and program implications of the family as a social support system.

440   Shore, Barbara. (1985). Extended kin as helping networks. In Sauer, William, and Coward, Ray (Eds.), Social support networks and the care of the elderly, pp. 108-120. New York: Springer Publishing Company, 284p.

The author indicates that the general notion that older Americans are alone, with no family or other supports, is not upheld by research findings. The older person's first source of help almost always is a family member or friends and neighbors. "Family networks persist in the face of institutions and norms that result in treating people as commodities rather than human beings."

441   Silliman, Rebecca, and Sternberg, Josef. (1988). Family caregiving: impact of patient functioning and underlying causes of dependency. The Gerontologist, 28(3), 377-382.

Illustrations of the different demands placed on family caregivers by different physical, social, psychological, and cognitive disabilities of the dependent persons. Hip fracture, dementia, and stroke are used as examples.

442   Simmons, Kathryn; Ivry, Joann; and Seltzer, Marsha. (1985). Agency-family collaboration. Gerontologist, 25(4), 343-346.

Reports on Family-centered Community Care for the Elderly, a research and demonstration project intended to strengthen and structure the relationship between informal and formal support systems. Describes how family members are trained in case management techniques by the social worker for their elderly relatives, and then share case management with the social worker.

443   Soldo, Beth; and Myllyluoma, Jaana. (1983). Caregivers who live with dependent elderly. Gerontologist, 23(6), 605-611.

Uses a nationally representative data base to construct statistical profiles of intrahousehold caregivers in three types of households. Examines the potential for disruption of each type of caregiving arrangement in terms of the care needs of the older person and the competing demands on the caregivers. "Situations where care is provided to a dependent, unmarried relative appear to be most vulnerable to dissolution."

444   Tennstedt, Sharon; McKinlay, John; and Sullivan, Lisa. (1989). Informal care for frail elders: the role of secondary caregivers. Gerontologist, 29(5), 677-683.

Describes the identity and activities of secondary caregivers (often spouse and children the primary caregiver). Secondary caregivers provide a wide variety of help, but much less than the primary caregiver, and the help is provided in a supplementary pattern, rather than complementary, to that of the primary caregiver.

445   Toseland, Ronald; Rossiter, Charles; and Labrecque, Mark. (1989). The effectiveness of peer-led and professionally led groups to support family caregivers. Gerontologist, 29(4), 465-471.

Subjects in professionally-led and peer-led groups "experienced significant improvements in psychological functioning, increases in informal support networks, and positive personal changes in handling of the caregiving role when compared with control participants. Professionally-led groups produced the greatest improvement in psychological functioning, and peer-led groups produced the greatest increases in informal support networks."

446   Toseland, Ronald; and Rossiter, Charles. (1989). Group interventions to support family caregivers: a review and analysis. Gerontologist, 29(4), 438-448.

Reviews 29 evaluative studies. Reveals that there is no clear link established "between participants' satisfaction and other outcomes for caregivers, such as improving coping skills, preventing psychological disturbances, increasing caregiver support systems, or improving caregivers' ability to care for themselves."

447   Vandivort, Rita.   (1985).   Caring for disabled
         elders. In Browne, Colette, and Onzuka-Anderson,
         Roberta (Eds.), Our aging parents: a practical
         guide to eldercare, pp. 30-38.   Honolulu:
         University of Hawaii Press, 278p.

Caregivers at home were found to be doing a physically and
psychologically demanding job with little assistance either
from the government or from their communities. "Most do so
because of love and affection for the elder and because they
wish to avoid nursing home placement. Survival strategies for
caregivers include setting limits, building a support network,
minimizing special efforts, maximizing independence, and
utilizing community services."

448   Viscusi, W. Kip.   (1981).   An assessment of aid to
         the elderly: incentive effects and the elderly's
         role in society.   In Fogel, Robert; Hatfield,
         Elaine; Kiesler, Sara; and Shanas, Ethel (Eds.),
         Aging, stability and change in the family, pp. 169-
         183. New York: Academic Press, 341p.

Analysis of the choice of the family structure and the role of
government policy in decisions concerning aid to the elderly.
Looks at how information obtained from the elderly's actions
can be used to target assistance more effectively, and
summarizes broader policy implications.   Authors recommend,
"There should be a continuing reexamination of government
programs to determine which [impact] has a substantial,
deleterious effect on the aged's welfare and which provisions
can be altered to improve the effectiveness of policies."

449   Wenger, G. Clare.   (1990).   Elderly carers: the
         need for appropriate intervention.   Aging and
         Society, 10, 197-219.

Focus on elderly caregivers. At least one-third of elderly
people can expect to become carers during retirement.
Differences between elderly and younger carers include:
"elderly care for shorter periods, are more likely to provide
intimate personal care and heavy nursing tasks associated with
terminal care, and to be caring for their most significant
other, usually a spouse." The author suggests that "elderly
carers represent a sub-group of carers with special needs not
necessarily met by present service provision."

450   Winfield, Fairlee. (1987). Workplace solutions for
         women under eldercare pressure. Personnel, 64(7),
         31-32, 34-39.

Author indicates that caring for elderly relatives is being
added to women's traditional roles of wife, mother, and
homemaker, as well as the new role of worker.   Trends are
cited, including the aging of the population, as well as
problems, such as loss of worker productivity. Presents model
corporate solutions.

451   Young, Rosalie, and Kahana, Eva.   (1989).
         Specifying caregiver outcomes: gender and

> relationship aspects of caregiving strain.
> *Gerontologist*, **29**(5), 660-666.

Analyzes gender and relationship of 183 heart patient-caregiver dyads with regard to process and outcome of caregiving. The finding was a consistent pattern of strain for caregivers. "Women, nonspousal caregivers, and daughters, in particular, experienced the most severe aftereffects."

452   York, Jonathan; and Caslyn, Robert. (1986). **Family involvement in nursing homes.** In Troll, Lillian (Ed.), **Family issues in current gerontology**, pp. 178-188. **New York: Springer Publishing Company, 382p.**

Study of some of the factors that affect family involvement in nursing home care. Data collected on the extent of the problem (i.e., the quality of family-resident interactions), availability and utilization of existing services, and willingness of family members to use services that might be offered in the future. The findings were that families did not separate themselves from their elderly relatives, but visited and talked frequently with older relatives prior to placement in the nursing home and often helped them with a variety of household tasks. When a crisis occurred, families did not use alternatives to nursing home care, and families were not very sophisticated in choosing nursing homes. Families visited their relatives after they entered the nursing home, but often did not enjoy the visits. For emotional support, families relied on nursing home personnel, and were willing to take part in programs offered by the nursing home staff.

453   Zarit, Steven; and Toseland, Ronald. (1989). **Current and future direction in family caregiving research.** *Gerontologist*, **29**(4), 481-483.

Symposium suggests ways to improve measurement of treatment effects in studies of group interventions for family caregivers: "better specification of goals and outcomes, development of measures less likely to have floor and ceiling effects, and determination of whether specific treatment processes have been implemented and goals attained."

Films

454   Brigham Young University. (1977). **The mailbox.**

An elderly woman waits each day to receive a letter from her children. Film depicts the loneliness of older persons when family members do not communicate meaningfully with them.

455   CBS News, Reemstma, Judy, and Carousel Film and Video. (1980). **What shall we do about mother?**

Experiences of two families deciding what to do about their aging parents. CBS News Correspondent Marlene Sanders narrates this documentary look at the plight of the elderly through the heartbreak suffered by two families as they make emotional and financial decisions about what to do about their parents.

456   **Cohen, Susan, and Whiteford, William.** (1984). Living with Grace.

Shows experiences of one woman with Alzheimer's disease who is cared for at home by her husband. Her husband affirms Grace's need for security and compassion and is shown as remarkably loving and companionate to his wife.

457   **Mann, Delbert, director.** (1978). Home to stay.

Story of elderly male stroke victim whose son wants to have him declared incompetent and placed in a nursing home. Sarah, a teenaged granddaughter, is violently opposed, and eventually becomes responsible for his care.

458   **Metromedia Producers Corp.** (1982). Someone I once knew.

Case studies of Alzheimer's disease patients. Validates the humanity of the Alzheimer's patient.

459   **Regional Video Network.** (1983). Parenting the parent.

Discusses the common problems encountered when caring for an elderly parent.

460   **Terra Nova Films.** (1984). My mother, my father.

Four families from different socioeconomic and ethnic backgrounds deal with an aging parent. "The fact that different options are chosen by the four families reflects that families are indeed unique, and need the freedom to choose the caregiving arrangement that is best for everyone involved . . . . These four families try to make their choices with the interests of the aging parent as well as their own best interests in mind."

461   **WITF-TV; Cohen, E.; and Stanaway, A.** (1981). Alzheimer's disease: you are not alone.

Shows experiences of four Alzheimer's victims and their families.

462   **WNET.** (1972). The aged.

A young Vietnam veteran returns home to find his parents are not able to care for themselves. Focus is on the problem of helping loved ones when they become old and helpless.

Documents

463   **Brody, Elaine.** (1987). Women-in-the-middle: the mental health effects of parent care, women's mental health occasional paper series. Washington, D.C.:

National Institute of Mental Health, U.S. Department of Health and Human Services, 40p.

Describes issues of "women-in-the-middle," women helping a disabled elderly relative. These women most often are in middle age and are caught in the middle by multiple responsibilities that compete for their time and energy. Concludes that "attention to filial caregivers is in the interests of the mental health of all generations, since the well-being of each family member is interlocked with that of the other family members."

464   Church Council of Greater Seattle, Washington. (1987). How to hire helpers: a guide for elders and their families. Seattle, Washington: Task Force on Aging, Church Council of Greater Seattle, 16p.

A guide for use by older persons and their families in hiring someone to assist periodically with household routines and personal care. Offers suggestions and lists steps needed to hire a worker. Covers determining what help is needed, setting up a job description/contract, sample contract, contract form advertising, interviewing, interview checklist, questions to ask references, hiring, financial and legal considerations, keeping your worker, and a flowchart describing the hiring process.

465   Day, Alice. (1985). "We can manage": expectations about care and varieties of family support among people 75 years and over. Melbourne, Australia: Institute of Family Studies, 176p.

Explores the significance of family support to people in old age. Presents data from interviews with 23 elderly persons living in the community in Sydney, Australia. A key finding from the study was that many old people are reluctant to ask their children to help.

466   Heald, Jane. (1986). Families and aging: resources for individuals and groups. Swarthmore, Pennsylvania: National Support Center for Families of the Aging, 16p.

A document originally prepared for participants at a "Helping Families of the Aging" workshop. Contains annotated lists of advice books, personal accounts, group manuals, and periodicals about caregiving.

467   Montgomery, Rhonda, and Borgatta, Edgar. (1985). Family support project: final report to the Administration on Aging. Washington, D.C.: Administration on Aging, Office of Human Development Services, U.S. Department of Health and Human Services, 163p.

Objective of this project was to implement and assess family support services that were aimed at enhancing the ability and willingness of families to retain the primary responsibility for caring for aged family members. An experimental design was used to assess the impact of family support programs that provided family training and education services, volunteer respite services, and family training in conjunction with volunteer respite services.

468   Smith, Bert. (1986). **Widening the generational circle: family caregivers**. Austin, Texas: Hogg Foundation for Mental Health, 17p.

Addresses the problem faced by families with an aging or disabled member and the stress associated with the family's role in caregiving. Discusses emotions experienced by family caregivers, especially when the caregiver is an adult child caring for an elderly or frail parent, and the trauma of placing a relative in a nursing home. Provides guidelines to help caregivers cope with the stresses associated with the caregiver role and gives suggestions on sources of help.

469   U.S. Congress. House. (1987). Report by the Chairman of the Subcommittee on Health and Long-term Care of the Select Committee on Aging. **Abuses in guardianship of the elderly and infirm: a national disgrace**. Washington, D.C.: U.S. Government Printing Office, 95p.

Presents a report on the guardianship of the elderly and the disabled and on abuses that may occur in such guardianship situations. Presents a set of 12 questions and answers about guardianship, including such issues as a definition of guardianship, who can be a guardian, the legal process for developing a guardianship, and some of the most frequently cited problems with the current American guardianship system.

470   U.S. Congress. House. (1986). Hearing before the Select Committee on Aging. **Alzheimer's Disease and related disorders: the government's response**. Washington, D.C.: U.S. Government Printing Office, 75p.

Presents testimonies and prepared statements from a Congressional hearing on Alzheimer's Disease, its treatment, funding for research, legal aspects, and support for families of Alzheimer's victims.

471   U.S. Congress. House. (1988). Hearing before the Subcommittee on Human Services of the Select Committee on Aging. **Caregiving: new approaches to an old tradition**. Washington, D.C.:   U.S. Government Printing Office, 95p.

This publication reports an oversight hearing held so that subcommittee members can assess the issues involved in caregiving and develop a federal response in terms of legislation and programs.   "Of particular interest is the respite care program as a caregiving service."

472   U.S. Congress. House. (1988). Hearing before the Select Committee on Children, Youth, and Families.

Double duty: caring for children and the elderly.
Washington, D.C.: U.S. Government Printing Office,
139p.

Text of a Congressional hearing on the concerns of members of
the "baby boom" generation who find themselves caring for both
their elderly parents and their own children at home.

473   U.S. Congress. House. (1988). A study by the
       Subcommittee on Human Services of the Select
       Committee on Aging. **Exploding the myths:**
       caregiving in America. Washington, D.C.: U.S.
       Government Printing Office, 79p.

This Congressional study underscores the continuing
contribution of the family in providing care to the frail and
disabled elderly. Distills existing information, provides new
data based on national estimates, and highlights both public
and private sector initiatives targeted at caregiving. Covers
status of current public policies, public sector support for
informal caregivers, federal legislation, and private sector
response.

Dissertations

474   Bakaly, John. (1989). **Appraisal of stressful**
       encounters, coping responses, and family role change
       as predictors of stress and burden in spousal
       caregivers of cancer patients. Unpublished doctoral
       dissertation, University of Southern California,
       number of pages not given.

Assessed appraisals of stressful encounters, coping responses,
and family role changes as predictors of stress and burden in
spousal, primary caregivers to pre-terminal and terminal cancer
patients. Subjects ranged from 36 to 85 years old.
Maintaining a sense of humor was explained as a method for
reducing stress and burden.

475   Barusch, Amanda. (1985). **Who cares: the**
       relationship between family assistance and formal
       services provided to the frail elderly in case-
       managed and traditional service environments.
       Unpublished doctoral dissertation, University of
       California, Berkeley, 144p.

Considers relationship between services and family assistance
to the elderly, and the impact of case management on that
relationships. Findings were that by coordinating service
delivery, the case manager reduces the substitution of services
for family support; however, by relieving the family of
responsibility for care management, the case manager reduces
family involvement in care. Case managers are less inclined
than service allocators in the traditional system to substitute
family assistance for services.

476   Bowers, Barbara. (1984). **Intergenerational**
       caretaking: processes and consequences of creating

knowledge.   Unpublished doctoral dissertation, University of California, San Francisco, 457p.

Analyzes processes by which knowledge about intergenerational caretaking is created, and demonstrates the use of dimensional analysis to discover these processes. The conceptualizations of caretakers and aged parents interviewed were subjected to a dimensional analysis to reveal the conceptual processes by which these families create knowledge about caretaking.

477   Brieff, Robert.   (1986).   **Correlates of demoralization/depression and related conditions in primary support persons caring for dependent elderly relatives**.   Unpublished doctoral dissertation, Columbia University Teachers College, 384p.

Analysis of impact of caretaking on primary support persons assuming varying degrees of task assistance and other responsibilities for elderly relatives.

478   Castro, Concepcion.   (1984).   **Family member caregivers of chronically ill elderly persons: their stressors and social support**.   Unpublished doctoral dissertation, Boston University, 125p.

Examines the stressors of caregiving and the influences social support have on the feeling of stress experienced by the caregiver of the chronically ill elderly person.   The functional ability of the patient cared for was found to be a more potent influence and a better predictor of the caregiver's feeling of stress than the social support received.

479   Cole, Ellan. (1983). **Old folks at home: who cares for the frail elderly?**   Unpublished doctoral dissertation, Columbia University, 175p.

Analyzes social networks as a resource for coping with failing strength and other disabilities.   Examines the contributions their family, friends, and others are making to the care of frail elderly in a particular community. The primary caretaker role emerged as the most outstanding feature of network organization.   In the rural community studied, kinship norms had a great deal of strength in determining who assumed the role and its comprehensiveness.

480   Dundon, Margaret.   (1987).   **Distress and coping among caregivers of victims of Alzheimer's disease and related disorders**.   Unpublished doctoral dissertation, State University of New York at Buffalo, 129p.

Explores the variables thought to influence the levels of distress and subsequent adaptation experienced by caregivers of family members with Alzheimer's disease or a related disorder. The variance in distress was accounted for by the use of escape-avoidance coping strategies, caregiver health, and family relations.

481   Edelman, Perry. (1986). **The impact of formal services to the homebound elderly on informal caregivers and the level and types of services they provide**. Unpublished doctoral dissertation, Loyola University of Chicago, 154p.

Investigates impact of community care to the homebound elderly on informal caregivers (family and friends) and the types of services they provide. "Formal services which provided respite to the informal caregiver were found somewhat less frequently than formal services which simply replaced informal services."

482   Fischgrund, Ellen. (1981). **Coping with terminal illness: a case study of primary caregivers in a hospice home care program**. Unpublished doctoral dissertation, Case Western Reserve University, 247p.

Examines the role of family members designated as primary caregivers and the key elements in hospice home care. General conclusions and discussion about issues affecting hospice home care processes, including family functioning, medical delivery system, and the philosophy of hospice care.

483   Fitting, Melinda. (1984). **Caregivers for dementia patients: a comparison of men and women**. Unpublished doctoral dissertation, University of Denver, 182p.

Families are the primary caregivers for two-thirds of dementia victims. Compares males and females to determine if there were significant sex and age differences in a population of caregivers for dementia patients. "While there were statistical differences noted between male and female caregivers, these two groups did appear to be remarkably similar as caregivers."

484   Fox, Mary. (1986). **Social support and psychological distress among spouse caregivers of dementia patients**. Unpublished doctoral dissertation, The University of Arizona, 114p.

Examines informal support systems of spouse caregivers of dementia patients in relation to two variables associated with maintaining their patient at home--caregiver's experience of psychological distress and caregiver's need for formal support. Level of caregiver anxiety was found to be significantly related to perceived need for counseling services.

485   Gibeau, Janice. (1986). **Breadwinners and caregivers: working patterns of women working full-time and caring for dependent elderly family members**. Unpublished doctoral dissertation, Brandeis University, The F. Heller Graduate School for Advanced Studies in Social Welfare, 313p.

Examines how working women manage their work lives while serving as primary caregivers for dependent elderly family members. Findings were that working caregivers have significant, longstanding, and competing attachments to both their elderly family members and their employment.

486   Gray-Shelgrove, Rosemary. (1982). **The experience of giving care to a parent dying of cancer: meanings reflected through the process of shared reflection**. Unpublished doctoral dissertation, University of Toronto, 448p.

Attempt to understand what is meaningful in having given care to a parent dying of cancer and in talking about that event with another person who has had a similar experience. An image of the intentional person derives from four key understandings: "hopefulness emerged out of suffering, relationship was fundamental to meaningfulness, pre-reflecting knowing was grasped through talking, and mutual affirmation of persons occurred as they shared reflection."

487   Hasselkus, Betty. (1987). **Family caregivers for the elderly at home: an ethnography of meaning and informal learning**. Unpublished doctoral dissertation, The University of Wisconsin-Madison, 191p.

Describes meaning of caregiving to family caregivers for the frail elderly in the community and identifies patterns of informal learning imbedded in the caregiving experience.

488   Herman, Shirley. (1986). **Enabling relationships between female pre-teenagers and elderly women in the congregations**. Unpublished doctoral dissertation, Drew University, 139p.

Format of Saturday morning programs for nine weeks helped "to initiate and nourish the growth of mutual understanding and caring relationships between the members of the group."

489   Horowitz, Amy. (1982). **Adult children as caregivers to elderly parents: correlates and consequences**. Unpublished doctoral dissertation, Columbia University, 423p.

Systematically examines the caregiving relationship in order better to understand its causes and consequences. The typical caregiving child is a late middle-aged daughter who holds concurrent responsibilities to other family members as well as working outside the home. Emotional support was the most universal caregiving activity, although substantial proportions also assisted with linkage tasks and instrumental services, as well as financial assistance. The primary strains of caregiving were found to be the result of the emotional aspects of providing care and the restrictions on time and freedom necessitated by caregiving responsibilities. The most salient independent predictors of caregiving involvement were: the parent's level of impairment, the quality of the parent-child affective relationship, the child's sex and marital status, and the degree of anticipatory planning for caregiving. The child's employment status did not impinge upon fulfilling caregiving responsibilities.

490   Houlihan, Mary. (1986). Family caregivers of the terminally ill elderly and the terminal illness home care experience. Unpublished doctoral dissertation, Fordham University, 315p.

Explores nature and needs of caregivers. Findings suggested increased provider focus on caregivers' as well as patients' needs, outreach to homeland and solitary caregivers, initial preparation of caregivers for unfamiliar role responsibilities, continued monitoring of home caregiving situations, and reevaluation of current restrictive financial guidelines for care at home for the terminally ill elderly.

491   Ishii-Kuntz, Masako. (1987). The impact of informal social support on the subjective sense of well-being: comparisons across stages of adulthood. Unpublished doctoral dissertation, Washington State University, 140p.

Looks at whether support given by family, friends, and neighbors differentially influences one's well-being and whether the relationship between social support and well-being change across stages of adulthood. Over the life cycle, support from neighbors may play a complementary role for family and friends' support.

492   Ivry, Joann. (1985). Social service agencies and family members: an attempt at partnership through training of family members as case managers. Unpublished doctoral dissertation, The Ohio State University, 229p.

Attempts to develop and evaluate a partnership strategy between a family service agency and family members--sharing responsibility for case management functions. An unanticipated finding was that control group elderly clients performed more case management tasks than experimental group elderly clients, suggesting that capable elderly clients can assume case management responsibility for themselves.

493   Janas, Monica. (1988). Control, introversion, and social support: a model of loneliness in Alzheimer's caregivers. Unpublished doctoral dissertation, Virginia Polytechnic Institute and State University, 141p.

Examines loneliness in caregivers of Alzheimer's family members. Results were that introversion, control, social support, and income account for almost two-thirds of the variance in loneliness. Higher income was associated with higher levels of loneliness in the caregiver.

494   Jones, Beverly. (1986). Relationship, social support, appraisal, coping, and meaning in life in predicting stress in spousal caregivers of dementia patients. Unpublished doctoral dissertation, University of Southern California, number of pages not given.

Cognitive-phenomenological and existential perspectives of caregiver stress for those caring for dementia patients at home. Concluded that a synthesis of cognitive, behavioral, and existential perspectives is possible in planning interventions to alleviate caregiver stress.

495   Kahn, L. Louise. (1987). **Family of origin experiences and selected factors as predictors of adult child caregiving to an aged parent**. Unpublished doctoral dissertation, The Florida State University, 152p.

Examined influence of family of origin experiences of autonomy and intimacy and other selected variables as predictors of adult children choosing the roles of caregiver or non-caregiver for their aged dependent parent. Females and youngest females were caregivers.

496   Kauffman, Janice. (1982). **The caring role of middle-aged employed women with elderly mothers: an exploratory study with implications for home economics educational programming**. Unpublished doctoral dissertation, Michigan State University, 233p.

Explores the caring roles of adult unemployed women with elderly mothers and identifies scientific approaches as to how home economics education could support these roles. Concludes that the majority of the daughters felt that their employment limited the amount of time they were able to spend with their mothers. Many of the daughters felt guilty that they could not spend more time with their mothers.

497   Kayser, Lynda. (1984). **Women caregivers: stresses, coping mechanisms, and the effectiveness of respite care**. Unpublished doctoral dissertation, University of Maine, 273p.

Investigated areas of satisfaction, stress, and coping mechanisms among women caregivers of older relatives, and the use of respite care as a tool in the reduction of stress. Caregivers were satisfied that they had accepted the caregiver role and prevented the institutionalization of the elder. Causes of stress for the caregivers were role fatigue, worry, communication with hearing impaired elders, arguments with elders, emotional dependency of elders upon caregivers, and relationships with other family members, especially siblings. Caregivers coped by relying on social sources, seeking active and passive diversions, taking firm action, thinking positively, and professing a belief that they would not someday become dependent upon their children. Caregivers with respite care appeared to have lower levels of stress than those without it.

498   Kinney, Jennifer. (1987). **Development and evaluation of a scale to assess the stress of caring for an older adult with Alzheimer's disease**. Unpublished doctoral dissertation, Kent State University, 188p.

Developed and evaluated the data quality of a scale designed to assess the stress of caring for a family member with Alzheimer's disease. Scale was based on transactional theories of stress, which hold that individuals' appraisals of events are more strongly associated with well-being than are the objective events themselves.

499   Krach, Margaret. (1985). **Rural adults' perceptions of filial responsibility for and affectional bonds with their aged parents.** Unpublished doctoral dissertation, The Ohio State University, 148p.

Perceived levels of filial responsibility of rural, adult children for their elderly parents were found to be significantly related to their perceived levels of affection for their parents. The mean level of filial responsibility and affection was lower for females than it was for males.

500   McCrory, Audrey. (1984). **The impact of caregiving on the marital need satisfaction of older wives with dependent husbands.** Unpublished doctoral dissertation, The University of North Carolina at Greensboro, 149p.

Investigated influence of caregiving on the marital need satisfaction of older women who were caring for their dependent, functionally impaired husbands at home. Concluded that marital need satisfaction is unrelated to the caregiving status. However, the marital need satisfaction scores of both caregivers and noncaregivers decrease as the husbands' level of functional impairment increases. Social support, health, and socioeconomic status are of no relative importance to the marital need satisfaction of either caregivers or noncaregivers. Subjects characterized their marital status as "long-term marital limbo."

501   Mederer, Helen. (1982). **The transition to a parent caring role by adult children: a model case of role transition and difficulty of role performance.** Unpublished doctoral dissertation, University of Minnesota, 261p.

A study of the effects of adult children providing help to older parents. Describes and predicts the ease with which adult children were able to change their helping role vis-a-vis their parents from reciprocal help between parents and children to a "parent caring" role, and to assess effects of ease of role transition on subsequent ease of parent caring role performance. Results were not supportive of the theory. Anticipatory socialization and adult children's household incomes were inversely correlated with ease of role transition, contrary to the expected direction. Degree of filial responsibility was directly correlated with ease of role transition. Data did not support any effect of ease of role transition on difficulty of helping.

502   Polansky, Elinor. (1982). **Caregiving of the chronically ill at home: the social, physical, and financial impact on the family caregiver.**

Unpublished   doctoral   dissertation,   Columbia
University, 375p.

Describes caregiving families, their caregiving functions,
financial resources, availability of services, and impact of
caregiving tasks on the family caregivers.   Provides an
assessment tool for early identification of high risk family
caregiving situations and provides basis for ordering priority
of the distribution of needed services. Types of services most
required: decentralized distribution of information and
services; training and support groups; financial support for
home care services, drugs, and equipment; tax exemptions and
cash grants.   Many well-intentioned caregivers lack the
capacity to assume full caregiving responsibility, but
supportive structures, if placed early enough, can sustain them
as an essential part of the health care system.

503   Rau, Marie.   (1986).   **Elderly stroke patients and
        their partners: a longitudinal study of social
        support and well-being changes associated with a
        disabling   stroke**.   Unpublished   doctoral
        dissertation, Portland State University, 517p.

Explored relationship of demographic, social network, social
support,   and   stroke-related   factors   to   depressive
symptomatology and well-being in 50 elderly individuals who had
recently suffered a first, completed stroke and their partners.

504   Rowe, Jan.   (1982).   **An ethnography of women's
        experiences with a dying husband and their grief and
        redefinition   of   self**.   Unpublished   doctoral
        dissertation, Georgia State University, 252p.

Ethnographic study exploring the relationship between women's
anticipation between women's anticipations of their husband's
deaths and their grief and redefinition of self after he dies.
Three   themes--caretaking,   coping,   and   communication--were
associated with their grief and redefinition of self.   Choices
of themes were influenced by commitment to being available to
the husband and his needs.   The women who had the least
difficulty with their grief and redefinition of self were those
who made a realistic appraisal, experienced their involvement
in the husband's care as strengthening, and communicated openly
with him.

505   Scharlach, Andrew.   (1985).   **Filial relationships
        among women and their elderly mothers**.   Unpublished
        doctoral dissertation, Stanford University, 137p.

Examines proposition that strain experienced by an adult
daughter can interfere with the nature of her relationship with
her aging mother, and have a potentially deleterious impact on
the mother. "Findings provide support for the hypothesis that
mother-daughter relationships in later life can be improved
when daughters are helped to resolve potentially conflictual
personal expectations regarding their responsibilities to their
aging mothers."

506   Sharma, Sushil.   (1985).   **A study of chronic
        diseases and family burden**. Unpublished doctoral
        dissertation, University of Maryland Baltimore
        County, 218p.

"A matched case comparison design study conducted to determine
whether female caregivers of elderly persons suffering dementia
experience different levels of burden than their counterparts
caring for elderly persons with chronic physical diseases
. . . . Caregivers of chronic physically ill patients were
found to experience significantly greater sense of social,
physical, and overall burden. . . . Dependency level was found
to be associated with burden among physically ill patients, but
behavioral characteristics were associated with burden among
caregivers of demented elderly patients."

507   Shuman, Susan. (1988). **Mothers' attributions about
        daughters' caregiving: an application for Kelley's
        personal relationships model**. Unpublished doctoral
        dissertation, The Pennsylvania State University,
        151p.

Applied Kelley's theory of attributional processes in personal
relationships to the mother-daughter caregiving relationship in
later life to learn more about mothers' perceptions of
caregiving and the association between those perceptions and
the quality of the relationship.   Study shows that
attributional processes exist in parent-child relationships and
are related to relationship quality.

508   Simon-Rusinowitz, Lori.   (1987).   **Government
        participation in long-term care of the elderly**.
        Unpublished doctoral dissertation, University of
        Illinois at Chicago, 267p.

Examines views of home care agency administrators and
policymakers regarding a policy to pay family caregivers. Most
participants thought government involvement in caring for the
elderly was appropriate; however, they varied about the extent
of responsibility.

509   Stanley, Renee. (1987). **The value of support
        groups for caregivers of a patient with Alzheimer's
        disease: a family systems perspective**. Unpublished
        doctoral dissertation, Texas Woman's University,
        number of pages not given.

Uses family systems theory to examine whether or not primary
caregivers of a patient with Alzheimer's disease perceive
support groups to be valuable means for assisting them in
dealing with their feelings of stress and burden, stress-
related symptoms, family relationships, and coping and adapting
strategies; and how this decision has been influenced by their
particular family system.

510   Stueve, Charlotte. (1985). **What's to be done about
        Mom and Dad? Daughters' relations with elderly
        parents**.   Unpublished doctoral dissertation,
        University of California, Berkeley, 239p.

Daughters were found to be more attentive when they lived near parents and the parents were in poor health. Feelings were associated with experiences of stress. Full-time workers tended to see and help their parents less.

511   **Tennstedt, Sharon.** (1984). **Informal care of frail elders in the community.** Unpublished doctoral dissertation, Boston University, 287p.

Explores role of informal caregivers in the care of frail elders in the community and determines the role of caregiving network characteristics in explaining the variability of care provided. Primary caregivers were usually spouses for males and offspring for females. Type and amount of care were related to gender and availability of the caregiver. Familial responsibility was a strong motivation for caregiving.

512   **Van Winkle, Nancy.** (1987). **Primary caregivers of relatives with dementia: the stressful experience of spouses and adult children.** Unpublished doctoral dissertation, University of Kentucky, 265p.

Uses transactional view of stress to consider similarities and differences between spouses and adult children who are caring for a relative with dementia along six dimensions: characteristics of the caregivers, characteristics of the dependent relatives, appraisal, coping resources, coping responses, and caregiver well-being. Spouses and adult children have more similarities than differences in their caregiving experiences.

513   **Walker, Ella.** (1987). **Influences on the decision of black middle-aged career women to provide care for elderly parents.** Unpublished doctoral dissertation, Texas Woman's University, 128p.

A qualitative study investigating the influences on the decision of black middle-aged career women to provide care for their elderly parents. Findings were that there was need for more care service options for career women who provide care to their elderly parents.

514   **Wilcox, Julie.** (1986). **Impact of assessor values on measurement of family care provided to the impaired elderly.** Unpublished doctoral dissertation, University of Illinois at Urbana-Champaign, 230p.

Study of influence of values on eligibility decisions in social service agencies. Examines association between individual values of professionals and their decisions related to the allocation of community services to the impaired elderly.

515   **Wright, Scott.** (1986). **The relationship of personal and social resources on coping and individual well-being in caregivers of dementia patients.** Unpublished doctoral dissertation, Oregon State University, 307p.

Constructed and assessed a theoretical model which investigates the effects of patient functioning, personal and social resources on coping behaviors, and adaptational outcomes (caregiver well-being) in caregivers of dementia patients. Findings showed support for development of intervention programs which assist caregivers in developing specific skills necessary for coping with the potential long-term role of careprovider. Findings indicate strong relations between social support and a caregiver's ability to adapt to the caregiving role.

9

Racial and Ethnic Minority Groups

Books

516   Coles, Robert. (1989). <u>The old ones of New Mexico</u>. Albuquerque: University of New Mexico Press, 74p.

A sympathetic and sensitive treatment of the elderly Mexican-Americans of Northern New Mexico. Coles, a physician, tries to understand the target population within their culture and geographic context, combining oral history and commentary.

517   Gelfand, Donald, and Kutzik, Alfred (Eds.). (1979). <u>Ethnicity and aging: theory, research and policy</u>. New York: Springer Publishing Company, 372p.

An anthology with sections ranging from theoretical and historical discussions to those dealing with particular minorities--blacks, Chicanos, Puerto Ricans, American Indians, Mormons, Japanese, and Jews.

518   Palmore, Erdman. (1975). <u>The honorable elders</u>. Durham, North Carolina: Duke University Press, 148p.

Based on data gathered in Japan in 1973. A purpose of the research was to find out whether the status of older Japanese had declined with industrialization or had maintained relatively high levels. Most evidence shows the status of Japanese elders has suffered little decline and is substantially higher than that of the aged in other industrialized countries. Another purpose was to examine the evidence from Japan bearing on the controversy between disengagement and activity theory. Palmore indicates that, "Evidence from Japan tends to support activity theory rather than disengagement theory." A third purpose of this investigation was to determine patterns of attitudes and behaviors in Japan which might suggest ways that the West could adopt to improve the situation of its elders. The author identifies respect for elders and self-respect among elders, as well as other options.

519   Ragan, Pauline, and Simonin, Mary (Eds.). (1977).
         Black and Mexican American aging: a selected
         bibliography. Los Angeles: University of Southern
         California Press.

A selected bibliography of references on socio-cultural aspects
of aging among blacks and Mexican Americans. Included are
doctoral dissertations, papers presented at professional
meetings, published articles and books. Items are those of
"fairly general interest, sufficient length, and significance."

520   Valle, Ramon, and Mendoza, Lydia. (1978). **The**
         elder Latino. San Diego, California: Center on
         Aging, San Diego State University, distributed by
         Campanile Press, 103p.

This study of Latino older persons is part of a larger cross-
cultural study of minority elders of Dan Diego County. Among
the objectives of the study were: to explore and describe the
characteristic lifestyles and primary interactional networks of
ethnic minority elderly, to identify perceptions and attitudes
of ethnic minority elders toward formal programmatic assistance
and use of formal assistance. Two overall conclusions were:
"it was critical to record and analyze information in terms of
the situational conditions in which the information was
obtained, and the researchers were struck with the varieties of
natural network resources among the Latino populations."

Articles/chapters

521   Bastida, Elena. (1978). Family structure and
         intergenerational exchange of the Hispanic American
         elderly. Gerontologist, 18(5), 48.

Summary of a study of 210 elderly Mexican-Americans, Puerto
Ricans, and Cubans--especially considering family and
intergenerational exchange. Preliminary findings suggest that
multigenerational households are infrequent and varied.

522   Bastida, Elena. (1987). Sex-typed age norms among
         older Hispanics. Gerontologist, 27(1), 59-65.

Examines age identification and age-appropriate behavior among
160 older Hispanics of Mexican, Puerto Rican, and Cuban origin.
Extensive use among all three groups and both sexes of
realistic qualifiers about one's age. Consensus on age- and
sex-appropriate behaviors, but greater strictures for women
than for men.

523   Block, Marilyn. (1979). Exiled Americans: the
         plight of the Indian aged in the United States. In
         Gelfand, Donald, and Kutzik, Alfred (Eds.),
         Ethnicity and aging: theory, research and policy,
         pp. 184-192.   New York: Springer Publishing
         Company, 372p.

An introductory and general overview of the subject of elderly
American Indians. Considers the status of research on the

situation of the Indian aged, the role played by family in their culture, and proposes directions for public policy and government agencies in addressing this group's needs.

524   Carp, Frances. (1969). Housing and minority-group elderly. (1969). The Gerontologist, 9(1), 20-24.

Reports the study of under-utilization by Mexican-Americans of public housing for the elderly in one city. Concludes that Mexican society makes staying with relatives more desirable than living among seniors.

525   Chow, Nelson. (1983). The Chinese family and support of the elderly in Hong Kong. Gerontologist, 23(6), 584-588.

Chinese family in Hong Kong is "the most fundamental unit in society." However, effectiveness of the family in caring for itselderly members is rapidly declining. "The question facing Hong Kong is the form of care that should be adopted and the ways in which the family can continue to be a source of support."

526   Fadel-Girgis, Mary. (1983). Family support for the elderly in Egypt. Gerontologist, 23(6), 589-592.

Looks at the emerging problem of the elderly in Egypt, including degree of involvement and interactions with family and society and the elderly's expectations of the role of their families, society, and the government.

527   Gibson, Rose. (1986). Outlook for the black family. In Pifer, Alan, and Bronte, D. Lydia (Eds.), Our aging society: paradox and promise, pp. 181-197. New York: W. W. Norton, 438p.

Includes discussion of blacks at midlife (divorce and separation, mental health status, reconceptualizing work and retirement) and the Black elderly. "The renowned strengths of the Black family will be put to a severe test as our society ages, and as larger and more powerful groups compete for limited resources."

528   Gibson, Rose. (1987). Reconceptualizing retirement for black Americans. Gerontologist, 27(6), 691-698.

Examination of a subsample of nonworking older black Americans (294) from the National Survey of Black Americans. Four factors contributed significantly to subjects' unretired-retired status: indistinct line between lifetime and old age work patterns, the view that occasional work is necessary, income from other than private pensions, and benefits that accrue from identifying as disabled rather than retired.

529   Heller, Tamar, and Factor, Alan. (1988). Permanency planning and black and white family caregivers of older adults with mental retardation. Mental Retardation, 26(4), 203-208.

Describes differences among older families (25 black, 75 white) regarding permanency planning for their mentally retarded dependents. Finding was that black families were less likely to want outside residential placements and were less likely to make future financial arrangements for their mentally retarded relative following their own lifetimes.

530   James, Alice; James, William; and Smith, Howard. (1984). Reciprocity as a coping strategy of the elderly: a rural Irish perspective. Gerontologist 24(5), 483-489.

Study of the aging process and the mechanisms used by the elderly to cope with age in rural Ireland. Identifies reciprocity as one of the major strategies that reinforce independence, shown in the stem family, sibling relations, pets, neighbors, parental caretakers, financial resources, and family configurations.

531   Koh, James, and Bell, William. (1987). Korean elders in the United States: intergenerational relations and living arrangements. Gerontologist, 27(1), 66-71.

Koreans 60 years of age and over in New York City were interviewed about living arrangements, service needs, and orientation to filial and formal support systems. These subjects were compared with elders in South Korea. Findings indicated that changes have occurred in intergenerational relations and living arrangements for older Koreans in the U.S., that both Korean elders and their adult children in the U.S. have accepted a pattern of coexistence more characteristic of the U.S. than of Korea.

532   Little, Virginia. (1983). International symposium: the family as a source of support for the elderly: introduction: cross-national reports on elder care in developed and developing countries. Gerontologist, 23(6), 573-575.

Presents discussion from a symposium on aging and the family, looking at information for certain developed and developing countries and the policy implications. "The chief goal was to present the research being conducted in several countries as a tool in analyzing persisting myths and stereotypes about nuclear versus extended or 'joint' families and the reverence for old people held to exist more in some cultures than others."

533   Maeda, Daisaku. (1983). Family care in Japan. Gerontologist, 23(6), 579-583.

Family continues to be "the most important source of support for the elderly in Japan." The author concludes that the relative importance of family support of the elderly will inevitably decrease because: "the proportion and real number of frail and impaired older people who are no longer independent in their daily living will greatly increase and the capability of families to care for older parents will decrease due to industrialization and urbanization."

534   Maldonado, David. (1979). Aging in the Chicano context. In Gelfand, Donald, and Kutzik, Alfred (Eds.), Ethnicity and aging: theory, research and policy, pp. 175-183. New York: Springer Publishing Company, 372p.

Examines the Chicano family, male and female roles, ethnic self-identity, ethno-cultural centrism, and cultural incongruence.

535   Maldonado, David. (1977). The Mexican-American grows old. In Kalish, Richard (Ed.), The later years: social application of gerontology, pp. 37-42. Belmont, Wadsworth Publishing Company, 402p.

Examines factors that separate the Mexican-American elderly from their majority counterparts. The extended family and its changing structure are among variables examined to explain the relative lack of attention Hispanic gerontology problems have received.

536   Malson, Michelene. (1983). The social-support systems of black families. In Lein, Laura, and Sussman, Marvin (Eds.), The ties that bind: men's and women's social networks, pp. 37-57. New York: Haworth Press, 111p.

Explores the literature on social networks of black families. Discusses theories of black families' support networks and black families' economic maintenance. "Work showing evidence of social-support systems among black families of different types supports the hypotheses that self-help systems, especially among kin, are characteristic of them."

537   Markides, Kyriakos, and Vernon, Sally. (1984). Aging, sex-role orientation, and adjustment: a three-generation study of Mexican-Americans. Journal of Gerontology, 39(5), 586-591.

Investigates the effect of sex-role orientation on psychological well-being, using data from a three-generation study of Mexican-Americans.

538   Martinez, Maria. (1979). Family policy for Mexican-Americans and their aged. Urban and Social Changes Review, 12(2), 16-19.

Emphasizes the need of Mexican-American elderly to receive support within their family system to insure continued familial integration, as well as support that is related to their culture.

539   Mindel, Charles. (1983). The elderly in minority families. In Brubaker, Timothy (Ed.), Family relationships in later life, pp. 193-208. Beverly Hills: Sage Publications, 272p.

Describes patterns and variations which are distinctive to
ethnic minority families and their relationships with the
elderly. The variations are categorized into three areas--the
nuclear family's structure and organization, the relationship
between nuclear family units and their interdependence, and the
relationship of the nuclear and extended family unit with
society.   Presents the special family patterns of the two
largest ethnic minority groups--American blacks and Mexican-
Americans.

540   Mirande, Alfredo. (1977). The Chicano family: a
         reanalysis of conflicting views. Journal of
         Marriage and the Family, 39, 747-756.

Examines two conflicting views of the Chicano family--rigid,
male-dominated, and authoritarian structure that breeds
passivity and dependence; and a warm, nurturing, and supportive
structure that gives its members a strong sense of security.
Presents an objective view of the Chicano family.

541   Mitchell, Jim, and Register, Jasper. (1986). An
         exploration of family interaction with the elderly
         by race, socioeconomic status, and residence. In
         Troll, Lillian (Ed.), Family issues in current
         gerontology, pp. 313-328. New York: Springer
         Publishing Company, 382p.

Discusses the extendedness of the black family. Data from the
1975 Harris and Associates study are presented. (There is more
representation of blacks in the United States in these data
than in the majority of similar studies.) Authors cite the
need for policymakers and practitioners to focus upon the needs
of individuals and to disregard stereotyped views of black
family structure. Hypotheses emphasizing the extendedness of
black family relationships with the elderly were not uniformly
accepted and racial differences were minimal. "Although black
elderly were more likely to receive help from family members
and also to take children into the home to live with them, this
could be due to a more pronounced need for help among black
elderly people and a tendency for black elderly to help family
members who are working elsewhere by caring for their
children."

542   Mutran, Elizabeth. (1986). Intergenerational
         family support among blacks and whites. In Troll,
         Lillian (Ed.), Family issues in current gerontology,
         pp. 189-203. New York: Springer Publishing
         Company, 382p.

Questions remain about racial differences in how families
respond to needs of their elderly members. This study
considers racial differences in family helping behavior and
whether the difference results from socioeconomic variables or
cultural factors. Black families appear to be more involved in
exchanging help across generations. "The slope for blacks on
both giving and receiving of help is significantly higher, even
considering differences in age and sex composition for the two
groups. There are arguments for socioeconomic factors and for

culture as causes of differences." Further investigation is called for.

543   Penalosa, Fernando. (1968). Mexican family roles.
        Journal of Marriage and the Family, 30, 680-688.

This study found the wife playing a subordinate role to the husband; father-son relationships distant and severe; father-daughter relationships conflict-free; mother-son relationships a preparation for dominance. These still represent the dominant patterns in Mexican families.

544   Richman, Harold, and Stagner, Matthew. (1986).
        Children: treasured resource or forgotten minority.
        In Pifer, Alan, and Bronte, D. Lydia (Eds.), Our
        aging society: paradox and promise, pp. 161-179.
        New York: W. W. Norton, 438p.

"The aging society poses two possible consequences for America's children. They may become a treasured resource, nurtured all the more for their scarcity and importance to the nation's future. Or they may come to be regarded, amid the increasing clamor for resources and attention by other dependent groups, as only another needy minority." The authors discuss both optimistic and pessimistic views and possible strategies.

545   Rosenthal, Carolyn. (1986). Family supports in
        later life: does ethnicity make a difference?
        Gerontologist, 26(1), 19-24.

The author indicates that "a lack of conceptual clarity has hampered research on ethnicity and family supports in later life, that ethnicity has been conceptualized as culture, inequality, and ways of thinking and behaving."

546   Shebani, Bashir; Wass, Hannelore; and Guertin,
        Wilson. (1986-1987). Correlates of life
        satisfaction for old Libyans compared with the
        judgments of Libyan youth. International Journal of
        Aging and Human Development, 24(1), 19-28.

Questionnaires measuring life satisfaction in old age were administered to Libyan undergraduates (106) and their aged relatives (109). Younger subjects rated social relationships outside the family and having basic physical needs met in old age as more important than did older subjects.

547   Stanford, E. Percil, and Lockery, Shirley. (1984).
        Aging and social relations in the black community.
        In Quinn, William, and Hughston, George (Eds.),
        Independent aging: family and social systems
        perspectives, pp. 164-181. Rockville, Maryland:
        Aspen Systems Corporation, 300p.

Presents a demographic profile and fairly structural characteristics of the black family. Cites black elderly as community volunteers and in engendering greater awareness in

service delivery of the cultural and socioeconomic history of
these families.

548   Stephans, Richard; Oser, George; and Blau, Zena.
           (1980).   To be Hispanic and female: the triple
           risk.   In Melville, Margarita (Ed.), Twice a
           minority: Mexican-American women, pp. 249-258. St.
           Louis: C. V. Mosby Co., 270p.

Reports data based on telephone interviews. Concludes that the
Mexican-American woman's plight arises from her sex, ethnicity,
and age.

549   Taylor, Robert.   (1985).   The extended family as a
           source of support to elderly blacks. Gerontologist,
           25(5), 488-495.

Study of the impact of family and demographic factors on the
frequency of support from family members among 581 blacks aged
55 years of age and above.   Data were obtained from the
National Survey of Black Americans.   Findings indicate that
income, education, region, degree of family interaction,
proximity of relatives, and having adult children were
determinants of frequency of support. Black elderly are active
participants in family networks, with over half the subjects
receiving assistance from family members.

550   Tobin, Joseph.   (1987).   The American idealization
           of old age in Japan. Gerontologist, 27 (1), 53-58.

American images of Japanese aging were studied through
interviews with Americans living temporarily in Japan and
through questionnaires administered to Americans living in
Chicago and Honolulu.   The finding was that Americans idealize
Japanese old age and this idealization reflects Americans'
ambivalence about dependence across the life cycle.   The
American tendency   is to idealize Japanese old people as
happily dependent honored elders.

551   Torres-Gil, Fernando. (1986). Hispanics: a special
           challenge.   In Pifer, Alan, and Bronte, D. Lydia
           (Eds.), Our aging society: paradox and promise,
           pp. 219-242. New York: W. W. Norton, 438p.

Hispanics are becoming the largest minority in the country, and
are very diverse--Puerto Ricans, Chicanos, Mexican-Americans,
and Central and Latin Americans.   Covers political power and
competition, resource allocation, financial security,
consequences of current programs, policy, redefining ethnicity,
bilingualism-biculturalism.

552   Wenger, G. Clare.   (1984).   Adapting to old age in
           rural Britain. International Journal of Aging and
           Human Development, 19(4), 287-299.

Discusses adaptation and coping with aging among 500 rural
elderly persons in Great Britain.   Describes residence and
household composition changes, access to services, and support

from family and friends. Social service implications are discussed.

553   **Weihl, Hannah. (1983). Three issues from the Israeli scene.** Gerontologist, **23(6), 576-578.**

Addresses familial support of the aged in Israel--effect of cultural norms on family support systems, effect of modernization on Arab families, and the development of intergenerational support over a period of 12 years.

554   **Worach-Kardas, Halina. (1983). The Polish family tradition.** Gerontologist, **23(6), 593-596.**

"In Poland the tradition of support based on family ties has always existed as an element of our historical and cultural norms. The Polish family has continued that tradition, providing support in difficult periods such as the partitions of Poland, wars, and occupations. For the family unit to survive intergenerational ties continue to be essential. . . . The family, and especially a family living in a joint household, feels morally obliged to provide personal care and emotional support for its senior members."

555   **Zambrana, Ruth; Melino, Rolando; and Santana, Sarah. (1979). Health services and the Puerto Rican elderly. In Gelfand, Donald, and Kutzik, Alfred (Eds.),** Ethnicity and aging: theory, research and policy, **pp. 308-319. New York: Springer Publishing Company, 372p.**

Examines use of health services among Puerto Rican elderly in East Harlem and the different types of delivery systems they can use effectively.

Films

556   **Andrus Gerontology Center, University of Southern California. (1979).** Housing for the minority elderly.

Looks at issues which confront planners, policymakers, and administrators in providing housing for minority elderly, and offers insights into the potential consequences of choices made in the housing development process.

557   **EBEC (1977). Pamela Wong's birthday for Grandma.**

Presents an urban Chinese-American family and a young girl's perspective as she participates in a family party.

558   **Institute of Gerontology, Federal City College (Producer). (1974).** The black elderly: toward a better understanding.

Explores many problems confronting black elderly such as income, health, sociopsychological status, and housing. Also emphasizes the strengths of the black elderly.

559   Kaplan, Richard, Productions.   (1972).   Happy
         birthday, Mrs. Craig.

Shows Lulu Sadler Craig celebrating her 102nd birthday. She
talks about her father, a slave who swam the Missouri River to
join the Union Army. She receives many telegrams, one from
then-President Nixon. Mrs. Craig embodies a special black and
American experience.

560   Nunez, Victor/Perspective Films and Video.   (1978).
         Taking care of mother.

Captures the special relationship between an old black woman
and a young black boy who does her chores.

Documents

561   Cordova, Dorothy; Kang, Gay; Kang, Tai; Leung, Paul;
         Liem, Nguyen; and Suzuki, Peter; National
         Pacific/Asian Resource Center.   (1985). Guide to
         the utilization of family and community support
         systems by Pacific/Asian elderly. Washington, D.C.:
         National Pacific/Asian Resource Center, 212p.

Shows the dramatic growth of the Korean community in the United
States during the past 10 years. Thus, elderly are faced with
adult children who themselves are just becoming acculturated to
the American lifestyle and a developing community unable fully
to address the seniors' needs. "The family remains the basic
resource for the elderly, with the church playing a significant
role in supporting the social and psychological needs of the
elderly, but churches lack adequate knowledge and resources for
providing access to social welfare agencies. Many community
organizations are still emerging and represent a limited
resource, inasmuch as many of the members have only been in the
U.S. a few years and are unfamiliar with the social service
system." The document defines and describes the nature and
functions of informal support systems for five Pacific/Asian
ethnic groups, identifies similarities and differences in the
communities and strengths and weaknesses among the various
support systems, and presents policies and methods for
strengthening and using the systems to enhance delivery of
services to the elderly.

562   Cubillos, Herminia.   (1987).   Los ancianos: the
         aging of the Hispanic community, a preliminary
         demographic profile. Washington, D. C.: National
         Council of La Raza, Office of Research Advocacy and
         Legislation, 31p.

Presents a demographic profile of the aged Hispanic community.
Topics presented include: changes in the population, living
arrangements, education, employment, income, poverty status,
and health. Findings show that most of the Hispanic elderly
live in households, rather than in nursing homes. One-fourth
of elderly Hispanics do not receive any form of Social Security
benefits. The poverty rate is twice as high as for the white

elderly. This population is also experiencing the feminization of poverty.

563   **Garza, Jose.** (1979). <u>**Housing Hispanic America**</u>.
        Washington, D.C.: National Hispanic Housing
        Coalition, Department of Housing and Urban
        Development, 37p.

Presents a perspective on Hispanic housing concerns that highlight the relationship among Hispanics between a need for shelter and other social issues. Discusses general needs of Hispanics in housing and other issues affecting the migrant and seasonal farmworker families and the Hispanic elderly.

564   **Ghelfi, Linda.** (1986). <u>**Poverty among black**</u>
        <u>**families in the nonmetro South**</u>. **(Rural Development**
        Research Report No. 62, U.S. Department of
        Agriculture). Washington, D.C.: U.S. Government
        Printing Office. 35p.

Analyzes sources of income and income problems of black families in the nonmetropolitan South, using 1980 data. Describes some characteristics of family householders and adult family members related to income-earning capacity, such as age, education, work disability,. labor force status, occupation, and weeks worked. Compares blacks and whites by poverty status and family type in order to illustrate how the characteristics of these families differfrom or coincide with those of the majority of southern nonmetropolitan families. Black families are three times as likely to be poor as are white families. There is a high incidence of poverty among southern nonmetropolitan black families, especially female-headed households. There are much higher unemployment rates among black family members in all poverty status and family type categories.

565   **LaCayo, Carmela.** (1980). <u>**A national study to**</u>
        <u>**assess the service needs of the Hispanic elderly**</u>.
        Los Angeles: Asociacion Nacional Pro Personas
        Mayores, 400p.

A final report on the first national needs assessment on the Hispanic elderly. Reports data on status and needs of older Hispanics, including health and housing. Provides recommendations for aging policies and programs as they affect Hispanic elders.

566   **LaCayo, Carmela (Ed.).** (1981). <u>**A research,**</u>
        <u>**bibliographic and resource guide on the Hispanic**</u>
        <u>**elderly**</u>. **Los Angeles: Asociacion Nacional Pro**
        Personas Mayores, 421p.

A research, bibliographic, and resource guide providing a comprehensive, annotated listing of available contemporary literature on the Hispanic elderly. This guide may help researchers, service deliverers, and policymakers in formulating relevant studies and policies concerning Hispanic elders.

567   Montiel, Miguel (Ed.). (1978). Hispanic families:
           critical issues for policy and programs in human
           services. Washington, D.C.: National Coalition of
           Hispanic   Mental   Health   and   Human   Service
           Organizations, 113p.

Collection of papers on historical processes, cultural values,
and socioeconomic conditions which contribute to the present
status of Hispanic families--including Mexicans, Puerto Ricans,
and Cubans in the United States.

568   Tobias, Cynthia; Ide, Bette; and Kay, Margarita.
           (1987).   Identifying Anglo, Mexican American and
           American Indian respondents for a study of recent
           widows: suggestions   for   future   researchers.
           Tucson, Arizona: University of Arizona, Southwest
           Institute for Research on Women, 13p.

Describes innovative methods used to obtain the desired number
of Anglo, Mexican American, and American Indian women for a
study of the health of recently widowed, low-income women.
Social and health service agencies proved generally unable to
assist by contacting their clients.   Among the successful
techniques in recruiting and retaining members of different
ethnic groups were newspaper advertisements and letters sent in
response to obituary notices (Anglo widows), churches (Mexican
American widows and American Indian widows).   None of the
widows considered the interview process intrusive.

569   U.S. Congress. Senate. Special Committee on Aging.
           99th Congress. (1986). The Older Americans Act and
           its application to Native Americans (Oklahoma City,
           Oklahoma), 214p.

Three panels appearing before the Senate Special Committee on
Aging discuss the sensitivity of the Administration on Aging to
Native Americans, coordination of services between Title II and
Title VI of the Older Americans Act, and availability of
services under the act. Experts report on analysis of computer
data from a needs assessment of 813 older Indians in the U.S.
and trends of a survey which focused on decreasing funding
levels of Title VI grantees and the impact of these funds on
service to unserved and underserved older Indians.

570   U.S. Congress.   House.   Select Committee on Aging.
           100th Congress. (1987). The status of the black
           elderly in the United States, a report by the
           National Caucus and Center on Black Aged, Inc., for
           the Select Committee on Aging. Washington, D.C.:
           U.S. Government Printing Office, 79p.

Report on the status of the black elderly in the United States,
based on six issue forums that the National Caucus and Center
on Black Aged, Inc., conducted throughout the United States in
1986 and on three House Select Committee on Aging hearings on
this subject. Addressed are statistics related to income and
employment needs, health needs, budget issues, housing issues,
impact of crime, and service needs.   Older blacks are the
poorest group in the nation and among the most poorly housed

groups. They are more likely to experience health problems that are aged persons in general and are at greater risk of being criminal victims than are other Americans. "As a group, older blacks have borne more social, economic, and psychological damage than other groups because of racial discrimination." Offers recommendations for improving each aspect of the status of older blacks.

571   U.S. Congress. House. Select Committee on Aging.
        100th Congress. (1988). The chairman's report on
        the black elderly in America: a report by the
        chairman of the Select Committee on Aging, House of
        Representatives. Washington, D.C.: U.S. Government
        Printing Office, 16p.

Report on the status of black Americans over 65 years of age, based on nine public forums and hearings held in major cities throughout the country in 1986. Findings include that: older blacks are the poorest of the poor among the elderly, older blacks suffer more intense health care problems than other Americans, older blacks have suffered from recent federal budgetary cuts, older blacks are more likely to inhabit unsuitable housing, older blacks are more likely to be the victims of crime, and older blacks are underrepresented in Older Americans Act and other service programs. Recommendations include reforming the Federal Supplemental Security Income standards, establishing a mandatory pension system, resisting attempts to cut Medicare and Medicaid coverage, encouraging preventive medicine, enacting a universal and comprehensive national health insurance program, developing a more balanced method of reducing the federal deficit, repealing the Gramm-Rudman-Hollings Amendment, providing additional housing units for the elderly, combatting crime with preventive techniques, and encouraging minority elderly to participate in programs of the Older Americans Act.

572   U.S. Congress, House. Select Committee on Aging.
        99th Congress. (1986). The plight of the black
        elderly: a major crisis in America. Washington,
        D.C.: U.S. Government Printing Office, 129p.

Suggests that solutions for the gap in the quality of life between elderly blacks and elderly whites must be closed "through the joint efforts of individuals; religious and community organizations; political institutions; and the private sector." Among suggestions offered are insuring accessibility to quality health care, improving housing and its affordability, and controlling poverty.

Dissertations

573   Ashley, Laurel. (1985). Self, family, and
        community: the social process of aging among urban
        Mexican-American women. Unpublished doctoral
        dissertation, University of California, Los Angeles,
        306p.

Depicts process of aging among Mexican-American older women in Southern California. Many subjects were not deeply involved in families or in labor-intensive grandmothering, but were not familial or social rejects. This study found that the senior center was a major means of self-enhancement and a social arena in which to create new roles and to demonstrate and expand the nurturant role, previously confined to relatives, to their peers and to the community-at-large.

574   Bastida, Elena.   (1979).   **Family integration and adjustment to aging among Hispanic American elderly.** Unpublished doctoral dissertation, University of Kansas, 219p.

Examines the relative impact of ethnic and sociodemographic factors on family integration and adjustment to aging in later life. A weak correlation was found between sociodemographic variables and the two dependent variables, family integration and adjustment to aging. The author suggests that ethnic factors may be better indicators of family integration and adjustment to aging. The majority of subjects in this study were not living in multi-generational households. "Data indicate that permanent residence in children's households is seriously considered only in the event of widowhood and/or incapacitation." It is suggested that "the contribution of ethnicity, measured along various dimensions, to sub-cultural patterns of aging may be greater than that suggested by ethnicity as strictly a classificatory variable."

575   Boldt,   Joanne.   (1985).   **Patterns   for intergenerational helping among Mexican-Americans: a three generation study**. Unpublished doctoral dissertation, University of Kentucky, 278p.

Description of helping patterns among three generations of Mexican-Americans. Examination of the effect of transmitted similarities in values and behaviors in certain life areas on intergenerational helping. General support was found for the hypotheses that there were generational differences in help exchanged, received, and perceived as received among three generations of Mexican-Americans. Through multiple regression analysis, it was shown that marital status, age, self-rated health, income, and sex-linkage (especially female same sex-linkage) among the generations were significantly associated with intergenerational helping.

576   Brown, Addie.   (1983) **Grandparents' perceived roles in urban extended black family relationships.** Unpublished   doctoral   dissertation,   U.S. International University, 125p.

Examination of perceived roles of black grandparents who resided in three-generation extended family homes. Description, analysis, and clarification of these roles as they relate to family survival and stability. "The shift to a three-generation family arrangement represented a dramatic change, with emotional overtones and economic problems for several grandparents. The roles described indicated that the subjects carried on the tradition of care and concern for their extended family as suggested by previous investigators."

577   Burton, Linda.   (1985).   Early and on-time grandmotherhood in multi-generation black families. Unpublished doctoral dissertation, University of Southern California, number of pages not given.

Explores the consequences of "early" versus "on-time" entry into the grandmother role.   Examines timing of role entry, intergenerational cohesion, and grandparental role satisfaction.   Finding was that early grandmothers are significantly less satisfied with their role than are on-time grandmothers.   There is "a complex relationship between lineage timing and cohesion which appears to have an impact on satisfaction by early grandmothers in the grandmother role."

578   Coe, Sherri.   (1982).   A study of identity patterns among three generations of black women.   Unpublished doctoral dissertation, Northwestern University, 277p.

Exploration of identity patterns (developmental issues, values, self-views) across and within three generations of black women. Six patterns described the developmental character of black women: first generation emphasis on religion and the maternal role; second generation expression of aspirational values in the family and work systems; third generation a maturational transition into adulthood.   Shared by all generations were humanistic values and self-reliance.   The three fundamental principles which explained essential meanings of identity for each generation were the principle of survival (for older); of upward mobility (for second generation); and of personal mobility (for younger).

579   Graves, Conrad.   (1981).   Family and community support networks and their utilization by the black elderly.   Unpublished doctoral dissertation, New York University, 237p.

Description of needs and responses to social services of black elderly.   Focus on obtaining more information on the black aged (especially differences between urban and rural); information about methods and techniques of service delivery that result in the most effective utilization of service by the poor, black elderly; more information on whether social services that are offered and used have a positive effect on the social health of the client population.

580   Jarrett, Robin.   (1985).   The maternal role in multi-generational families.   Unpublished doctoral dissertation, The University of Chicago, number of pages not given.

Analysis of the maternal role in multi-generational black families--normative orientations, patterns of interaction, and patterns of female socialization in extended families.   Each subject family had at least three generations of grandmothers,

mothers, and daughters who had forged strong, interdependent bonds.

581   John, Robert. (1986). **Aging in a Native American community: service needs and support networks among Prairie Band Potawatomi elders.** Unpublished doctoral dissertation, University of Kansas, 425p.

Investigates the role of formal and informal support networks, including family, friends, and social service agencies in the lives of Prairie Band elders. Analyzes service utilization. The analysis showed the importance of the informal support network as a service provider in all areas.

582   Koo, Jasoon. (1982). **Korean women in widowhood.** Unpublished doctoral dissertation, University of Missouri, Columbia, 269p.

Describes consequences of modernization for the social integration of widows in a modernizing society, Korea. Indicates the impact of rural versus urban living and age on the social integration of widows. Four hundred widows were included in this study. "Older urban widows were less integrated, depended on children, did not have authority over the family in modern, urban situations. Older rural widows had higher degrees of social integration."

583   Langston, Esther. (1982). **Kith and kin: natural support systems: their implications for policies and programs for the black aged.** Unpublished doctoral dissertation, The University of Texas at Arlington, 102p.

Examines accessibility and utilization of informal support systems by the black aged and on whom the black aged can call in a crisis. Secondary analysis of National Senior Citizen Survey. "Residential environment (urban, semi-urban) was found to be a major factor in examining the use of informal support systems. The kith system had the highest frequencies of visits and lived closer to the respondent in all geographic areas. The kin system was found to be the first choice for support in time of crisis such as illness, except in the semi-urban area, where the formal system was the first choice."

584   Laurel, Noel. (1976). **An intergenerational comparison of attitude toward the support of aged parents: a study of Mexican-Americans in two South Texas communities.** Unpublished doctoral dissertation, University of Southern California, number of pages not given.

Testing of the assumption that familism and care for the aged constitute core values in Mexican-American culture. This quantitative-descriptive study provides a comparison of two generations of Chicanos in their attitudes toward filial responsibility. Rural subjects scored significantly higher in filial responsibility than did urban subjects.

585   Martinez, Maria, de. (1980). **Los ancianos: a study of the attitudes of Mexican Americans regarding support of the elderly**. Unpublished doctoral dissertation, Florence Heller Graduate School for Advanced Studies in Social Welfare, Brandeis University, 261p.

"Los ancianos are confronted with the issues of the larger, low-income, elderly population: diminishing health, inadequate housing, poor nutrition, cumulative effects of the discrimination they have experienced throughout their lifetime." This publication considers five questions: 1) Is the Mexican American family still viewed as the central supportive mechanism for its elderly?, 2) Among five areas of care--economic aid, health care, emotional support, daily living aid, and advocacy--what areas are supported less by the family than others?, 3) What is the influence of acculturation on traditional support stances for the aged?, 4) How do the descriptive data characterize family household makeup, geographic and emotional closeness, age, sex and nativity differences?, 5) What key value concepts are viewed as integral for culturally relevant services for ancianos? The author recommends policies that would "buttress the Mexican American family system in its social service role for the aged . . . and continue to delineate avenues by which . . . cultural integrity can be maintained, thus insuring the integrity of Los Ancianos into our family systems in a meaningful manner."

586   Mason, Theresa. (1987). **Experience and meaning: an interpretive study of family and gender ideologies among a sample of Mexican American women of two generations**. Unpublished doctoral dissertation, The University of Texas at Austin, 406p.

Used strategic and interactional theory of culture to interpret perspectives on family relationships by a sample of Mexican American women. Explores how these women have used ideologies of family roles to express and moderate the pressures and contradictions constituted by their class, generational, and gender related interests.

587   Nkweti, David. (1982). **The aged in black middle class families: a study in intergenerational relations**. Unpublished doctoral dissertation, The American University, 184p.

Examination of how the elderly in black middle class and upper income families relate with their kin, how the middle generation copes with aging problems of their parents, and the family context where youthful and elderly attitudes are formed. The author found that middle class families maintained a dynamic relationship with their elderly members in spite of numerous factors and demands which tended to impede ongoing social interaction. Intergenerational relationships were not ruptured by attitudinal discrepancies between the elderly and the young and a feeling of social distance by the elderly.

588   Novero, Evangelina. (1985). **Perceptions of filial**
           responsibility by elderly Filipino widows and their
           primary caregivers. Unpublished doctoral
           dissertation, Kansas State University, 248p.

Assessment of filial expectations and perceptions of filial
behaviors by both generations. Comparison of reports for
within generations and between generations. Assessment of the
degree to which selected demographic and personal variables
predicted these filial responsibility dimensions. Finding was
that "widows held significantly higher expectations for respect
than for other types of support. Mothers received
significantly more financial and material aid, service
provision, and warmth and affection than they expected. Their
expectations for respect and personal care were congruent with
amounts received. Filial responsibility data for primary
caregiving daughters were similar to those of the widows.
However, caregivers provided significantly less instrumental
support than they believed they should give to their mothers."

589   Pacheco, Sandra. (1984). **Adult children's feelings**
           toward their aging parents: a comparative study
           between Anglo and Mexican-American adult children.
           Unpublished doctoral dissertation, The University of
           Texas at Austin, 347p.

Questions if Anglo and Mexican-American adult children behave
and feel differently toward their aging parents. Finding was
that there were no differences in the way males and females
behave and feel toward their mothers and fathers. But Mexican-
Americans and subjects living closer to parents visited and
phoned mothers and fathers more frequently than did Anglo
subjects.

590   Rosebud-Harris, Mary. (1982). **A description of the**
           interactional and subjective characteristics of the
           relationships between black grandmothers and their
           grandchildren enrolled in the University of
           Louisville. Unpublished doctoral dissertation, The
           University of Iowa, 449p.

Describes interactional and subjective characteristics of the
relationships between black grandmothers and their adult,
college-educated grandchildren, as perceived by both
grandmothers and grandchildren. "The interactional and
subjective relationships were extremely strong. Maternal
grandmothers, granddaughters, younger grandmothers, and younger
grandchildren interacted with greater frequency than paternal
grandmothers, grandsons, older grandmothers, and older
grandchildren, but differences were insignificant."

591   Sanchez, Carmen. (1985). **Strengthening the**
           informal support system of the Hispanic elderly:
           group program for caregivers and potential
           caregivers. Unpublished doctoral dissertation, City
           University of New York, 285p.

Reports a project designed to supply the Hispanic adult
caregiver (relatives, friends, and neighbors) with information

and social support through a group approach. "The project offered experiential learning and facilitated the formation of an informal support network in which the participants explored their personal feelings toward their caregiving role, shared problems and concerns, and engaged in mutual problem-solving activities." The program was found to be effective in meeting needs of participants for educational and emotional support.

592   Sotomayor, Marta. (1973). **A study of Chicano grandparents in an urban barrio.** Unpublished doctoral dissertation, University of Denver, number of pages not given.

Presents an exploratory field study of status and role perceptions of 38 Chicano grandparents. Strong support was found for the grandparents perceiving themselves as important in raising grandchildren, feeling a sense of responsibility when a crisis hits the family, and seeing themselves as having credible authority in the family. There was less support for perceiving grandmothers as responsible for the grandchildren's religious training and seeing themselves as responsible for cultural transmission.

593   Taylor, Robert. (1983). **The informal social support networks of the black elderly: the impact of family, church members and best friends.** Unpublished doctoral dissertation, The University of Michigan, 356p.

Examination of informal social support networks of the black elderly, focusing on the support which they receive from family, church members, and best friends. Used the National Survey of Black Americans. Black elderly were found to be extensively involved in their friendship networks. Religion and the church were important. Church members represented an important source of social support. The family also played a crucial role in the informal social support network.

594   Tuck, Inez. (1980). **An analysis of the intergenerational patterns in two African-American families.** Unpublished doctoral dissertation, The University of North Carolina at Greensboro, 333p.

Examination of culture found in two rural, average African-American families as they were reconstructed for genealogical charts to determine generational patterns, study interaction between economic/political institutions and the two families, and analyze families to determine the degree of retention of African cultural remnants. General findings supported the theory of cultural pluralism. These families were found to have an ethnic culture rooted in Africanism. The conclusion was that "African-American families have used strategies for coping with societal changes which are characteristic of the ethnic-racial group."

10

Living Arrangements
of Older Persons

Books

595   American Association of Homes for the Aging.
       (1984). <u>Continuing care retirement community: a
       guidebook for consumers, second edition</u>.
       Washington, D.C.: American Association of Homes for
       the Aging, 13p.

Guide to help persons entering a life care community and their
families to evaluate contractual arrangements offered by the
community.

596   Dobkin, Leah. (1983). <u>Shared housing for older
       people: a planning manual for match-up programs</u>.
       Philadelphia: Shared Housing Resource Center, 91p.

Describes success and failure factors of existing shared
housing programs. Includes forms needed to operate a match-up
program.

597   Lawton, M. Powell, and Hoover, Sally (Eds.).
       (1981). <u>Community housing choices for older
       Americans</u>. New York: Springer Publishing Company,
       326p.

Focus on housing of the majority of older Americans who live in
self-chosen homes in cities, towns, and rural areas. Most
chapters originally were presented as papers at a conference
directed by the Philadelphia Geriatric Center on "Community
Housing Choices for Older Americans." The book covers a
variety of housing situations for older persons. The editors
conclude that, "The reluctance of older people to move is
demonstrated once more. . . . Success is most likely when the
subsidy is applied to the residence where the older person
presently lives, rather than forcing the person to move.
However, the last words are not yet in on the success of the
program in meeting its basic goal of elevating the quality of
the housing."

598   Shared Housing Resource Center, Inc.   (1983).
           National Directory of Shared Housing Programs.
           Philadelphia: Shared Housing Resource Center, Inc.,
           50p.

Lists housing according to state and city of location.   Each
listing is categorized as group residence, match-up program,
etc.

599   Streib, Gordon; Folts, W. Edward; and Hilker, Mary.
           (1984).   Old homes--new families: shared living for
           the elderly. New York: Columbia University Press,
           316p.

Shared living households for older people are viewed as social
experiments in creating "families"--primary group environments
that provide services and companionship in a noninstitutional
setting.   These households have organizational linkages to
formal organizations--churches, nonprofit corporations, welfare
agencies, governmental bodies.   Topics covered include: the
need for shared housing, the continuum of living arrangements,
share-a-homes, diversity in sponsorship, structure, and cost,
alternative housing using existing households, problems and
dilemmas in established shared living facilities, sociological
interpretations, and policy implications of shared housing.

Articles/chapters

600   Beland, Francois.   (1987).   Living arrangement
           preferences among elderly people.   Gerontologist,
           27(6), 797-803.

Elderly living alone or with a spouse only are more likely than
those living with a child, relative or friend to move into
alternate setting (senior housing or nursing home).

601   Brody, Elaine, and Leibowitz, Bernard.   (1981).
           Some recent innovations in community living
           arrangements for older people.   In Lawton, M.
           Powell, and Hoover, Sally (Eds.), Community housing
           choices for older Americans, pp. 245-258. New York:
           Springer Publishing Company, 326p.

Presents information on such innovative living arrangements for
older people as group homes or residences, cooperatives, and
communes.   These types of housing are usually small and serve
no more than 20 people under one roof and provide one or more
supportive services.   They are viewed as noninstitutional and
as promoting independence and continued community living.
"Despite demonstrated appeal, so few have developed probably
because they are not easy to develop and require ingenuity and
persistence to surmount assorted obstacles along the way to
completion."

602   Carlin, Vivian, and Fox, Richard. (1981).   An
           alternative for elderly housing: home conversion.
           In Lawton, M. Powell, and Hoover, Sally (Eds.),
           Community housing choices for older Americans, pp.

259-266. **New York:** **Springer Publishing Company,** 326p.

Describes a pilot project of the New Jersey Division on Aging to help low-income elderly homeowners remain in their own homes by providing non-interest bearing loans to convert their dwellings to include an income-producing apartment. This method increased the supply of suitable apartments for low-income elderly renters at a cost far below that of a new unit in a multi-unit project. The author concludes that, "The home conversion program can have significant impact on older people's lives. Choices of where to live for the elderly must be increased, particularly for low-income persons who presently have few, if any, housing alternatives. The extension of this and similar programs can be the stimulus that will directly impact the presently unfavorable housing for older people."

603   Connell, Terrence. (1981). An overview of the elderly experience in the experimental housing allowance program. In Lawton, M. Powell, and Hoover, Sally (Eds.), Community housing choices for older Americans, pp. 299-313. New York: Springer Publishing Company, 326p.

The chapter is a summary report of how older people have responded to the Experimental Housing Allowance Program, conducted over a period of years by the U.S. Department of Housing and Urban Development. The experiment has provided data on "how individuals, housing markets, and whole communities respond to the opportunity to pay a lesser proportion of one's income on housing."

604   Connor, Patrick. (1981). Long-term-care facilities and organization theory: some research suggestions. In Fogel, Robert; Hatfield, Elaine; Kiesler, Sara; and Shanas, Ethel (Eds.), Aging, stability and change in the family, pp. 233-249. New York: Academic Press, 341p.

Suggests research directions which organization theorists might take in the area of institutionalized care, long-term-care facilities. Five foci of research interest noted include: "conceptualizing long-term-care organizations, organizational goals, organization-environment relationships, organization-individual relationships, and definitions and measurement of overall institutional effectiveness."

605   Crimmins, Eileen, and Ingegneri, Dominique. (1990). Interaction and living arrangements of older parents and their children. Research on Aging, 12(1), 3-35.

Examines availability of and interaction with children among elderly Americans over the past two decades. Uses causal models to explore the effects of social, economic, and demographic change on family interaction and living with a child. Between 1962 and 1984 there was a decrease in the percentage of parents and children co-residing and there was continued reduction in the number of days/year that parents and their children who do not co-reside saw one another.

"Interaction among parents and children who do not co-reside seems to be most influenced by child availability as indexed by distance."

606   Danigelis, Nicholas, and Fengler, Alfred. (1990).
        Homesharing: how social exchange helps elders live
        at home. Gerontologist, 30(2), 162-170.

Uses social exchange theory to analyze the relationships in traditional and caregiving homesharing arrangements. In both arrangements, there was high satisfaction with basic money and service exchanges.   "In traditional matches, client satisfaction is also related to life style fit, amount of social interaction desired and received, and amount of lodger access in the provider's home.   In caregiving matches, satisfaction is also related to the intensive interpersonal relationship developed between sharers; stress is a particular problem for the caregiver."

607   DeVos, Susan. (1990). Extended family living among
        older people in six Latin American countries.
        Journal of Gerontology, 45(3), S87-S94.

Examines demographic and urban/rural residence underpinnings to people 60 and over living in extended family households in six Latin American countries. A majority of the elderly lived in extended family households.   In all countries studied, unmarried people were more likely to live in extended family households than were married people and for unmarried elderly, there was a greater likelihood for women than for men. Neither urban/rural residence nor age among the elderly themselves tended to be important.

608   Felton, Barbara; Lehman, Stanley; and Adler, Arlene.
        (1981).   Single-room occupancy hotels: their
        viability as housing options for older citizens. In
        Lawton, M. Powell, and Hoover, Sally (Eds.),
        Community housing choices for older Americans, pp.
        267-285. New York: Springer Publishing Company,
        326p.

"Older people constitute a substantial proportion of the SRO hotel population." Single-room occupancy (SRO) hotels include hotels, rooming houses, and converted apartment buildings, and contain furnished rooms, usually without kitchens, frequently without bathrooms, and most often in old and deteriorated physical facilities located in or near commercial areas of cities. "These hotels are usually inhabited by single adults who, by virtue of their status as mental patients, their skid row lifestyle, or their relative social isolation, are considered 'socially marginal'." The author indicates that planning is needed and that research is needed to determine what kinds of services can be provided that do not threaten the natural support systems that operate in hotels. Policy goals are recommended which would preserve the integrity of the SRO lifestyle, while also providing SRO tenants with the basic amenities necessary for health and happiness.

609   Gutowski, Michael. (1981). Housing-related needs
        of the suburban elderly. In Lawton, M. Powell, and
        Hoover, Sally (Eds.), Community housing choices for
        older Americans, pp. 109-122. New York: Springer
        Publishing Company, 326p.

Suburban households represent nearly 30% of all elderly
households. Usually, the suburban elderly have higher incomes
and higher rates of home ownership than their central city
counterparts.

610   Hoover, Sally. (1981). Black and Spanish elderly:
        their housing characteristics and housing quality.
        In Lawton, M. Powell, and Hoover, Sally (Eds.),
        Community housing choices for older Americans, pp.
        65-89. New York: Springer Publishing Company,
        326p.

While there are fewer older black homeowners than there are
older white homeowners, blacks are more likely to remain in a
home once it is purchased. Older Spanish persons are less
likely to be either property owners or long-term residents if
the property is owned. The study found no trend toward greater
home ownership.

611   Klopf, Beverly. (1985). From care at home to
        nursing home. In Browne, Colette, and Onzuka-
        Anderson, Roberta (Eds.), Our aging parents: a
        practical guide to eldercare, pp. 199-212.
        Honolulu: University of Hawaii Press, 278p.

The dependency of many older persons on other people to manage
their daily lives may increase to the point where a nursing
home placement provides the most appropriate care. Family
members may improve the quality of care in the nursing home
through visiting and by discussing concerns with the staff.

612   Krivo, Lauren, and Mitchler, Jan. (1989). Elderly
        persons living alone: the effect of community
        context on living arrangements. Journal of
        Gerontology, 44(2), S54-S62.

Incorporates the community context into an aggregate
explanation of intermetropolitan variation in rates of living
alone among elderly persons. Authors contend that three
crucial community resources influence the rate of living alone:
demographic and normative environment, economic affordability,
and community social services.

613   Lawton, M. Powell, and Hoover, Sally. (1981).
        Housing for 22 million older Americans. In Lawton,
        M. Powell, and Hoover, Sally (Eds.), Community
        housing choices for older Americans, pp. 11-27. New
        York: Springer Publishing Company, 326p.

Sketches the new construction programs in federally-assisted
housing and provides an overview of housing occupied by most
older Americans, who do not live in planned housing. Describes
housing-related services and existing public program serving

housing needs. Authors conclude that "greater attention is required for the housing problems of community-resident, aged owners and renters. Existing programs are too few, too capricious in coverage, lacking in technical expertise, and poorly coordinated."

614   Mellinger, Jeanne. (1989). Emergency housing for frail older adults. Gerontologist, 29(3), 401-404.

Describes an emergency housing program which provides immediately available beds in private homes for homeless, impaired elderly adults. Twenty-four-hour care is provided for from two to four weeks. The environment was found to provide more positive social support and to save money, compared to traditional programs for the homeless. After one year, "clients were significantly less likely to be institutionalized than were comparable nonparticipants."

615   Mullins, Larry, and Dugan, Elizabeth. (1990). The influence of depression, and family and friendship relations, on residents' loneliness in congregate housing. Gerontologist, 30(3), 377-384.

Examines impact of various social relationships on levels of loneliness reported by 208 elderly residents of 10 senior housing apartments. The loneliest were those who were less satisfied with the quality of their relationships and had less contact with close friends. Having children, grandchildren, siblings, or neighbors had no significant effect on reported loneliness.

616   Namazi, Kevan; Eckert, J. Kevin; Kahana, Eva; and Lyon, Stephanie. (1989). Psychological well-being of elderly board and care residents. Gerontologist, 29(4), 511-516.

Examines effect of several social and physical environmental features of small, unregulated board and care homes on the psychological well-being of elderly residents. Social aspects, such as peer relationships, "had a more significant impact on residents' psychological well-being than aspects of the physical environment."

617   Netting, F. Ellen; and Unks, Raymond. (1984). Life care: an emerging industry in need of professional security. Journal of Applied Gerontology, 3(1), 20-33.

Discusses issues surrounding life care and continuing care communities.

618   Noelker, Linda, and Bass, David. (1989). Home care for elderly persons: linkages between formal and informal caregivers. Journal of Gerontology, 44(2), S63-S70.

Investigates how personal care and home health services are used in relation to assistance from primary kin caregivers. Develops a typology based on task sharing or segregation between kin caregivers and service providers. Identifies four types of informal-formal linkages around these tasks--kin independence, formal service specialization, dual specialization, and supplementation. Finding was that predictors of the types showed that caregiver and care recipient need variables were most significant in differentiating among them, although caregiver gender also had some discriminatory power. Caregiver need or stress is predictive of in-home service use.

619   **Noll, Paul. (1981). Federally assisted housing programs for the elderly in rural areas: problems and prospects. In Lawton, M. Powell, and Hoover, Sally (Eds.), Community housing choices for older Americans, pp. 90-108. New York: Springer Publishing Company, 326p.**

Many older Americans live in rural areas, are not highly mobile, and are not likely to move to bigger cities in order to improve the quality of life. They may own land or homes, but are not usually well off or well housed. Compared to urban-dwelling elders, rural elders are more likely to have substandard housing, lower incomes, and older housing valued at 50% of urban housing values. The author identifies deficiencies in national housing policy for rural areas: "no agreement on which government agency is responsible, inadequate delivery systems, urban bias, inadequate subsidies, underfunding and disproportionate distribution."

620   **Ramsey, Mildred. (1985). Providing a safe home environment. In Browne, Colette, and Onzuka-Anderson, Roberta (Eds.), Our aging parents: a practical guide to eldercare, pp. 176-185. Honolulu: University of Hawaii Press, 278p.**

Describes specific steps for making outside the home and rooms inside safer for frail elderly persons. "Most homes can be made safe and comfortable for the elderly at various levels of dependency. The safest method of carrying out an activity is usually the most efficient one. By making appropriate changes in the home, caregivers are also helped to conserve their physical and mental resources."

621   **Regnier, Victor, and Bonar, James. (1981). Recycling buildings for elderly housing. In Lawton, M. Powell, and Hoover, Sally (Eds.), Community housing for older Americans, pp. 286-298. New York: Springer Publishing Company, 326p.**

Presents the consensus of a team of service planners and designers dealing with issues of providing housing for the elderly, using still-sturdy building stock, and upgrading an off-central-city core area in Los Angeles. Provides a model to estimate the positive and negative features of any proposed conversion.

622   **Rubinstein, Robert. (1989). The home environments of older people: a description of the psychosocial**

processes linking person to place.   **Journal of Gerontology**, 44(2), S45-S53.

Describes the meaning with which older people endow the home environment.   Suggests that the home environment is given meaning through three classes of psychosocial process relating the person to the sociocultural order, the life course, and the body.

623   **Ruchlin, Hirsch, and Morris, John.   (1987).   The congregate housing services program: an analysis of service utilization and cost.   Gerontologist, 27(1), 87-91.**

Estimates cost of services provided to tenants participating in the Congregate Housing Services Program.   "Community services accounted for 50% of costs, medical care accounted for 42%, and 8% represents the imputed cost of informal care."

624   **Sixsmith, Andrew.   (1986).   Independence and home in later life.   In Phillipson, Chris; Bernard, Miriam; and Strang, Patricia (Eds.), Dependency and interdependency in old age: theoretical perspectives and policy alternatives, pp. 338-347. London: Croom Helm, 371p.**

Presents the results of an interview-based study on the meaning and experience of home in later life.   Questions addressed were: What is the everyday meaning of the word "independence"? and How does an older person's home contribute to independence? Independence was seen in three modes: not being dependent, self-direction, and obligation.   "Home seems to contribute toward maintaining independence in later life, and thus provides a material context for independence."

625   **Soldo, Beth, and Brotman, Herman.   (1981).   Housing whom?   In Lawton, M. Powell, and Hoover, Sally (Eds.), Community housing choices for older Americans, pp. 36-55.   New York: Springer Publishing Company, 326p.**

Reviews the literature showing that: 1) living arrangements are the outcome of a life cycle process, and 2) living arrangements are the outcome of a complex life cycle process. Since living arrangements are the end product of a process, effects of intervention strategies will permeate the entire system.   Programs providing direct cash subsidies to the family with whom an older person lives may undermine, for example, the preference of older persons to live alone and independently. Previous research suggests that efforts to modify current patterns of living arrangements will be successful only if they give attention to a comprehensive life-course perspective.

626   **Soldo, Beth; Sharma, Mahesh; and Campbell, Richard. (1984).   Determinants of the community living arrangements of older unmarried women.   Journal of Gerontology, 39(4), 492-498.**

Examines the joint effects of age, marital status, personal income, and the need for functional assistance on living arrangements of older unmarried white women.

627   Steinfeld, Edward. (1981). The scope of residential repair and renovation services and models of service delivery. In Lawton, M. Powell, and Hoover, Sally (Eds.), Community housing choices for older Americans, pp. 201-220. New York: Springer Publishing Company, 326p.

There is increasing emphasis on providing ways for people to remain in their present homes and to improve their current living conditions. The chapter describes a variety of residential repair and renovation services and presents some models of service delivery.

628   Struyk, Raymond, and Devine, Deborah. (1981). Determinants of dwelling maintenance activity of elderly households. In Lawton, M. Powell, and Hoover, Sally (Eds.), Community housing choices for older Americans, pp. 221-244. New York: Springer Publishing Company, 326p.

Analyzes the determinants of dwelling maintenance and repair activity of elderly homeowners located in both urban and rural areas. This study analyzes what causes or prevents elderly owner-occupants from maintaining their homes. Examination of the effects that income, household structure, health, assets, the ratio of housing expenses to income, the proximity of grown children living in separate households, and the physical condition of the dwelling and the area in which it is located have on the likelihood of repairs being made and how the repairs are made (i.e., done by the elderly household itself, by a friend or relative outside of the elderly household, or by hired labor or under contract).

629   Struyk, Raymond, with Greenstein, Deborah. (1981). Research in housing for the elderly: the U.S. Dept. of Housing and Urban Development. In Lawton, M. Powell, and Hoover, Sally (Eds.), Community housing choices for older Americans, pp. 28-35. New York: Springer Publishing Company, 326p.

At the publication of this book, the general thrust of research on housing was for the "independent elderly." There was a concern for supporting the desires of older persons to stay in their own homes. Six research tasks described in this chapter include: 1) monitoring what is happening to the quality of housing for the elderly and the income portions devoted to housing, 2) investigating the demand side of housing programs, 3) examining the determinants of housing-maintenance activities by elderly homeowners, 4) researching the relationships between explicit housing services and housing-related supportive services, 5) evaluating the provision of maintenance services to elderly-headed households in Baltimore, and 6) describing the process by which elderly households adjust to their changing housing needs.

630   Wallace, Edward.   (1981).   Housing for the black elderly--the need remains.   In Lawton, M. Powell, and Hoover, Sally (Eds.), <u>Community housing choices for older Americans</u>, pp. 59-64.   New York: Springer Publishing Company, 326p.

Based on data from limited surveys, except for public housing, elderly blacks have been virtually excluded from federally financed elderly housing.   The authors notes that elderly blacks are the ones who need that help most.   Author concludes that poor elderly blacks should be provided a choice of housing--decent, affordable housing.

631   Walsh, Thomas.   (1981).   Cost of home services compared to institutionalization.   In Lawton, M. Powell, and Hoover, Sally   (Eds.),   <u>Community housing choices for older Americans</u>, pp. 125-134. New York: Springer Publishing Company, 326p.

The lack of community-based, home-delivered services may bring about premature or unnecessary transfer of an older individual to an institution.   The past decade has seen growth in the search for community alternatives to institutionalization. Data from a Cleveland, Ohio, study show that about 60% of elderly who are extremely impaired live outside of institutions, but they receive a wide array of in-home services (personal care, meal preparation, nursing care, homemaker service, continuous supervision) and transportation, housing, social, and recreational services.   The home services are provided in combination to help maintain health, activity, and independence.   At all impairment levels, the value of services provided by families and friends greatly exceeds the cost of services provided by public agencies.   The total cost of home services becomes greater than the cost of institutionalization for older people who are greatly or extremely impaired.   In the Cleveland study, family and friends provided over half of the services received by older persons at all impairment levels and almost three-fourths of the services received by the greatly or extremely impaired.

632   Worobey, Jacqueline, and Angel, Ronald.   (1990). Functional capacity and living arrangements of unmarried elderly persons.   <u>Journal of Gerontology</u>, <u>45</u>(3), S95-S101.

Used 1986 Longitudinal Study of Aging to consider the impact of functional capacity, gender, race and ethnicity, and various socioeconomic characteristics on changes in living arrangements among unmarried elderly persons over a two-year period.   The finding was that "a decline in functional capacity greatly increases the likelihood that an elderly person will move in with others, or become institutionalized."

Films

633   American Journal of Nursing.   (no date).   <u>Entering a nursing home: a critical time</u>.

Part of a four-program series to aid nurses in providing sensitive, professional guidance to families and clients who decide on nursing home placement.

634   **American Journal of Nursing.** (1970). <u>The homebound aged</u>.

Special problems of the old person who is homebound are discussed. The principles of teaching health care to homebound persons are covered, with emphasis on the nurse's role in planning and developing home care services for the aged.

635   **American Journal of Nursing.** (1970). <u>The institutionalized aged</u>.

A discussion of the patho-physiological and psychosocial needs that have implications for geriatric nursing practice.

636   **American Journal of Nursing.** (1983). <u>What now?</u>

Discusses the various ways to help family members cope during nursing home placement.

637   **Barbre Productions, for Visiting Nurse Association of Denver Area, Inc.** (1977). <u>There's no place like home</u>.

Covers the importance of the home as a health care institution. Examples shown are a 92-year-old woman who still lives in her own home and an older woman who has had a stroke, both of whom receive needed help from a visiting nurse and a home health aide.

638   **Carousel Films.** (1972). <u>SRO (Single room occupancy)</u>.

Describes a welfare hotel, where the pervasive and hopeless air of decay extend to the residents themselves. However, residents show an "obdurate spirit of survival."

639   **Churches TV and Radio Center in Great Britain.** (1977). <u>Aunt Harriet (handle with care series)</u>.

Aunt Harriet is an eccentric old aunt struggling to avoid being sent to an old people's home. Her niece and her niece's boyfriend can't be married until they find a home of their own and they have their eyes on Aunt Harriet's flat--but will Aunt Harriet cooperate and move into an old people's home?

640   **Cornell University.** (1974). <u>Housing options for older people</u>.

Discusses several people at various stages in their search for appropriate housing. Offers practical information. Does not cover nursing homes as an option, but includes residential apartments, service-oriented congregate care, and health-oriented multilevel care.

641   **DYNC.** (1955). <u>Place to live</u>.

Presents the need for suitable accommodations and useful activity for the aged. Gives examples of problematic situations. Points out community responsibility.

642   **Indiana University. (1979). Adaptation and aging: life in a nursing home.**

Profiles adjustments of a group of elderly people to life in a nursing home in a look at a typical day in one such home.

643   **Indiana University. (1974). The occupant in the single room.**

In New York City, more than 200,000 elderly are living on fixed incomes below national poverty level in single-room occupancy hotels in deplorable living conditions.

644   **International Center for Social Gerontology. (1977). Assisted residential living (a form of congregate housing).**

Presents information about a type of living environment that fills the gap between housing for the fully independent elderly and medically-oriented institutions for elderly persons who require continuous care. It shows how housing can be combined with supportive services to make it possible for residents to continue an independent lifestyle despite some limitations imposed by increasing age.

645   **Jeffries Films International. (1978). They used to call 'em trailers.**

Depicts the lifestyle of older Americans who live in mobile home parks. Interviews with residents show why mobile home parks fulfill the social and housing needs of older Americans.

646   **Klein, Walter, Co. (1976). American nursing homes: a study in progress.**

Provides questions that one should ask in choosing a nursing home for an aged relative. Views of modern nursing homes are discussed.

647   **London Department of Environment. (1983). Housing for the elderly.**

Elderly people explain what kind of housing they want. The film considers ways in which needs are being met by local authorities and housing associations, and increasingly by the private sector, often by all of them working together.

648   **Losak, Stanley; Swaybill, Marion; Films, Inc. (1979). Share-a-home.**

Share-a-home is a family concept bringing together old people in love and friendship. From the series, "American Family: An Endangered Species."

649   **Maimonides Hospital and Home for the Aged.** (1975).
        Beyond shelter.

Film emphasizes independent living as opposed to confinement in
institutions for older people. Denmark, because it is widely
recognized as a world leader in care for the aged, is presented
as a possible model for alternatives to the institutions
available in the United States and Canada. The facilities and
social programs depicted in the film reflect "Denmark's active
concern that the elderly, even those with handicaps, should
remain independent as long as possible."

650   **Michigan Media.** (1979). **New concepts in housing
        for older adults**.

Looks at housing needs of the elderly and offers some
innovative and well-considered solutions, including assisted
residential living, developing a "human" design, financing,
managing, and an architect's perspective.

651   **NIMH.** (1977). **It can't be done**.

Presents nine short sequences dramatizing the problems of
managing the elderly patient. Includes admission procedures,
the dehumanizing ward routines, handling death.

652   **Pennsylvania State University/WPSX-TV.** (1975). **The
        faces of "A" wing (To age is human series)**.

This documentary presents a series of vignettes of staff,
residents, and relatives--how they relate on a personal and on
an institutional level. From ages 18 to 97, each person
provides a different perspective on life in the nursing home.

653   **Tachhella, Charles.** (1978). **The last winters**.

Shows the relationship between two residents of a county rest
home--Charles and Marguerite. Marguerite commits herself to
meaningful activities. Charles is not engaged with his present
life. He reveals himself as a lonely man, dependent on
Marguerite. The viewer thinks of the self-imposed limitations
that hinder his development as a character.

654   **Temaner, Gerald.** (1967). **Home for life**.

Explores experiences, adjustments, and problems of two elderly
people in a home for the aged. One is a man who is unwillingly
isolated from the world he knew, and the other is a woman who
was wrenched from her family setting.

655   **TRANSIT MEDIA.** (1976). **Beyond shelter**.

Compares North American total care institutions for the elderly
and the handicapped with Denmark's sheltered flats and in-home
services.

656   **UMI.** (1981). **Aging in the future, no. 4--living
        arrangements and services**.

Considers various types of housing and living arrangements for older Americans in the 1980s. Explains types of financing that are available now and what older Americans can expect in the future.

657   UMI. (1978). **New concepts in housing for older adults--the architect's vision.**

Interview with architect William Kessler. Provides guidelines for construction of housing for the aged. Gives examples of housing this architect has designed for the aged.

658   UMI. (1978). **New concepts in housing for older people, no. 1--assisted residential living.**

Explains the assisted residential environment concept of housing for older persons. Shows how this housing is replacing the multi-family living style, and why it is a more economical alternative to nursing homes.

659   UMI. (1978). **New concepts in housing for older people, no. 2--design must be human.**

Interviews with senior citizens, photographs of actual residences, and conceptual drawings to consider factors that are important in humanizing dwellings for older adults.

660   UMI. (1978). **New concepts in housing for older people, no. 3--financing.**

Eugene Hackler, finance lawyer, discusses how to obtain funds for housing for older adults, tells of the kinds of programs available from the government and in the private sector, emphasizes knowing terminology and resources, and stresses the importance of patience in obtaining funding.

661   University of Kansas, Bureau of Child Research. (no date given). **A place to call home.**

Filmed on location in a nursing home which has adapted its programs and activities to include the mentally retarded. Shows the warm atmosphere that is possible in the nursing home and the sense of well-being that the residents keep. Demonstrates additional benefits acquired by uniting the young and the old.

662   University of Southern California, School of Cinema/Television. (1980). **Golden age.**

Emphasizes the fears which older people attach to living in a nursing home.

663   VNI. (1970). **The homebound aged.**

Outlines special problems faced by an older patient who is homebound.

664   VNI. (1970). **The institutionalized aged.**

Discusses the patho-physiological and psycho-social needs of geriatric patients in a nursing home for the aged.

665   VWA. (1982). **Aging and health in a five-generation family**.

Synthesizes various parts of the human life span through a common experience. Participants are women, aged 87, 69, 51, 27, and 4--all related as mothers and daughters.

666   WCNY. (1980). **Old folks at home**.

This part of the "U.S. Chronicle" series examines the housing situations of senior citizens and how they deal with them.

667   WNET. (1974). **The occupant in the single room**.

A look at the plight of New York's elderly living below the poverty level in deplorable hotels.

Documents

668   U.S. Congress. House. Subcommittee on Housing and Consumer Interests of the Select Committee on Aging. 98th Congress. (1984). **Homelessness in Nashville**, 193p.

Report on homeless elderly in Nashville, Tennessee. The elderly problems addressed include: aging, failing health, lack of job training with no prospect of correcting the deficiency, lack of basic life-skills in many cases, and chronic depression.

669   U.S. Congress. House. Subcommittee on Housing and Consumer Interests of the Select Committee on Aging. 98th Congress. (1984). **Homeless older Americans**, 184p.

Examines problems of homeless older Americans, estimated from 40,000 people to 400,000. The hearing was held "to help identify an aggressive, coordinated program of action to deal with this staggering problem." For homeless, older Americans who have mental illnesses, emergency food and shelter programs can be life-sustaining. However, these programs provide only temporary relief. "The mentally ill and the homeless with extensive physical problems require permanent housing arrangements that are linked to services capable of meeting their physical and mental needs."

670   U.S. Congress. House. Subcommittee on Housing and Consumer Interests of the Select Committee on Aging. (1985). **Senior citizen housing: an emerging crisis in America**, 91p.

The first federal housing program targeted to needs of the elderly is Section 202 of the Housing Act--authorizing direct, low-interest loans to provide housing for the elderly. Congregate housing services provide supportive services for those seniors who are frail or disabled and who live in Section 202 or public housing projects. "The need for additional units of housing for older Americans is skyrocketing. Up to one-third of older Americans in are in substandard or inadequate housing."

671   U.S. Congress. House. Subcommittee on Housing and Consumer Interests. (1986). **Maximizing supportive services for the elderly in assisted housing: experiences from the congregate housing services program**, 87p.

Examines the current status of the Congregate Housing Services Program. The goal of congregate housing is "to provide environments that encourage support to a maximum degree of the independent." Highlights congregate housing services as representing "a holistic and rational approach to providing care for the elderly."

672   U.S. Congress. Senate. Special Committee on Aging. (1982). **Alternative approaches to housing older Americans**, 94p.

Explores alternative approaches to meeting housing needs of older Americans, including shared housing, accessory apartments, and home equity conversions.

673   U.S. Congress. House. Subcommittee on Housing and Consumer Interests. (1983). **Housing the elderly: alternative options (Erie, Pennsylvania)**, 51p.

For elderly persons, housing costs are the single greatest expense in their budget. For older persons, housing cost is much more acute and represents a far greater proportion of their monthly budget. However, the elderly can't get jobs to help meet the growing cost of housing. "Suitable housing for our elderly today and in the future is becoming scarce, but the number of elderly continues to climb dramatically and there is no parallel increase in the federal government's efforts to match this increase." This hearing looked at future availability of housing for senior citizens and the various types of living arrangements that keep the elderly out of nursing homes, except when such care is medically necessary.

674   U.S. Congress. Senate. Special Committee on Aging. (1983). **Community alternatives to institutional care**, 66p.

Looks at the types of alternatives to institutional care which might be implemented on a broader scale. "Given . . . medical progress, we should be striving to maximize self-care and allow all citizens to lead normal lives in the least restrictive setting."

675   U.S. Congress. House. Subcommittee on Housing and Consumer Interests of the Select Committee on Aging. (1980). **Housing needs of the elderly**, 52p.

Recommends improving housing for older persons and developing and improving the programs which are an essential part of the daily life of older Americans.

676   U.S. Congress. House. Subcommittee on Housing and Consumer Interests of the Select Committee on Aging. 97th Congress. (1981). Shared housing, 52p.

Exploration of ways in which shared housing could provide a partial answer to the housing crisis of older Americans--what barriers would need to be met by senior citizens while developing shared housing and investigating the role the Federal government can play in promoting shared-housing alternatives.

Dissertations

677   Michaels, Francine. (1986). Perspectives: a study of boarding home life for aging adults. Unpublished doctoral dissertation, Union for Experimenting Colleges/University Without Walls and Union Graduate School, 256p.

Study of the life of aging boarding home residents. Emerging themes included losses, specific behavior problems, food, problem solving, and aging.

678   Reschovsky, James. (1982). Aging in place: an investigation of the housing consumption and residential mobility of the elderly. Unpublished doctoral dissertation, The University of Michigan, 228p.

Housing adjustments should be prompted by declines in income, family size, and physical capabilities which accompany old age. However, among older persons, adjustments in housing consumption through moving are rare. "Costs to moving were found to deter mobility. Psychological costs were not found to be a predominant impediment to mobility. [There is] evidence that perhaps costs of searching for new dwellings are greater for the elderly, a likely result of lower income and poorer access to transportation."

679   Rose, Linda. (1983). Activity patterns and life satisfaction among residents of an old age home. Unpublished doctoral dissertation, University of California, Los Angeles, 221p.

Investigation of activity and life satisfaction in a total institution for the aging. Significant correlations were not found between life satisfaction and most of the activity and nonactivity variables studied. Continuity (from pre-institutionalization to post-institutionalization) of activities which were important to residents was not correlated with life satisfaction. There were no significant correlations between residents' perceptions of institutional totality and life satisfaction. "Perceived health, exercise, and total number of activities were significantly correlated with life satisfaction.   Activity profiles of residents indicated that those high in participation valued work, helping others, being active, and/or keeping busy."

680   Schreter, Carol.   (1983).   <u>Room for rent: sharing housing with non-related Older Americans</u>. Unpublished doctoral dissertation, Bryn Mawr College, The Graduate School of Social Work and Social Research, Bryn Mawr, Pennsylvania, 210p.

Compares self-initiated home sharers, clients of a housemate matching service, and group household members to examine the role, extent, and function of the homesharing programs.

681   Stanford, Barbara.   (1982).   <u>Shared housing for the elderly</u>.   Unpublished doctoral dissertation, The Fielding Institute, 243p.

Considers whether house-sharing improves the life satisfaction of low- and moderate-income people, especially taking into account the economic distress and the isolation felt by the aged.   "There was no observable pattern of a change in the feelings of isolation among subjects, matched, matchended, or not matched.   Pre and post measures on the Life Satisfaction Index indicated no major changes of any significance between the means of any of the groups examined."

682   West, Sheree.   (1985).   <u>Sharing and privacy in shared housing for older people</u>.   Unpublished doctoral dissertation, City University of New York, 379p.

Studies small-scale shared housing which offers security, economy, and modest services in a community setting.   "Most subjects believed they could have adequate privacy and a private life.   Three important themes of privacy were: protecting freedom and autonomy, defining and regulating social boundaries, and validating individual identity and status."

683   Wilson, Bernice.   (1983).   <u>Major issues of older adults confronting institutional living: "what to keep and what to give away"</u>.   Unpublished doctoral dissertation, University of Toronto, number of pages not given.

An interpretive study of how five older persons, applying to an institutional setting, try to come to terms with a major change in living arrangement.   Exploration of "the nature of the search for meaning, the movement or process of the questioning, the shifts in perspective . . . the dynamic nature of the struggle. . . . The goal of maintaining the integrity of self and life purpose over a long life becomes clarified as the person makes the existential choice about living fully the years that are left."

11

General

Books

684   Atchley, Robert. (1983). <u>Aging: continuity and</u>
        <u>change</u>. Belmont, California: Wadsworth Publishing
        Company, 325p.

This text on aging is centered on "creating empathy and
providing information for diagnosis and helping." Includes
sections on relating to others and the environment (such as
with adult children, with other kin), and major transitions in
later life (such as launching the children, midlife career
changes, and widowhood).

685   Bastida, Elena (Ed.). (1984). <u>Older women:</u>
        <u>current issues and problems</u>. Kansas City, Kansas:
        Mid-America Congress on Aging, 136p.

Considers the societal changes which impact older women's
lives. Provides a comprehensive description of social and
economic conditions affecting the older woman. Topics include
health, crime prevention, social services, personal growth, and
older women in rural areas and small towns.

686   Brubaker, Timothy (Ed.). (1983). <u>Family</u>
        <u>relationships in later life</u>. Beverly Hills: Sage
        Publications, 272p.

"Families in later life" refers to families who have members
who are beyond the childrearing years and who have launched
their children. This book provides an overview of family
relationships in later life, presents research on specific
family relationships, focuses on specific issues concerning
families in later life, and discusses practice and policy
concerns. The book focuses on the idea that there is a viable
family network for many older persons, that later life family
relationships are important to older people <u>and</u> other family
members, that such relationships have both positive <u>and</u>
negative aspects, and that policy and practice concerning older
people must recognize how important the family network can be
for older individuals.

687   Brubaker, Timothy.   (1985).   <u>Later life families</u>.
           Beverly Hills: Sage Publications, 144p.

Reviews studies on later life family patterns. This book
examines research that supports the contention of
gerontologists that the later life family is alive and well.
Later life families represent responsive social relationships
that deal with the various changes associated with aging.
Generally, younger family members do not ignore older family
members.   At the same time, some components of these
relationships do need support and assistance. The later life
family involves long-term relationships, and is characterized
by "mutual interaction, respect, and support."

688   Gwyther, Lisa; Gold, Deborah; and Hinman-Smith,
           Elizabeth. (No date given). <u>Older people and their
           families: coping with stress and conflict</u>. Durham,
           North Carolina: Duke University Medical Center,
           Center for the Study of Aging and Human Development,
           number of pages not given.

Curriculum for workshop presentations to help the general
public resolve stress and conflict within their family systems,
especially involving the aged. Aim of the curriculum is to
prevent elder abuse/neglect before detectable problems occur.
Topics include general aging issues, focusing on helping
families learn conflict resolution strategies and identifying
formal and informal helping networks.

689   Harbert, Anita, and Ginsberg, Leon. (1979). <u>Human
           services for older adults: concepts and skills</u>.
           Belmont, California: Wadsworth Publishing Company,
           345p.

Includes a chapter on serving older adults and their families.
"Thinking about the older client means thinking about the
client's family, too. For almost all older adults, the family
is a crucial reference point. Many older people's lives have
meaning primarily in the context of their families; failing to
take the family of the older client into account may cause a
human-service worker to neglect the most important parts of
that client's life."

690   Illinois State Department on Aging.   (1986).   <u>The
           status of older women in Illinois today: a report
           by the Task Force on Older Women in Illinois</u>.
           Springfield, Illinois: Illinois State Department on
           Aging, 23p.

Report of an Illinois task force formed to examine issues that
make it different to grow older as a woman than as a man and to
develop a set of recommendations to help meet the needs of
women in Illinois. Focus is on housing, health care, and
economic security of older women. Responses from over 1,300
older women attending public hearings, speak-outs, and
roundtable discussions revealed that lack of financial security
and a fear of the inability to pay for housing and health care
in their later years were major concerns. Includes a
conclusion and recommendations.

691   Lein, Laura, and Sussman, Marvin (Eds.). (1983).
        **The ties that bind: men's and women's social
        networks**. New York: Haworth Press, 111p.

A new importance of social networks as functional service
systems "is a result of decreasing support for institutional
professionalized human services--a turn to self-help and
increased involvement in caring and other helping activities by
members of such primary groups as families." Sussman notes
that it may be easy to conceptualize the family as the unit of
linkage and analysis in social network research and extremely
difficult to characterize and measure family networking. "The
situation, purpose, rationale, motivation, and interest of the
network participant determine who are the potential
beneficiaries of network activities and the proportional
distribution of benefits for the individual or the group."

692   Manney, James. (1975). **Aging in American society:
        an examination of concepts and issues**. Ann Arbor,
        Michigan: The Institute of Gerontology, The
        University of Michigan--Wayne State University,
        231p.

Includes section on major social roles of people, including
widows, spouse, grandparent, etc.

693   National Institute on Aging. (no date). **Health
        resources for older women**. Gaithersburg, Maryland:
        National Institute on Aging Information Center, 76p.

Provides women over 65 with up-to-date information on major
health issues affecting them today. Intended as a resource
tool for women seeking information on locating services for
better medical and health care.

694   Pifer, Alan, and Bronte, D. Lydia (Eds.). (1986).
        Our aging society: paradox and promise. New York:
        W. W. Norton, 438p.

Considers societal aging from the perspectives of particular
areas. Explores major demographic phenomenon of aging that
will, into the next century, "profoundly affect every one of
our nation's institutions and individuals."

695   Rich, Bennett, and Baum, Martha. (1984). **The
        aging: a guide to public policy**. Pittsburgh:
        University of Pittsburgh Press, 400p.

Interdisciplinary introduction to major concepts and issues of
gerontology. Includes section on the family and its elders.

696   Troll, Lillian; Miller, Sheila; and Atchley, Robert.
        (1979). **Families in later life**. Belmont,
        California: Wadsworth Publishing Company, 168p.

Describes variations in family structure, family relationships,
and family life that exist in the United States now. Covers
issues, perspectives, problems, older couples, on being
unmarried in later life, parents and their adult children,

being a grandparent or great-grandparent, siblings and other kin, and implications.

697   Troll, Lillian (Ed.).   (1986).   Family issues in
         current gerontology. New York: Springer Publishing
         Company, 382p.

Collection of reprints of 20 articles from The Journal of Gerontology and The Gerontologist. Covers changes in marital relations over time, widowhood, parent-adult child relations, caregiving, living arrangements, kinship networks, childlessness, and divorce.

Articles/chapters

698   Back, Kurt.   (1987).   Age segregation.   In Maddox,
         George (Ed.), The encyclopedia of aging, pp. 19-20.
         New York: Springer Publishing Company, 890p.

Author indicates that the primary problem of age segregation today is "the separation, real or imagined, of the core of the conjugal family the remainder of the population, particularly from the aged. . . . The effects of the current trend toward age segregation are ambiguous with the extremes becoming daily more onerous and adversely affecting costs and benefits for each group."

699   Beckman, Linda, and Houser, Betsy.   (1986).   The
         consequences of childlessness on the social-
         psychological well-being of older women.   In Troll,
         Lillian (Ed.), Family issues in current gerontology,
         pp. 333-349.   New York: Springer Publishing
         Company, 382p.

Examines the effects of childlessness on the social-psychological well-being of married and widowed women aged 60 to 75 years. The results of the study were that childlessness has a greater effect on well-being for widowed than for married women. Childless widows had lower overall well-being and were lonelier and more dissatisfied with their lives than were widows with grown children. Authors suggest that "women who are widowed, childless, Jewish, nonreligious, and without social support or satisfying social interactions are likely to evidence low social-psychological well-being. Women who represent combinations of such risk factors should be targeted for intervention strategies that can improve the quality of their lives."

700   Belle, Deborah.   (1983).   The impact of poverty on
         social networks and supports.   In Lein, Laura, and
         Sussman, Marvin (Eds.), The ties that bind: men's
         and women's social networks, pp. 89-103. New York:
         Haworth, 111p.

Discusses relationship between social networks and stress, psychological well-being, and family economic maintenance among poor families. "Since the natural helping networks of the poor are often emotionally costly, they should not be viewed as a substitute for formal helping networks or for economic security."

701   Campbell, Shirley.   (1984).   The fifty-year-old woman and midlife stress. International Journal of Aging and Human Development, 18(4), 295-307.

Suggests that women in their fifties are susceptible to many stresses.   "The possibilities of widowhood, divorce, or poverty, combined with intra- and interpersonal strains, make this a time of insecurity about aging for many women." Provides suggestions as to why women cope successfully with aging.

702   Chibucos, Thomas.   (1984).   Role of children and childhood in independence of the aged.   In Quinn, William, and Hughston, George (Eds.), Independent aging: family and social systems perspectives, pp. 243-255.   Rockville, Maryland: Aspen Systems Corporation, 300p.

Presents a model for examining the role of children in the independence and the development of old people.   Considers thinking about children and older persons related to socialization patterns and reciprocal influences around interdependence.   Proposes fostering "more interconnectedness among generations throughout the life span, with an emphasis on uniqueness and diversity."

703   Clark, C. Roberta.   (1984).   Aging and the family. Canadian Home Economics Journal, 34(1), 24-26.

Considers emotional, social, medical, and nutritional needs of older people, and stresses the need for education of the families of older persons and the need for a coordinated approach to service delivery to the elderly.

704   Cohen, Pennie.   (1983).   A group approach for working with families of the elderly. Gerontologist, 23(3), 248-250.

Describes a group approach used for working with families of the elderly as an effective treatment tool for adults who were responsible for aging family members.   "The group process encouraged information sharing, support, and working through emotional and practical problems associated with care of the elderly."

705   Connidis, Ingrid, and Davies, Lorraine.   (1990). Confidants and companions in later life: the place of family and friends.   Journal of Gerontology, 45(4), S141-S149.

Considers the importance of various family members to a sample of 400 older persons.   "Distinction regarding availability of kin must be made among those who never had a particular kin tie (e.g., childless and single), those who had lost a previous tie (e.g., widowed), and those whose ties live far away."   The finding was that single and previously married individuals without children, especially males, may be at risk of not having diverse enough social networks to insure that these needs are met regularly.

706   Dorfman, Lorraine, and Hill, Elizabeth.   (1986).
        Rural housewives and retirement: joint decision-
        making matters.   Family Relations, 35(4), 507-514.

Describes reactions of rural housewives (95) to their husbands' retirement and factors associated with satisfaction of rural wives during the retirement years. Finding was that there was a highly consistent relationship between joint decision-making by husband and wife and satisfaction of the wife in retirement.

707   Eisler,   Terri.   (1984).   Career   impact   on
        independence of the elderly.   In Quinn, William, and
        Hughston, George (Eds.), Independent aging: family
        and social systems perspectives,   pp.   256-264.
        Rockville, Maryland: Aspen Systems Corporation,
        300p.

Looks at the impact of career on independence and society by the identification of the intrinsic and the extrinsic rewards. Outlines positive consequences of mid-life career change. Concludes that career provide both intrinsic and extrinsic rewards;   that   careers   affect   personal,   private,   and professional lives; that careers involve thoughtful planning and movement along a continuum; that career development and choice are lifelong and continuous.

708   Fallo-Mitchell, Linda, and Ryff, Carol.   (1982).
        Preferred timing of female life events.   Research on
        Aging, 4(2), 249-267.

Examination of cohort differences in the preferred timing of events in the female life cycle. Middle-aged or old-aged women preferred earlier ages for family life events and later ages for general life events than did young adult women.

709   Fillenbaum, Gerda, and Wallman, Laurence.   (1986).
        Changes in household composition of the elderly: a
        preliminary investigation.   In Troll, Lillian (Ed.),
        Family issues in current gerontology, pp. 284-300.
        New York: Springer Publishing Company, 382p.

Presents longitudinal data from a small sample on household composition of the elderly--economic status (representing environmental circumstances), self-care capacity (representing individual life cycle matters), marital status, and extent of help available from family and friends (representing family life cycle matters).   Substantial change in household composition occurs. There was no apparent relationship between change in economic status and change in self-care capacity to change in household composition.   The flexibility of residential arrangements was confirmed. Authors suggest that "capacity to remain in a particular setting may depend less on the individual's personal capabilities than on the supportive services available, services that may, but do not have to be, provided by another resident."

710   Friedman, Ariella. (1987). Getting powerful with age: changes in women over the life cycle. Israel Social Science Research, 5, 76-86.

Presents results of a series of eight empirical studies of changes in women over the life cycle, which indicate that women in the later years are happier, more powerful, and less vulnerable in their marriages than they are in their earlier years. The trend is related to a change in the balance of power in the relationship between spouses. As their parental role demands are reduced, women become less dependent on their husbands and find other types of support and satisfaction, while men move in an opposite direction. "With the years, and especially after retirement, the family becomes more dependent on the wife." Author suggests that female traits are evaluated more positively in the later years than in the earlier years.

711   Gold, Deborah; Woodbury, Max; and George, Linda. (1990). Relationship classification using grade of membership analysis: a typology of sibling relationships in later life. Journal of Gerontology, 45(2), S43-S51.

Compares two typologies of sibling relationships in old age in terms of number of types generated, characteristics of each type, factors influencing typological construction, and the utility of empirical results.

712   Greenberg, Jan, and Becker, Marion. (1988). Aging parents as family resources. Gerontologist, 28(6), 786-791.

Investigates extent to which aging parents experience stress when problems arise in the lives of their adult children and how they serve as resources to their children in need. Mothers experienced significant stress, while fathers experienced stress indirectly through the stress caused their wives. Parents were active in helping their children cope.

713   Hagestad, Gunhild. (1987). Able elderly in the family context: changes, chances, and challenges. Gerontologist, 27(4), 417-422.

Discusses differences between past and future young-old populations. Describes changes in mortality, work, and family patterns that represent new potential for families and life careers. "While demographic and cultural changes could create new chasms between worlds of men and women, they could also lead to increased convergence in their experience."

714   Hagestad, Gunhild. (1987). Family. In Maddox, George (Ed.), The encyclopedia of aging, pp. 247-249. New York: Springer Publishing Company, 890p.

Defines family. Discusses family roles, family structure and patterns of contact, exchange of support, socialization and consensus, the affective quality of ties, and neglected issues.

715   Hagestad, Gunhild. (1986). The family: women and
         grandparents as kin-keepers. In Pifer, Alan., and
         Bronte, D. Lydia (Eds.), Our aging society: paradox
         and promise, pp. 141-160. New York: W. W. Norton,
         438p.

Considers altered patterns of family deaths, durable bonds, a
new uniformity on childhood experiences, the changing age
structure of kin networks, the lack of cultural rules, new
forms of interdependence, who has the right to be old, kinkeeping and its costs, the old as resources, the effects of
divorce and remarriage, increased matrilineality, and contrasts
between men's and women's social networks.

716   Hansson, Robert; Jones, Warren; Carpenter, Bruce;
         and Remondet, Jacqueline. (1987). Loneliness and
         adjustment to old age. International Journal of
         Aging and Human Development, 24(1), 41-53.

Examines loneliness in older adults in a sample of 177 persons.
Finding was that loneliness was related to poor psychological
adjustment and to dissatisfaction with family and social
relationships.   Loneliness was also related to fears,
expectations, and personality characteristics likely to inhibit
the restoration of personal support networks after a stressful
life event such as widowhood and to maladaptive behavior
patterns.

717   Haraven, Tamara. (1981). Historical changes in the
         timing of family transitions: their impact on
         generational relations. In Fogel, Robert; Hatfield,
         Elaine; Kiesler, Sara; and Shanas, Ethel (Eds.),
         Aging, stability and change in the family, pp. 143-
         165. New York: Academic Press, 341p.

Examines basic concepts of the life-course framework as they
describe changing historical conditions affecting aging and the
family, historical developments in timing of life transitions
as they affect the family relationships of older persons,
timing patterns and intergenerational relations among American
families in the late 19th and early 20th centuries and the
implications of the timing patterns for generational relations
in later life.

718   Hess, Beth, and Waring, Joan. (1983). Family
         relationships of older women: a women's issue. In
         Markson, Elizabeth (Ed.), Older women, pp. 227-251.
         Lexington, Massachusetts: Lexington Books/D.C.
         Heath and Co., 351p.

Discusses family relationships of women in old age, old-age
dependency, familial resources, women without children, parent-
child bonds, caregivers to the elderly, family caregiving in
the future, and social policies affecting family relationships.

719   Iris, Madelyn. (1988). Guardianship and the
         elderly: a multi-perspective view of the decision-
         making process. Gerontologist, 28, 39-45.

Describes case studies from a study of judicial decision-making on guardianship for elderly persons to describe four decision-making roles: family, attorneys, physicians, and judges. Focus was on conflicting roles of guardian ad litem and interface between legal and medical standards of competency. The finding was that "societal attitudes and beliefs about aging had great impact on guardianship decision-making process."

720   Jeter, Kris.   (1983).   Analytic essay: the ties that bind.   In Lein, Laura, and Sussman, Marvin. (Eds.), The ties that bind: men's and women's social networks, pp. 105-111. New York: Haworth, 111p.

"Family ties have various strengths, weaknesses, meanings, and knots . . . supportive networks have been built around families and kin from time immemorial and where non-family and non-kin are involved and they are apt to be treated 'like family'." Individuals count on family and kin networks when in trouble or needing affection, help, love, etc.

721   Kuypers, Joseph, and Bengston, Vern.   (1984). Perspectives on the older family.   In Quinn, William, and Hughston, George (Eds.), Independent aging: family and social systems perspectives, pp. 2-20.   Rockville, Maryland: Aspen Systems Corp., 300p.

Discusses the ways in which family life, conceptualizations of family competence, and social breakdown syndrome are understood.

722   Kuypers, Joseph, and Bengston, Vern.   (1983). Toward competence in the older family. In Brubaker, Timothy (Ed.), Family relationships in later life, pp. 211-228.   Beverly Hills: Sage Publications, 272p.

Focuses on the older family as an aging system. Explores predictable passages, strains, and issues facing older families.   Discusses differences between older and younger families and identifies special concerns which practitioners may have as they attempt to help older families in corrective action. Concludes that "as economics and policy shifts combine to encourage the family to assume more responsibility for its elder members, the limits of the family's capacity will be revealed. In our efforts to assist, we must become informed as to the unique strengths and weaknesses that unfold in older families."

723   Lein, Laura.   (1983).   The ties that bind: an introduction. In Lein, Laura, and Sussman, Marvin (Eds.), The ties that bind: men's and women's social networks, pp. 3-7. New York: Haworth Press, 111p.

Describes the various chapters in this book which explores the implications of social networks and men and women in different

social contexts. Explains that each section illustrates the
links between network structure and network functioning and the
changes in networks as individuals change circumstances. The
book "explores aspects of men's and women's social networks:
the important functions of networks and the ways social
networks shape adult lives at different points in the life
cycle and for men and women in different kinds of families."

724   **Little, Virginia. (1983). International symposium:
        the family as a source of support for the elderly.
        Gerontologist, 23(6), 573-596.**

Reviews research on the family as a source of support for the
elderly in Israel, Japan, Poland, Hong Kong, and Egypt. Focus
is on cultural norms, changes in intergenerational support over
time, family relationships, lack of social services, social
change, and stress factors.

725   **Longino, Charles, and Lipman, Aaron. (1982). The
        married, the formerly married and the never married:
        support system differentials of older women in
        planned retirement communities. International
        Journal of Aging and Human Development, 15, 285-297.**

Explores the informal support given to older women, depending
upon their marital status and the presence of living children.
Those women who were presently or formerly married received
more emotional, social, and instrumental support from their
family members. The never married experienced the greatest
informal support deficits, seen to be a result from the lack of
children.

726   **Mancini, Jay. (1984). Leisure lifestyles and
        family dynamics in old age. In Quinn, William, and
        Hughston, George (Eds.), Independent aging: family
        and social systems perspectives, pp. 58-71.
        Rockville, Maryland: Aspen Systems Corporation,
        300p.**

Four assumptions about leisure, the family, and old age are the
bases for this review--that the interplay between the leisure
and the family domains is potentially substantial, that leisure
participation and family interaction can influence well-being
in old age, that relational dimensions of leisure participation
must be understood to understand adequately the impact of
leisure on well-being, and that the leisure context should be
considered to understand adequately the impact of family
interaction on well-being.

727   **Mancini, Jay. (1984). Research on family life in
        old age: exploring the frontiers. In Quinn,
        William, and Hughston, George (Eds.), Independent
        aging: family and social systems perspectives, pp.
        265-284. Rockville, Maryland: Aspen Systems
        Corporation, 300p.**

Discussion of frontiers of research on family life in old age.
Identifies myths and theoretical issues. Suggests that "the
importance of family life may be overestimated, that the

criterion 'well-being' is not always the appropriate choice; that research has tended to address the alienation, enrichment, and empty nest hypotheses; that qualitative approaches are underutilized; that concerted theory development efforts are advised; and that the field still lacks a cumulative body of knowledge."

728   Nydegger, Corinne. (1986). Family ties of the aged in cross-cultural perspective. In Troll, Lillian (Ed.), Family issues in social gerontology, pp. 145-161. New York: Springer Publishing Company, 382p.

Presents an anthropological perspective--"the value of bringing a cross-cultural perspective to bear on family ties of the elderly is not simply in the cataloguing of other societies' practices but in placing our own practices into the larger context which is generated by such studies." The author looks at American institutions in light of other cultures' practices. The author recommends accepting negative aspects of family ties as natural outcomes and looking at the structural features that encourage conflict in order to understand older persons and their family ties.

729   O'Donnell, Lydia. (1983). The social worlds of parents. In Lein, Laura, and Sussman, Marvin. (Eds.), The ties that bind: men's and women's social networks, pp. 9-36. New York: Haworth Press, 111p.

Discusses social networks of men and women during the parenting years. Reviews literature on parents' needs for social supports, on the kinds of supports they customarily receive through social networks, on the contributions made by parents to social networks, and on the role of children in the social networks of their parents.

730   Oppenheimer, Valerie. (1981). The changing nature of life-cycle squeezes: implications for the socioeconomic position of the elderly. In Fogel, Robert; Hatfield, Elaine; Kiesler, Sara; and Shanas, Ethel (Eds.), Aging, stability and change in the family, pp. 47-81. New York: Academic Press, 341p.

Treatise on economic squeezes, situations in which the cost of achieving or maintaining an accustomed or desired life-style exceeds the income currently available to do so, pressures for additional income for families. The author identifies three essential components of an economic squeeze--the family life-style aspirations, cost of the aspirations, and income currently available to achieve the aspirations. When one or more components is out of balance with the others, certain types of behavior, such as the wife working outside the home, result. The author supports the use of a life-cycle squeeze model in studying the socioeconomic position of the elderly. Family (or societal) techniques for dealing with an older population may increasingly rely on purchase of goods and services from non-kin.

731   Orbach, Harold. (1983). Symposium: aging, families, and family relations: behavioral and social science perspectives on our knowledge, our myths, and our research. Gerontologist, 23(1), 24-50.

Presents four articles exploring the relationship between aging and family life and myths about treatment of the aged. Provides psychological perspectives of autonomy and interdependence in the adult family and examines research needs of the frail elderly and demonstrates the important role of intrafamily resource transfers.

732   Pinkston, Elaine, and Linsk, Nathan. (1984). Behavioral family intervention with the impaired elderly. Gerontologist, 24(6), 576-583.

Describes the Elderly Support Project that was designed to evaluate intervention procedures on teaching families better home care of the mentally and physically impaired elderly. Evaluates "intervention procedures derived from behavioral parent training research and adapted to teach families better home care of the mentally and physically impaired elderly." The finding was that these intervention procedures were valuable for promoting continuing home care, better mental status, and improved behavior of elderly clients by offering families alternative positive responses for use with their older relatives.

733   Quinn, William. (1984). Autonomy, interdependence, and developmental delay in older generations of the family. In Quinn, William, and Hughston, George (Eds)., Independent aging: family and social systems perspectives, pp. 21-34. Rockville, Maryland: Aspen Systems Corporation, 300p.

Discusses elements of interaction that become conducive or disturbing to the intergenerational relations of adult family members--quality in intergenerational relationships in affection, communication, filial expectations and filial responsibility; conceptual integration; and family transition.

734   Reno, Virginia. (1981). Family roles and social security. In Fogel, Robert; Hatfield, Elaine; Kiesler, Sara; and Shanas, Ethel (Eds.), Aging, stability and change in the family, pp. 185-210. New York: Academic Press, 341p.

Considers alternative approaches to exploring family roles in the Social Security system. Author argues that the present system, with adults as either workers or dependents of workers, lacks flexibility to consider the differences in family economic relationships that occur over the lifetime. The viability of various approaches may depend largely on estimates of their distributional effects, i.e., how many people in certain circumstances would experience a change in benefits or taxes.

735   Riley, Matilda. (1987). Age stratification. In
        Maddox, George (Ed.), The encyclopedia of aging,
        pp. 20-22. New York: Springer Publishing Company,
        890p.

The age stratification model offers a framework for developing
fundamental principles about age and aging and considering
policy implications of "an age stratification system where
individual lives and societal structures are subject to
change." Discusses the age stratification model, age
stratification studies, relation to other forms of
stratification, and contributions of this model to theory and
methodology.

736   Riley, Matilda. (1983). The family in an aging
        society: a matrix of latent relationships. Journal
        of Family Issues, 4(3), 439-454.

Focus is on the influence of increased longevity on the kinship
structure. "Today's kinship structure can be viewed as
continually shifting linkages that provide the potential for
activating and intensifying close family relationships, raising
issues such as the need for special approaches to family
research and practice."

737   Scott, Jean. (1983). Siblings and other kin. In
        Brubaker, Timothy (Ed.), Family relationships in
        later life, pp. 47-62. Beverly Hills: Sage
        Publications, 272p.

Addresses questions of what types of interaction and helping
behavior characterize sibling relationships in later life; how
sibling interaction in this stage of life compares with other
kinds of kin interaction, such as child and grandchild
relationships; how equitable exchanges of help are among older
siblings and how the sibling equitability compares with that of
child and grandchild relations. The author concludes that
sibling relationships for older, white, urban, middle-class
adults indicate high positive affect, sociability (e.g., brief
visits, getting together for special occasions), and limited
mutual assistance. According to Scott, siblings appear to
provide support for older adults, complementing their
relationships with children and grandchildren.

738   Seltzer, Marsha; Ivry, Joann; and Litchfield, Leon.
        (1987). Family members as case managers:
        partnership between the formal and informal support
        networks. Gerontologist, 27(6), 722-728.

Experimental/control groups with family members participated in
a case management training program. After training, the
families in the experimental group performed a significantly
greater number of case management tasks for elderly relatives
than the families in the control group. "Duration of service
was significantly shorter for the elderly in the experimental
group."

739   Seltzer, Mildred. (1989). Random and not so random
        thoughts on becoming and being a statistic:

professional and personal musings. **International Journal of Aging and Human Development**, **28**, 1-7.

Offers personal and professional thoughts of the author on becoming and being an old woman. Describes "daily confrontations with the chasm between science and personal experiences" of the author as subject (old woman) and researcher (gerontologist).

740   Silverstein, Nina; Gonyea, Judith; and King, Nancy. (1989). Family-professional partnerships for addressing Alzheimer's disease. **Gerontologist**, **29**(6), 830-834.

Partnership project for collaboration between families and professionals demonstrated in eight Massachusetts communities. Project was successful in its strategies to heighten public awareness, strengthen interagency networking, and improve community resources.

741   Smith, Daniel. (1981). Historical change in the household structure of the elderly in economically developed societies. In Fogel, Robert; Hatfield, Elaine; Kiesler, Sara; and Shanas, Ethel (Eds.), **Aging, stability and change in the family**, pp. 91-114. New York: Academic Press, 341p.

Contrasts the existing record of the historical documentation of the household structure of the elderly with the theoretical perspectives. Outlines three major theoretical notions relevant to household structure of the elderly, uses available historical evidence to fill in the framework, and comments on important problems suggested by realistic propositions.

742   Steinmetz, Suzanne, and Amsden, Deborah. (1983). Dependent elders, family stress, and abuse. In Brubaker, Timothy (Ed.), **Family relationships in later life**, pp. 173-192. Beverly Hills: Sage Publications, 272p.

Looks at the relationship between dependency measured by the frequency with which tasks or services need to be provided (by adult children) for older persons, stress as perceived by caregivers, and abusive techniques used to gain or maintain control. Concludes that family members provide many caregiving tasks for their older relatives and that there is an increase in the likelihood of abusive and disruptive family interaction because of the elder's dependence on the caregiver and the caregiver's overall sense of burden. The data herein indicate that social/emotional and mental health dependencies are the most likely to produce stress and violence. Families need support services to help them cope and to help them find alternative living arrangements, when needed.

743   Stueve, Ann. (1983). The elderly as network members. In Lein, Laura, and Sussman, Marvin. (Eds.), **The ties that bind: men's and women's social networks**, pp. 59-87. New York: Haworth, 111p.

Discusses the position of the elderly in each other's social networks and in the social networks of younger individuals. Looks at older persons as contributors of services as well as beneficiaries of services. Emphasizes older persons remaining active in their families, neighborhoods, and world communities. The elderly "participate, are diverse, and still have much to offer age peers and other generations in their roles as family members, friends, neighbors, natural helpers, and volunteers."

744   Voges, Wolfgang, and Pongratz, Hannelore. (1988). Retirement and the lifestyles of older women. Aging and Society, 8, 63-83.

Analysis of the impact of moving from a private household to a residential care facility on dimensions of lifestyle and the success with which adaptation to the new setting is made. Uses interviews with 13 female residents, ages 69 to 91, of residential care facilities in the Munich (West Germany) area. Supplements these data with interviews with a close relative of each woman subject and with a member of the care facility staff who knows the woman subject well. There was found a positive relationship between continuity in lifestyle and content with life situation. However, often compensation for a lifestyle dimension was disrupted by the transition with another dimension.

745   Ward, Russell. (1985). Informal networks and well-being in later life: a research agenda. Gerontologist, 25(1), 55-61.

Outlines a research agenda for understanding the contributions of informal social support to the quality of later life. Author suggests a conceptual model for investigating informal support networks and well-being for the elderly and offers suggestions for operationalizing the model.

746   Weiler, Stephen. (1981). Aging and sexuality and the myth of decline. In Fogel, Robert; Hatfield, Elaine; Kiesler, Sara; and Shanas, Ethel (Eds.), Aging, stability and change in the family, pp. 317-327. New York: Academic Press, 341p.

Facts about aging and sexuality are replacing myths about aging and sexuality. The author suggests that social scientists should learn "to become reasonably skeptical of statistical knowledge and increasingly sensitive to the experience of individuals. . . . Sexual expression continues late in life and continues in the context of the marital unit."

747   Whiting, John. (1981). Aging and becoming an elder: a cross-cultural comparison. In Fogel, Robert; Hatfield, Elaine; Kiesler, Sara; and Shanas, Ethel (Eds.), Aging, stability and change in the family, pp. 83-90. New York: Academic Press, 341p.

Presents the example of Kikuyu culture (in Nairobi, Africa) as a highly-developed age set, age grade system. Because that system no longer is functioning, the system was reconstructed as it existed in 1890 just before radical change from early

ethnographic reports.   The author says that such a system is
not compatible with a complex, industrialized society, but that
some features of modern society could be modified.

748   Wynne, Edward.   (1986).   Will the young support the
        old?   In Pifer, Alan, and Bronte, D. Lydia (Eds.),
        Our aging society: paradox and promise, pp. 243-
        261.   New York: W. W. Norton, 438p.

The United States is moving toward a period when fewer working-
age adults will need to provide goods, health care, and other
services to increasing number of older persons.   Discusses
rights versus reciprocity, principles of reciprocity, the
benefit system, defining society's obligations, caring for the
aged in a "transformed" society.

Films

749   Franciscan Communications.   (1981).   Aging Grace.

Describes needs and experiences of the aging.

750   Sacramento Community Commission for Women.   (1977).
        Women and aging.

A candid exploration of the aging process among women.
Stresses needs and concerns confronting older women, financial
and psychological difficulties encountered when a 25-year
marriage ends in divorce, the importance of family to a widowed
grandmother, the importance of continuing to be active in
retirement, and nursing home life.   Shows the diversity among
older women and the problems and benefits of old age.

751   Snyder, Patricia, and Marks, Harvey.   (Producers).
        (1985).   Silent pioneers.

Profiles eight gay and lesbian older men and women, depicting
their capacity for affection, the ability to maintain lasting
relationships, and the universal need for forming meaningful
human relationships.

752   Soho Cinema, Ltd.   (1976).   Mamma.

"Mamma" left Sicily, Italy, at age 19.   In this film, she
reminisces about her trip to the U.S.   "Hers is the voice of
the old ways in the New World.   We are her children and she
speaks to each one of us."

Documents

753   Butler, Robert.   (1984).   A generation at risk:
        when the baby boomers reach Golden Pond.   Austin,
        Texas: Hogg Foundation for Mental Health, 19p.

Author suggests that, as they reach retirement, baby boomers
will have to balance their own needs with those of living
parents and even grandparents.   At the same time, the baby

boomers will have fewer family members to turn to for help as a result of having fewer children, more divorce, and more social isolation. Butler suggests that society must spur institutional change in order to minimize dependency and maximize productivity.

754   Cohen, George, et al. (1986). Families: an expanding role for professional counselors. Alexandria, Virginia: American Association for Counseling and Development, 89p.

Contains papers from a conference targeting the needs and interests of counselors working with families. Includes section on families with aging members.

755   Fowles, Donald. (1986). A profile of older Americans. Washington, D.C.: American Association of Retired Persons, 11p.

Provides statistical data on the aging of the American population, including age cohort data, information on racial and ethnic groups, geographic migration, and income.

756   National Commission on Working Women. (1987). Women, work and age: a fact sheet. Washington, D.C.: Wider Opportunities for Women, 5p.

Provides statistics on various aspects of the special concerns of midlife and older women in the labor force. Looks at number of midlife and older women in the work force, marital status, displaced homemakers, and occupational categories represented by these women. Presents a profile of midlife and older women in the labor force, and discusses age discrimination. Reviews future trends for these women.

Dissertations

757   Aizenberg, Rhonda. (1979). Socio-familial involvements among aged nursing home residents. Unpublished doctoral dissertation, Duke University, 253p.

Examines the socio-familial involvements of aged residents in nursing homes. Includes an assessment of their patterns of participation in institutionally-sponsored activities and the contacts they maintain with family and non-family members not living in the facility. Functional health status is the primary determinant of internal involvement. Contacts with externally-based individuals also have significant, although conflicting, effects on the internal involvements developed by residents. When frequent and regular contact is not maintained with a spouse, residents tend to substitute by establishing extrafamilial involvements within the nursing home. Where there is much contact with other relatives and externally-based nonrelatives, there is more frequent and extensive institutional participation.

758   Bearon, Lucille.   (1982).   **No great expectations:**
         the nature of life satisfaction in a sample of
         elderly women. Unpublished doctoral dissertation,
         Duke University, 148p.

Identifies factors which older women consider when they are
making global assessments of their well-being, including the
objective conditions and evaluation criteria which are
important to them. Older women in this study were much more
likely than middle-aged women to aspire solely to maintain the
status quo and prevent deterioration, while middle-aged women
more frequently wanted to have positive changes in their lives.

759   Brown, Barbara.   (1982).   **Married, academic, women**
         in mid-life transition.   Unpublished doctoral
         dissertation, Temple University, 199p.

Investigates whether married, academic women in mid-life
transition follow the same developmental patterns as the men in
Levinson's 1978 study. The women subjects followed the same
developmental patterns as the men in Levinson's study.

760   Cassidy, Margaret.   (1982).   **The effects of**
         retirement on emotional well-being: a comparison of
         men and women. Unpublished doctoral dissertation,
         Washington State University, 171p.

Used premises of symbolic interaction theory and activity
theory to predict and interpret effects of retirement on
emotional well-being--self-worth and morale--in old age.
Retirement negatively affected the self-worth of women but not
men and positively affected the morale of men and women.
Retirees were more socially active than were employed persons.
Social activity enhanced emotional well-being. Health had the
strongest positive direct effect on emotional well-being, and
age had the strongest negative indirect effect on emotional
well-being.

761   Chelsvig, Kathleen.   (1982).   **Family interaction**
         patterns and life satisfaction among the elderly: a
         policy analysis. Unpublished doctoral dissertation,
         University of Maryland, 145p.

Examines three types of family interaction--service aid, money
aid, and interaction frequency, from younger to older persons.
The most likely to be involved in all types of family
interaction were blue collar, employed males, white collar
females, and non-employed females. High life satisfaction was
most likely to be reported by white and white collar
respondents.

762   Choi, Sung-Joe.   (1984).   **Modernization and social**
         integration of the aged into the family in Korea.
         Unpublished doctoral dissertation, Case Western
         Reserve University, 198p.

Study of how modernization exerts significant negative
influences upon social integration of the aged into their

families in Korea. The finding was that work roles were negatively associated with social integration.

763   Hatch, Laurie. (1986). **A structural analysis of men and women in retirement.** Unpublished doctoral dissertation, University of Washington, 327p.

Examines conditions under which sex differences in retirement attitudes and timing are likely to be observed. Results suggest that "the variable of sex is a poor proxy for life experiences and structural circumstances that are likely to covary with sex, such as work history."

764   Israel, Barbara. (1982). **Social networks and psychological well-being among elderly women.** Unpublished doctoral dissertation, The University of North Carolina at Chapel Hill, 210p.

Describes extent to which social network characteristics are related to psychological well-being. Reciprocal affective support, intensity, and affective support explained a significant amount of the variance in psychological well-being.

765   Kaye, Andrea. (1981). **An investigation of early adult and midlife structure for women living a traditional life pattern.** Unpublished doctoral dissertation, University of Pittsburgh, 183p.

In this study, traditional women were defined as women who were primarily home-centered and sustaining a full-time homemaker life pattern throughout their adult years. Seventeen generic life themes emerged in the lived-experiences of the subjects across the developmental phases.

766   Liss, Barbara. (1982). **Life satisfaction: a comparison of retired and employed women.** Unpublished doctoral dissertation, The University of Texas Health Science Center at Houston, 172p.

Study of life satisfaction for retired and employed women with long-term employment in a typically female occupational setting. Retired women's perceptions of their health and social participation were more positive than the employed women's. There was higher life satisfaction among traditional, retired women than among nontraditional, retired women. There was higher life satisfaction among retired and employed women who perceived continuity in life patterns than among women who perceived discontinuity. The greatest area of retirement concern for retired and employed women was in financial planning.

767   Luhmann, Frederick. (1984). **A study of the relationship between filial piety and age of urban residents in Korea and their attitude toward old people in general.** Unpublished doctoral dissertation, The Catholic University of America, 144p.

Uses modernization theory perspective to investigate whether the status of old people diminishes as a society becomes more technological.   College students were found to have less favorable attitudes toward old people than did senior center attendees.   Subjects who had higher filial piety scores had more favorable attitudes toward old people.   The findings were consistent with modernization theory.

768   MacKeracher, Dorothy.   (1982).   **A study of the experience of aging from the perspective of older women**.   Unpublished   doctoral   dissertation, University of Toronto, number of pages not given.

This qualitative study examines the aging experiences of 30 older women interviewed by the researcher.   Patterns of change were found in three aspects of experience--space, time, and energy.

769   Montgomery, Mary.   (1983).   **Structure and attributes of social support networks that affect health of the aged**.   Unpublished doctoral dissertation, University of California-Berkeley, 217p.

Examines uses of a social network analysis framework to explore the relationship between social support and health conditions and health perceptions among a sample of non-institutionalized elderly.   Describes specific aspects of the structure and function of elderly persons' personal support systems and explores how these are related to their health status.

770   Ojeda de la Rena, Norma.   (1987).   **Family life cycle and social classes in Mexico**.   Unpublished doctoral dissertation, The University of Texas at Austin, 314p.

Studies the life cycle of the contemporary conjugal Mexican family.   Uses the "life course" perspective as analytical framework.   "Every social class exhibits a peculiar time pattern in both the formation and expansion stages of the life cycle of the conjugal family."

771   Pelham,   Anabel.   (1980).   **"Plain-clothes" investigator in cockroach castles: toward a qualitative methodology and interactionist analysis of aging in the Tenderloin**.   Unpublished doctoral dissertation,   University   of   California-San Francisco, 140p.

This study suggests that aging is a complex biological, psychological, and social process of adaptation rendered problematic under certain conditions and within certain social contexts.   In this analysis, the person is at the center of a process of creating the social world.

772   Premo, Terri.   (1983).   **Women growing old in the New Republic: personal responses to old age, 1785-1835**. Unpublished doctoral dissertation, University of Cincinnati, 290p.

Examines women's personal responses to growing old in the 50
years following American independence. Continuity was a
dominant factor in the lives of aging women. Aging women
continued to depend upon husbands, sons, and brothers for
economic support, whatever the marital status of the women.
But older women preferred independent living arrangements and
enjoyed strong emotional attachments with female friends and
relatives.

773   Quam, Jean. (1981). **The utility of friendship for
        older women: an application of the task specific
        model.** Unpublished doctoral dissertation, The
        University of Wisconsin-Madison, 223p.

Examines relationship between characteristics of an older
woman's closest friendship and the utility that the friendship
will have for specific helping tasks. Friendships for older
women may substitute for a spouse. One of the few available
resources for all older women may be a natural helping network.

774   Sanchez-Ayendez, Melba. (1984). **Puerto Rican
        elderly women: aging in an ethnic minority aging in
        the United States.** Unpublished doctoral
        dissertation, University of Massachusetts, 333p.

Treats cultural value orientations as central to understanding
how minority elders approach growing old and dealing with
changes associated with aging. "Familial and community
networks, as well as social agencies, provide the respondents
with viable systems of support. The elderly women have a place
in the functional structure of their families and play
important roles in providing their families with assistance."

775   Shiang, Julia. (1984). **The significance of
        transactions: reciprocity between Chinese elderly
        and their adult children living in Boston and its
        suburbs.** Unpublished doctoral dissertation, Harvard
        University, 192p.

Shows the strength of the family as a support system for the
elderly. Mandarin-speaking families tended to conduct one-way
transactions; Cantonese-speaking families conducted two-way
transactions. "Parents would give to their children when they
were young and, in return, expect to be taken care of in old
age."

776   Spector, Carol. (1988). **An exploratory study of
        adult women born 1939-1944: their perceptions of
        self and self in relation to others.** Unpublished
        doctoral dissertation, Temple University, 235p.

Explores women's adult development, especially self-development
within a relational context, and how this affected their view
of responsibility to self and others throughout their adult
lives. The results were that "women, whether homemaker, carer,
or later work-oriented, view responsibility to themselves and
others within an interdependent relational context, if not from
early adulthood certainly by middle adulthood."

777   Tully, Carol.   (1983).   <u>Social support systems of a</u>
           <u>selected sample of older women</u>.   Unpublished
           doctoral   dissertation,   Virginia   Commonwealth
           University, 213p.

Examines social organizational structures and support systems
in the social world of the older lesbian woman.   Subjects seek
and receive support during crises from people who are aware of
the older lesbian's sexual orientation.   Those providing
support include homosexual and heterosexual women friends and
some family members, but rarely men.   "It is primarily within
the context of relationships with other women that those
surveyed gain support in times of crisis."

778   Tuttle, Robert.   (1987).   <u>Poverty over the family</u>
           <u>life cycle</u>.   Unpublished doctoral dissertation,
           University of Notre Dame, 153p.

Uses the Panel Study of Income Dynamics to investigate
families' vulnerability to poverty over the family life cycle.
Family size, race, and education of the head of the household
were highly correlated with poverty status.

Author Index

[Compiler's note: numbers in this index refer to the entry numbers of each annotation, not page numbers on which the annotations are found.]

Abel, E., 362
Adams, Rebecca, 26, 27, 28
Ade-Ridder, Linda, 58
Adler, Arlene, 608
Aizenberg, Rhonda, 757
Aldous, Joan, 191, 254
Allen, Katherine, 22, 47
Ames, Barbara, 307, 415
Amsden, Deborah, 742
Anderson, Donna, 30
Anderson, Roxanne, 286
Anetzberger, Georgia, 309
Angel, Ronald, 632
Arber, Sara, 391
Arens, Diana, 101
Arling, Greg, 363, 364
Arsenault, Anne, 144
Ashley, Laurel, 573
Atchley, Robert, 59, 684, 696
Atkinson, Lynn, 339
Atkinson, Maxine, 271

Back, Kurt, 298, 698
Bailey, Caroline, 1

Bain, Patrice, 365
Bakaly, John, 474
Baker, Diane, 216
Baldwin, Christine, 4
Banahan, Benjamin, 64
Bankoff, Elizabeth, 255
Barnett, Rosalind, 251
Barnewolt, Debra, 8
Barranti, Chrystal, 242
Barrell, Lorna, 145
Barresi, Charles, 104
Bartz, Karen, 299
Baruch, Grace, 2, 8, 251
Barusch, Amanda, 366, 475
Bass, David, 618
Bastida, Elena, 521, 522, 574, 685
Baum, Martha, 695
Baumhover, Lorin, 437
Beall, Colleen, 437
Bearon, Lucille, 758
Becker, Marion, 712
Beckman, Linda, 699
Beh, Hazel, 367
Beland, Francois, 600

Bell, William 308,
    531
Belle, Deborah 700
Bengston, Vern 29,
    189, 191, 192,
    193, 194, 195,
    198, 199, 202,
    204, 206, 207,
    208, 211, 213,
    721, 722
Bensel-Myers, Linda,
    146
Berger, Raymond, 23
Berkman, Sherry, 270
Berman, Leonard, 228
Berman, Raeann, 358
Bernard, Miriam,
    315, 356, 391,
    624
Biggers, Trisha, 147
Binstock, Robert, 29
Blau, Zena, 548
Block, Marilyn, 523
Blum, Michael, 217
Boldt, Joanne, 575
Bolland, John, 437
Bonar, James, 621
Borgatta, Edgar,
    256, 419, 467
Bottar, Karen, 148
Bowers, Barbara, 476
Boyd, Robert, 42
Braito, Rita, 30
Brawner, Debbie, 357
Brecher, Edward, 56
Breckenridge, James,
    124
Breneman, Mary, 368
Brewer, Mary, 149
Brieff, Robert, 477
Bright, Carole, 150
Brody, Elaine, 369,
    370, 371, 372,
    373, 377, 463,
    601
Bronte, D. Lydia,
    527, 544, 551,
    694, 715, 748
Brooks, Hildy, 280
Brooks-Gunn, Jeanne,
    2, 8
Brotman, Herman, 625
Brown, Addie, 576
Brown, Barbara, 759
Brown, Judith, 94
Browne, Colette,
    300, 348, 365,
    367, 368, 374,
    386, 447, 611,

    620
Brubaker, Ellie,
    375, 376
Brubaker, Timothy,
    32, 58, 59, 61,
    62, 107, 212,
    258, 360, 375,
    376, 390, 539,
    686, 687, 722,
    737, 742
Burton, Linda, 29,
    193, 577
Butler, Robert, 301,
    753
Bynum, Jerry, 437

Campbell, Richard,
    626
Campbell, Ruth, 377
Campbell, Shirley,
    701
Cantor, Marjorie,
    378
Carlin, Vivian, 602
Carp, Frances, 524
Carpenter, Bruce,
    716
Caslyn, Robert, 452
Cassidy, Margaret,
    760
Castro, Concepcion,
    478
Catalano, Donald,
    407, 408
Cate, Rodney, 402
Cauhape, Elizabeth,
    24
Cavanaugh, John, 379
Cavrell, Ira, 43, 44
Cavrell, Otis, 43,
    44
Chapleski,
    Elizabeth, 380
Cheal, David, 302
Chelsvig, Kathleen,
    761
Cherlin, Andrew,
    190, 194
Chibucos, Thomas,
    702
Chiriboga, David,
    31, 381
Choi, Sung-Joe, 762
Chow, Nelson, 525
Christianson, Jon,
    361
Cicirelli, Victor,
    257, 258, 382,
    383

Clark, C. Roberta, 703
Clark, Noreen, 384, 432
Clark, William, 355
Clary, Freddie Mae 151
Climo, Jacob 259
Clipp, Elizabeth 385
Coburn, Karen 3
Coe, Rodney 109
Coe, Sherri 578
Cohen, E. 461
Cohen, George 754
Cohen, Joan 3
Cohen, Pennie, 704
Cohen, Susan, 456
Cohler, Bertram, 296
Cole, Charles, 60
Cole, Ellan, 479
Coles, Robert, 516
Collado, Cathy, 386
Connell, Terrence, 603
Connidis, Ingrid, 705
Connor, Patrick, 604
Conroy, Donald, 195
Consiglio, Jeff, 219
Coon, Ann, 152
Cooney, Teresa, 42, 260
Cordova, Dorothy, 561
Cornman, John, 297
Costley, Delia, 312
Coward, Ray, 64, 261, 267, 383, 413, 440
Cozart, Carol, 95
Crimmins, Eileen, 605
Cubillos, Herminia, 562

Daatland, Svein, 387
Dale, Angela, 391
Daniels, Norman, 349
Danigelis, Nicholas, 606
Darnton, Frances, 75, 139
Davies, Lorraine, 705
Day, Alice, 465
Dean, Alfred, 262
DeBord, Beverly, 153
Deimling, Gary, 424
Deitrick, E., 423

DeLago, Louise, 11
Dellmann-Jenkins, Mary, 310
Dempsey, Norah, 370
Derenski, Arlene, 4
Desaulniers, Paul, 221
Devine, Deborah, 628
DeVos, Susan, 607
DiGiulio, Robert, 154
Dilworth-Anderson, Peggye, 388
Dobkin, Leah, 596
Dobson, Cynthia, 12, 61
Dobson, Judith, 263
Dobson, Russell, 263
Dorfman, Lorraine, 706
Dressel, Paula, 62
Dugan, Elizabeth, 615
Dundon, Margaret, 480
Dunn, Nancy, 379
Dura, Jason, 389
Dwyer, Jeffrey, 261

Eckert, J., 309
Eckert, J. Kevin, 616
Edelman, Perry, 481
Eisler, Terri, 707
Else, John, 85
Emery, Beth, 402
Engelhardt, Jean, 390
Enoch, Louise, 48
Ensel, Walter, 262
Erickson, Marji, 412
Estrin, Harriet, 155
Evandrous, Maria, 391
Eyde, Donna, 350

Factor, Alan, 529
Fadel-Girgis, Mary, 526
Fahey, Charles, 195
Fallo-Mitchell, Linda, 708
Farley, Joanne, 392
Farra, Robert, 156
Fay, Patricia, 392
Feinson, Marjorie, 102
Feld, Sheila, 106
Feller, Cathy, 379

Felton, Barbara, 608
Fengler, Alfred, 606
Ferrante-Wallace,
    Joan, 287
Ferraro, Kenneth,
    103, 104, 157
Fillenbaum, Gerda,
    709
Finch, Janet, 393
Finley, Nancy, 264
Fischgrund, Ellen,
    482
Fitting, Melinda,
    483
Floyd, James, 340
Foehner, Charlotte,
    95
Fogel, Robert, 63,
    67, 72, 301,
    304, 306, 439,
    448, 604, 717,
    730, 734, 741,
    746, 747
Fogler, Janet, 303
Folts, W. Edward,
    599
Forman, Stephen, 221
Fortier, Robert, 324
Fowles, Donald, 755
Fox, Mary, 484
Fox, Richard, 602
Franken, Mary, 269
Friday, Patricia,
    158
Friedman, Ariella,
    710
Friedman, Meredith,
    13
Friss, Lynn, 394
Fruchtman, Milton,
    222
Fruge, Ernest, 379
Fruit, Dorothy, 310
Fuhrmann, Max, 86
Fulcomer, Mark, 372,
    373
Funder, K., 196
Furstenberg, Frank,
    Jr. 190, 194,
    304

Gallagher, Dolores,
    108, 124, 395,
    396
Gander, Anita, 49
Garza, Joseph, 62
Garza, Jose, 563

Gelfand, Donald,
    305, 517, 523,
    534, 555
Gentry, Margaret,
    105
George, Linda, 29,
    385, 711
Ghelfi, Linda, 564
Gibbs, Jeanne, 159
Gibeau, Janice, 485
Gibson, Rose, 527,
    528
Gilbert, Bruce 76
Gilbert, G. Nigel
    391
Ginsberg, Leon 689
Gladstone, J., 197
Gladstone, James,
    243
Glass, J. Conrad, 7
Gold, Deborah, 265,
    688, 711
Goldman, Lorraine,
    417
Gonyea, Judith, 403,
    740
Goodman, Jane, 397
Gordon-Jackson,
    Patricia 50
Grana, Saverio, 324
Graves, Conrad, 579
Gray-Shelgrove,
    Rosemary, 486
Greenberg, Jan, 712
Greene, Ritsuko, 106
Greene, Vernon, 398
Greene, Victoria,
    365
Greenstein, Deborah,
    629
Griffitt, William,
    63
Gross, Zenith, 252
Grote, Nicholas, 437
Grunebaum, Henry,
    296
Guertin, Wilson, 546
Guest, Carol, 422
Guillory, Ann, 244
Gulle, Natividad,
    418
Gutmann, David, 198
Gutowski, Michael,
    609
Gwyther, Lisa, 688

Haddock, Cynthia,
    109

Hagestad, Gunhild,
    199, 266, 306,
    713, 714, 715
Haley, William, 399
Halpert, Burton, 400
Hanson, Sandra, 267,
    268
Hansson, Robert, 716
Haraven, Tamara, 717
Harbert, Anita, 689
Harmelink, Ruth, 401
Harris, Tamara, 411
Hasselkus, Betty,
    487
Hatch, Ruth, 269
Hatch, Laurie, 763
Hatfield, Elaine,
    63, 67, 71, 72,
    301, 304, 306,
    439, 448, 604,
    717, 730, 734,
    741, 746, 747
Hawkins, Barbara,
    288
Hawkins, Joellen, 57
Haywood-Niler,
    Elizabeth, 389
Heagerty, Bobby, 425
Heald, Jane, 466
Healy, David, 66
Heinemann, Gloria,
    107, 160
Heller, Tamar, 529
Hennon, Charles, 32
Henretta, John, 9
Henton, June, 402
Herman, Shirley, 488
Hess, Beth, 64, 718
Higgins, Loretta, 57
Hilker, M., 599
Hill, Connie, 108
Hill, Elizabeth, 706
Hinman-Smith,
    Elizabeth, 688
Hirshorn, Barbara,
    297
Hoelcl, Gisela, 77
Hoffman, Christine,
    371
Holahan, Carole, 65
Homan, Sharon, 109
Hoover, Sally, 597,
    601, 602, 603,
    608, 609, 610,
    613, 619, 621,
    625, 627, 628,
    629, 630, 631
Hooyman, Nancy, 351,
    403

Hornung, Karen, 161
Horowitz, Amy, 404,
    489
Hoskins, George, 14
Houlihan, Mary, 490
Houser, Betsy, 270,
    699
Howard, Judith, 341
Howard, Nelson, 51
Howell, Mary, 405
Hubbard, Richard, 87
Hubler, David, 431
Hudson, Cathie, 162
Hughston, George,
    60, 205, 276,
    277, 363, 376,
    402, 414, 431,
    435, 547, 702,
    707, 721, 726,
    727, 733

Ide, Bette 568
Ingegneri, Dominique
    605
Iris, Madelyn, 719
Ishii-Kuntz, Masako,
    491
Israel, Barbara, 764
Ivry, Joann, 442,
    492, 738

Jache, Ann, 289
James, Alice, 530
James, Jean, 342
James, Alice, 530
James, William, 530
Janas, Monica, 493
Janelli, Linda, 200
Jarrett, Robin, 580
Jarrett, William,
    406
Jarvik, Lissy, 352
Jeter, Kris, 720
John, Robert, 581
Johnsen, Pauline,
    372, 373
Johnson, Colleen,
    201, 202, 407,
    408
Jones, Beverly, 494
Jones, Laura, 39
Jones, Lind, 88
Jones, Warren, 716
Joyce, Rosemary, 245

Kahana, Eva, 451,
    616
Kahn, L. Louise, 495
Kalish, Richard, 535

Kang, Gay, 561
Kang, Tai, 561
Kaplan, Richard, 559
Katschke-Jennings,
    Bert, 66
Kauffman, Janice,
    307, 496
Kay, Margarita, 568
Kaye, Andrea, 765
Kayser, Lynda, 497
Keith, Judith, 163
Keith, Pat, 33, 34,
    35, 36, 37, 38
Kelley, Harold, 67
Kendig, Hal, 409
Kennedy, George, 203
Kiecolt-Glaser,
    Janice, 389
Kiesler, Sara, 63,
    67, 72, 301,
    304, 306, 439,
    448, 604, 717,
    730, 734, 741,
    746, 747
King, Nancy, 740
Kingson, Eric, 297
Kinney, Jennifer,
    410, 421, 498
Kivett, Vira, 123,
    271
Kivnick, Helen, 204,
    205
Kleban, Morton, 371
Klein, Walter, 646
Klopf, Beverly, 611
Knapp, Daniel, 228
Knott, Elizabeth, 7
Kofie, Vincent, 164
Koh, James, 308, 531
Kohen, Janet, 110
Kolody, Bohdan, 262
Koo, Jasoon, 582
Korbin, Jill, 309
Kornhaber, Arthur,
    206
Korthuis, Kathleen,
    52
Kovacs, Steven, 85
Kovar, Mary, 411
Krach, Margaret,
    290, 499
Krauss, Marty, 412
Krivo, Lauren, 612
Kutzik, Alfred, 517,
    523, 534, 555
Kuypers, Joseph,
    721, 722

Labrecque, Mark, 445

LaCayo, Carmela,
    565, 566
Ladd, Linda, 425
Lambert, Donna, 310
Lang, Abigail, 373
Lang, Martha, 246
Langston, Esther,
    583
Laurel, Noel, 584
Lawton, M. Powell,
    597, 601, 602,
    603, 608, 609,
    610, 613, 619,
    621, 625, 627,
    628, 629, 630,
    631
Learner, Richard,
    291
Leavitt, Priscilla,
    165
Ledesma, Bernadette,
    365
Lee, Gary, 311
Lehman, Stanley, 608
Leibowitz, Bernard,
    601
Leigh, Geoffrey, 343
Lein, Laura, 536,
    691, 700, 720,
    723, 729, 743
Leung, Paul, 561
Levine, David, 89
Lewis, Constance, 15
Liem, Nguyen, 561
Linsk, Nathan, 732
Lipman, Aaron, 413,
    725
Liss, Barbara, 766
Litchfield, Leon,
    738
Little, Virginia,
    532, 724
Litwak, Eugene, 353
Lockery, Shirley,
    547
Loeb, Leonard, 208
Logan, John, 10
Longino, Charles,
    413, 725
Lopata, Helena, 8,
    96, 97, 111,
    112
Lorenz, Frederick,
    37
Losak, Stanley, 648
Lovett, Steven, 396
Luhmann, Frederick,
    767

Lutzer, Victoria, 390
Lyon, Stephanie, 616

MacKeracher, Dorothy, 768
Maddox, George, 69, 70, 256, 266, 298, 381, 395, 430, 698, 714, 735
Maeda, Daisaku, 533
Maldonado, David, 534, 535
Malkinson, Ruth, 166
Malson, Michelene, 536
Mancini, Jay, 726, 727
Mann, Delbert, 457
Manney, James, 692
Maqashalala, Theophilus, 167
Mareth, Paul, 327
Margolin, Leslie, 68
Markides, Kyriakos, 312, 537
Marks, Harvey, 751
Markson, Elizabeth, 30, 69, 718
Martin, Mary, 344
Martinez, Maria, 538
Martinez, Maria de, 585
Masciocchi, Carla, 414
Mason, Edward, 133
Mason, Jennifer, 393
Mason, Theresa, 586
Massey, Veronica, 16
McAuley, William, 363, 364
McCord, William, 247
McCready, William, 207
McCrory, Audrey, 500
McCue, Fern, 418
McDonald, Donald, 231
McGloshen, Thomas, 168
McKinlay, John, 444
McMahon, Betty, 415
Mederer, Helen, 501
Melino, Rolando, 555
Mellinger, Jeanne, 614
Melville, Margarita, 548

Mendoza, Lydia, 520
Mercier, Joyce, 272
Michaels, Francine, 677
Miller, Baila, 416
Miller, Dulcy, 417, 418
Miller, Sheila, 59, 273, 696
Mindel, Charles, 313, 539
Mirande, Alfredo, 540
Mitchell, Jim, 541
Mitchler, Jan, 612
Moeller, Tamerra, 414
Monahan, Deborah, 398
Montgomery, Andrew, 416
Montgomery, Mary, 769
Montgomery, Rhonda, 70, 403, 419, 467
Montiel, Miguel, 567
Morgan, David, 113
Morgan, Leslie, 114, 115, 119, 120, 169, 314
Morgan, Susan, 357
Moroney, Robert, 354
Morris, Earl, 272
Morris, John, 623
Moss, Willodean, 170
Motenko, Aluma, 420
Mouser, Nancy, 171
Mowery, Doug, 379
Mullins, Larry, 615
Murayama, Diane, 367
Mutran, Elizabeth, 542
Myers, Jane 38, 274
Myers, Mary, 41
Myllyluoma, Jaana, 443

Nagy, Mary, 172
Namazi, Kevan, 616
Navin, Sally, 38
Nay, Tim, 425
Neale, John, 433
Netting, F. Ellen, 617
Niederehe, George, 379
Nkongho, Ngozi, 292
Nkweti, David, 587

Noelker, Linda, 618
Noll, Paul, 619
Norris, Virginia,
    421
Northcott, Herbert,
    116
Novak, Mark, 422
Novero, Evangelina,
    588
Nunez, Victor, 560
Nydegger, Corinne,
    728

O'Bryant, Shirley,
    117, 118, 119,
    120
O'Donnell, Lydia,
    729
O'Neill, Mary, 173
O'Rand, Angela, 9
Ojeda de la Rena,
    Norma, 770
Onzuka-Anderson,
    Roberta, 300,
    348, 365, 367,
    368, 374, 386,
    447, 611, 620
Oppenheimer,
    Valerie, 730
Orbach, Harold, 731
Oser, George, 548

Pacheco, Sandra, 589
Palmore, Erdman,
    112, 121, 518
Paulson, Lon, 272
Pearlman, Joan, 3
Pearson, M., 423
Pelham, Anabel, 355,
    771
Penalosa, Fernando,
    543
Peterson, James, 124
Phillipson, Chris,
    315, 356, 391,
    624
Pifer, Alan 527,
    544, 551, 694,
    715, 748
Pinkston, Elaine,
    732
Pinsker, Seth, 83
Polansky, Elinor,
    502
Pongratz, Hannelore,
    744
Poulshock, S.
    Walter, 424
Powers, James, 357

Pratt, Clara, 39,
    425
Premo, Terri, 426,
    772
Pruchno, Rachel,
    370, 427, 428

Quam, Jean, 773
Quayhagen, Margaret,
    429
Quayhagen, Mary, 429
Quinn, Joan, 430
Quinn, William, 60,
    205, 276, 277,
    363, 376, 402,
    414, 431, 436,
    547, 702, 707,
    721, 726, 727,
    733
Qureshi, Hazel, 315

Ragan, Pauline, 519
Rakowski, William,
    384, 432
Ramsey, Mildred,
    367, 620
Rasinski, Timothy,
    316
Rau, Marie, 503
Ray, Robert, 174
Reed, Bruce, 433
Reemstema, Judy, 455
Register, Jasper,
    541
Regnier, Victor, 621
Remnet, Valerie, 275
Remondet,
    Jacqueline, 716
Reno, Virginia, 734
Resch, Nancy, 428
Reschovsky, James,
    678
Rice, Susan, 53
Rich, Bennett, 695
Rich, Jay, 350
Richman, Harold, 544
Riley, Matilda, 735,
    736
Riley, Robert, 345
Rivera, Patricia,
    396
Rivers, Caryl 251
Robbins, Donna 296
Robbins, Martha 17
Roberto, Karen 276,
    434
Roberts, M. Diane
    264
Roberts, William 139

Robertson, Joan 189,
191, 192, 193,
194, 195, 198,
199, 202, 204,
206, 207, 208,
211, 213
Roche, B. 337
Rodriguez, Linda 312
Roebuck, Janet 209
Rogers, Jane 386
Rohr, Karen 18
Rose, Jonathon 396
Rose, Linda 679
Rosebud-Harris, Mary
590
Rosen, Rheta 346
Rosenthal, C. 29
Rosenthal, Carolyn
545
Rossiter, Charles
445, 446
Rothschild, Amalie
331
Rowe, Jan 504
Rowland, Don 409
Rubin, Allen 435
Rubinstein, Robert
40, 122, 436,
622
Ruchlin, Hirsch 623
Ryff, Carol 708

Samuelson, Kristine
85
Sanchez, Carmen 591
Sanchez-Ayendez,
Melba 774
Sanders, Gregory 90
Santana, Sarah 555
Sauer, William, 64,
267, 268, 383,
413, 440
Scharlach, Andrew,
293, 505
Schmall, Vicki, 317
Schnittger, Maureen,
91
Schoonover, Claire,
371
Schorr, Alvin, 285
Schreter, Carol, 680
Scogin, Forrest, 437
Scott, Jean, 123,
175, 276, 434,
737
Seagle, Audra, 347
Seelbach, Wayne,
268, 277
Segalla, Rosemary, 5

Seltzer, Marsha,
442, 738
Seltzer, Mildred,
739
Seskin, Jane, 6
Shabad, Peter, 92
Shanas, Ethel, 63,
67, 72, 301,
304, 306, 438,
439, 448, 604,
717, 730, 734,
741, 746, 747
Sharma, Mahesh, 626
Sharma, Sushil, 506
Sharp, Tessa, 400
Shea, Loretta, 248
Shebani, Bashir, 546
Sheehan, Susan, 98
Shiang, Julia, 775
Shin, Hwa-Yong, 39
Shore, Barbara, 440
Shulman, Arthur, 105
Shulman, Bernard,
358
Shuman, Susan, 507
Shuttlesworth, Guy,
435
Silliman, Rebecca,
441
Silverman, Phyllis,
99
Silverstein, Nina,
740
Simmons, Kathryn,
442
Simon-Rusinowitz,
Lori, 508
Simonin, Mary, 519
Sixsmith, Andrew,
624
Sloan, Bernard, 359
Small, Gary, 352
Smith, Bert, 468
Smith, Daniel, 741
Smith, Howard, 530
Snow, Robert, 19
Snyder, Patricia,
751
Soldo, Beth, 64,
443, 625, 626
Sonnek, Ida, 249
Soto, Richard, 332
Sotomayor, Marta,
592
Spaid, Wanda, 366
Spector, Carol, 776
Spitze, Glenna, 10
Springer, Dianne,
360

Stagner, Matthew, 544
Stanaway, A., 461
Stanford, Barbara, 681
Stanford, E. Percil, 547
Stanley, Arthur, 176
Stanley, Renee, 509
Steinfeld, Edward, 627
Steinmetz, Suzanne, 742
Stephans, Richard, 548
Stephens, Gretchen, 437
Stephens, Mary, 410, 421
Stephens, Susan, 361
Sternberg, Josef, 441
Sternberg, Malka, 177
Stiehl, Ruth, 317
Stoller, Eleanor, 278
Stone, Arthur, 433
Strang, Patricia, 315, 356, 391, 624
Streib, Gordon, 599
Strugnell, Cecile, 100
Struyk, Raymond, 628, 629
Stueve, Ann, 743
Stueve, Charlotte, 294, 510
Sullivan, Lisa, 444
Sundstrom, Gerdt, 318
Susskind, David, 238
Sussman, Marvin, 439, 536, 691, 700, 720, 723, 729, 743
Suzuki, Peter, 561
Swaybill, Marion, 648
Swihart, Judson, 250

Tachhella, Charles, 653
Taich, Arlene, 178
Talan, Roberta, 20
Talbott, Marie, 179
Tannenbaum, Robert, 180

Tanner, Mary, 181
Tappen, Ruth, 21
Tate, Nellie, 182
Taylor, Robert 549, 593
Temaner, Gerald, 654
Tennstedt, Sharon, 444, 511
Thomas, Adria, 414
Thomas, Jeanne, 210
Thompson, Larry, 108, 124, 396
Tice, Carol, 208
Tobias, Cynthia, 568
Tobin, Joseph, 550
Torres-Gil, Fernando, 551
Tortorici, Joseph, 295
Toseland, Ronald, 445, 446, 453
Traupmann, Jane, 71, 72
Troll, Lillian, 41, 65, 124, 211, 212, 255, 271, 313, 364, 382, 403, 424, 438, 452, 541, 542, 696, 697, 699, 709, 728
Tuck, Inez, 594
Tully, Carol, 777
Tuttle, Robert, 778

Uhlenberg, Peter, 41, 42
Unks, Raymond, 617

Vachon, Mary, 183
Valle, Ramon, 520
Vandivort, Rita, 447
VanWinkle, Nancy, 512
Vernon, Sally, 537
Vinton, Will, 143
Viscusi, W. Kip, 448
Voges, Wolfgang, 744
Volpendesta, Darci, 379

Waciega, Lisa, 184
Walker, Alexis, 39
Walker, Ella, 513
Wallace, Edward, 630
Wallman, Laurence, 709
Walsh, Thomas, 631
Walters, Judith, 185

Wambach, Julie, 186
Ward, Russell, 745
Waring, Joan, 718
Warner, Sandra, 187
Wass, Hannelore, 546
Waters, Elinor, 397
Watson, Mary, 93
Wattenberg, Esther,
    319
Wechsler, Harlan,
    213
Weihl, Hannah, 553
Weiler, Stephen, 746
Wenger, G. Clare,
    449, 552
Wentowski, Gloria,
    214
West, Sheree, 682
White, Lynn, 68
Whiteford, William,
    456
Whiting, John, 747
Whitlach, Carol, 73
Whitted, Mabel, 188
Wilcox, Julie, 514
Wilson, Bernice, 683
Wilson, Keren, 54
Winfield, Fairlee,
    450
Winner, Carol, 109
Wolinsky, Frederic,
    109
Wood, Patricia, 262
Woodbury, Max, 711
Worach-Kardas,
    Halina, 554
Worobey, Jacqueline,
    632
Wright, Fay, 253
Wright, Scott, 515
Wynne, Edward, 748

Yeager, Garry, 55
York, Jonathan, 452
Young, Rosalie, 451

Zambrana, Ruth, 555
Zarit, Steven, 73,
    453

Subject Index

Able elderly, 713
Abuse, 742
Academic women, 759
Activity patterns, 679
Adjustment to widowhood, 113
Adult children, 489, 501, 507, 512, 775
Adult day care 388
Aged parents/widowed daughters, 255
Age segregation, 698
Age stratification, 735
Aging in place, 678
Aging parents and favorite children, 254
Alternative housing options, 672, 673, 674
Alzheimer's disease, 389, 422, 429, 458, 461, 470, 480, 493, 498, 509, 740
Anticipatory bereavement, 108
Assisted residential living, 644, 671
Attitudes toward the aged, 7
Adult children, 14, 39, 191, 251, 252, 253, 254, 255, 256, 257, 258, 259, 260, 262, 263, 264, 265, 266, 267, 268, 269, 270, 271, 272, 273, 274, 275, 276, 277, 278, 279, 280, 281, 282, 283, 284, 285, 286, 287, 288, 289, 290, 291, 292, 293, 294, 295, 352, 589; aging parents, 254, 255, 257, 258, 259, 263, 267, 272, 273, 274, 275, 276, 288, 294; co-residence, 260; distant-living children, 259; elderly widows, 289; favorite children, 254; filial responsibility, 256, 264, 268, 271, 277, 282, 290, 291, 293; males as helpers, 278, 295; mothers, 252, 286; older rural parents, 276, 290; parenting, 266; parents in

nursing homes, 269;
sibling
    relationships,
    265, 287;
    widowed
    children, 255;
Australia, 409

Behavioral family
    intervention,
    732
Black caregivers,
    513
Black elderly, 182,
    193, 239, 340,
    519, 527, 528,
    529, 536, 542,
    547, 549, 558,
    564, 570, 571,
    572, 576, 577,
    578, 579, 580,
    583, 587, 590,
    593, 594, 610,
    630
Black grandmothers,
    193, 222, 239,
    322, 577
Board and care
    residents, 616,
    677
Brain-impaired
    adults, 394,
    425
Britain, 552

Caregiving, 39, 253,
    257, 261, 277,
    278, 279, 280,
    281, 282, 283,
    284, 285, 294,
    307, 348, 349,
    350, 351, 352,
    353, 354, 355,
    356, 357, 358,
    359, 360, 361,
    362, 363, 364,
    365, 366, 367,
    368, 369, 370,
    371, 372, 373,
    374, 375, 376,
    377, 378, 379,
    380, 381, 382,
    383, 384, 385,
    386, 387, 388,
    389, 390, 391,
    392, 393, 394,
    395, 396, 397,
    398, 399, 400,
    401, 402, 403,
    404, 405, 406,
    407, 408, 409,
    410, 411, 412,
    413, 414, 415,
    416, 417, 418,
    419, 420, 421,
    422, 423, 424,
    425, 426, 427,
    428, 429, 430,
    431, 432, 433,
    434, 435, 436,
    437, 438, 439,
    440, 441, 442,
    443, 444, 445,
    446, 447, 448,
    449, 450, 451,
    452, 453, 454,
    455, 456, 457,
    458, 459, 460,
    461, 462, 463,
    464, 465, 466,
    467, 468, 469,
    470, 471, 472,
    473, 474, 475,
    476, 477, 478,
    479, 480, 481,
    482, 483, 484,
    485, 486, 487,
    488, 489, 490,
    491, 492, 493,
    494, 495, 496,
    497, 498, 499,
    500, 501, 502,
    503, 504, 505,
    506, 507, 508,
    509, 510, 511,
    512, 513, 514,
    515, 529, 532,
    588, 591, 738;
    abuse, 437,
    469; adult
    daughters, 363,
    426, 489, 495,
    505, 507, 510;
    adult day care,
    388; affection,
    406;
    Alzheimer's
    disease, 389,
    422, 429, 458,
    461, 470, 480,
    493, 509, 512,
    515; Australian
    aged, 409;
    Blacks, 513;
    brain-impaired
    adults, 395,
    425; caregiving
    hassles scale,

410, 498;
childless
elderly, 407;
chronically ill
elders, 395,
478; community
services, 367,
375, 381, 387,
481, 492;
dementia
patients, 379,
389, 399, 405,
410, 420, 433,
484, 494, 506;
dependency,
356, 360, 402,
441, 443;
depression,
396, 428, 477;
disabled
elders, 447,
514;
educational
programming,
415; eldercare,
348, 351, 352,
358, 372,
373, 374, 383,
391, 450;
elderly carers,
449; family
context, 432,
435; family
management
model, 350;
family stress,
369, 378, 398,
451, 468, 474,
494, 497, 512;
family support,
438, 465, 467;
family
therapy,430,
446; filial
obligations,
349, 393, 499,
505; friendship
patterns, 434;
gender
differences,
366, 371, 377,
404; helping
skills, 384;
home care, 355,
368, 403, 411,
423, 424, 482,
487, 490;
hospice, 482;
impaired

elderly, 408,
414; informal
networks, 353,
361, 421, 419,
431, 435, 444,
491, 502, 511;
institutional-
ization, 365,
370, 376;
intergenera-
tional, 476,
488; knowledge
of services,
380; marital
need
satisfaction,
499; men alone,
436; mental
health, 370,
427; mental
retardation,
390, 412;
midlife crisis,
357; nursing
homes, 452;
policy, 354,
363, 439, 448,
508; positive
attitudes, 392;
public
payments, 364;
recovery from
stroke, 412,
503; research,
453; resources,
466; respite
services, 417,
418, 423, 464,
471; role
transition,
501; rural,
499; rural
caregiving,
400, 401;
sandwich
generation,
472; self-care,
386; siblings,
383; social
activity
limitations,
416; social
support, 385;
support systems
for women, 413;
women, 451,
463, 496, 497;
work, 397;

workplace, 450,
485, 496
Caregiving hassles
scale, 410
Caregiving strain,
451
Case management, 738
Childless elderly,
33, 38, 53,
407, 699
Chinese elderly,
525, 557, 775
Chronically ill,
elders 395,
502, 506
Church members, 593
Confidants and
companions, 705
Congregate housing,
615, 623, 644
Continuing care,
retirement
community, 595
Coping, 91, 158,
174, 178, 497,
515
Counseling, 754
Cross-cultural elder
care, 532
Cross-cultural
perspectives,
728, 747
Cross-cultural
perspectives on
widowhood, 121

Daughter caregivers,
507, 510
Death of parents, 17
Decisionmaking, 706
Dementia, 379, 389,
399, 420, 433,
483, 484, 494,
512, 515
Denmark, 649, 655
Dependent elderly,
402, 443, 485,
500, 742
Depression, 396
Divorce, 24, 31, 32,
40, 41, 42, 44,
49, 54, 55,
170, 181, 196,
197, 202, 243,
382
Dual-career couples,
91
Dying care
recipients,

482, 486, 490,
504

Effects of
bereavement on
physical
health, 124,
162
Egypt, 526
Elder abuse, 309,
437, 469, 742
Elderly caregivers,
449
Elderly couples
(types of), 59
Emergency housing,
614
Employed women, 766

Families and aging,
29, 107, 114,
205, 338, 374,
375, 376, 391,
408, 409, 421,
436, 438, 439,
440, 441, 442,
465, 466, 467,
468, 686, 687,
688, 696, 697,
703, 714, 720,
721, 722, 723,
724, 726, 736
Family therapy, 430
Federally assisted
housing
programs, 619
Filial
responsibility,
256, 257, 261,
264, 268, 271,
277, 285, 290,
291, 293, 294,
344, 346, 349,
354, 372, 372,
393, 406, 426,
499, 505, 588,
767
Filipino widows, 588
Finances
(economics),
34, 37, 94,
119, 148, 162,
314, 364
Formerly married
elderly, 725
Foster Grandparents,
218, 247
Frail elderly, 444,
511, 614

Friendships, 26, 27, 28, 434, 773

General, 684, 685, 686, 687, 688, 689, 690, 691, 692, 693, 694, 695, 696, 697, 698, 699, 700, 701, 702, 703, 704, 705, 706, 707, 708, 709, 710, 711, 712, 713, 714, 715, 716, 717, 718, 719, 720, 721, 722, 723, 724, 725, 726, 727, 728, 729, 730, 731, 732, 733, 734, 735, 736, 737, 738, 739, 740, 741, 742, 743, 744, 745, 746, 747, 748, 749, 750, 751, 752, 753, 754, 755, 756, 757, 758, 759, 760, 761, 762, 763, 764, 765, 766, 767, 768, 769, 770, 771, 772, 773, 774, 775, 776, 777, 778; able elderly, 713; abuse, 742; acadc _c women, 759; adult children, 775; age stratification, 735; aging parents, 712; Alzheimer's disease, 740; America, 692; baby boomers, 753; childhood, 702; childlessness, 699; Chinese, 775; confidants, 705; continuity, 684; counseling, 754; cross-cultural, 728, 747; decisionmaking, 706; family relationships, 686, 687, 688, 696, 697, 703, 714, 718, 721, 722, 724, 725, 726, 727, 728, 731, 734, 736, 738, 743; family transitions, 717; filial responsibility, 733, 767; formerly married women, 725; friendship, 773; gay men, 751; group process, 704; guardianship, 719; health resources, 693, 769; historical change, 741, 772; household composition, 709; human services, 689; impaired elderly, 732; independence, 702, 707; kinkeeping, 715; Korea, 762, 767; lesbian women, 751; life-cycle squeezes, 730; life satisfaction, 758, 761, 766; loneliness, 716; married women, 725; men, 691; nursing home residents, 757; policy, 695; poverty, 700, 778; Puerto Rican, 774; reciprocity, 748; retirement,

706, 763, 766;
744; rural,
706; sexuality,
746; sibling
relationships,
711, 737;
social
networks, 700;
stress, 688,
701, 742; well-
being, 745,
760; women,
685, 690, 691,
693, 699, 701,
706, 708, 710,
718, 744, 750,
751, 758, 763,
764, 766, 768,
772, 773
Grandfathers 216,
217, 219, 220,
221, 225, 227,
233, 235, 238,
240, 324, 330
Grandmothers 193,
197, 201, 209,
222, 224, 228,
229, 230, 232,
234, 236, 239,
241, 242, 245,
249, 296, 321,
322, 323, 329,
331, 332, 333,
557, 477, 590
Grandparenthood,
189, 190, 191,
192, 193, 194,
195, 196, 197,
198, 199, 200,
201, 202, 203,
204, 205, 206,
207, 208, 209,
210, 211, 212,
213, 214, 215,
216, 217, 218,
219, 220, 221,
222, 223, 224,
225, 226, 227,
228, 229, 230,
231, 232, 233,
234, 235, 236,
237, 238, 239,
240, 241, 242,
243, 244, 245,
246, 247, 248,
249, 250, 299,
321, 322, 323,
324, 329, 330,
331, 576, 592,
715;
adolescents'
attitudes, 244,
248; age
differences,
210; Black,
193; children's
literature,
200; Christian
perspective,
195; college
student
expectations,
203;
continuity,
199;
deculturation,
198; family
contact
patterns, 205;
family
watchdogs, 212;
Foster
Grandparents,
218, 247;
gender
differences,
199, 210;
grandfather,
215, 216, 217,
219, 220, 221,
225, 226, 227,
236, 238, 240;
grandmother,
201, 209, 222,
224, 228, 229,
230, 232, 234,
239, 241, 242,
245, 249;
grandmother-
grandchild,
197; great-
grandmother-
hood, 214;
Judaic
perspectives
213; mental
health, 204;
Native
American, 215;
new social
contract, 206;
older women's
perceptions,
214; parent-
adult child
status, 191;
policy, 208;
post-divorce

families, 196,
202, 243; role
diversity, 192;
styles, 194,
207
Grandparenthood and
mental health,
204
Grandparenting
styles,194, 207
Great-
grandmother-
hood, 214
Grief, 147, 150,
163, 165, 166,
179, 187
Guardianship, 719

Health, 555, 693
Homebased services,
411, 424, 481,
487, 502
Home care, 611, 618,
634, 637, 663
Home conversion, 602
Homelessness, 668,
669
Home services, 631
Homosexual men, 23,
751
Household
composition,
709
Housing allowance
program, 603
Husband/wife
networks, 64,
103

Impact of widowhood,
104
Impaired elderly,
514, 732
Independent living,
649, 655, 702,
707, 733
Institutionaliza-
tion, 631, 664,
679, 683
Intergenerational
relationships,
19, 21, 51,
196, 197, 203,
205, 223, 224,
227, 228, 229,
230, 231, 234,
235, 236, 237,
238, 239, 242,
242, 243, 244,

245, 248, 249,
250, 296, 297,
298, 299, 300,
301, 302, 303,
304, 305, 306,
307, 308, 309,
310, 311, 312,
313, 314, 315,
316, 317, 318,
319, 320, 321,
322, 323, 324,
325, 326, 327,
328, 329, 330,
331, 332, 333,
334, 335, 336,
337, 338, 339,
340, 341, 342,
343, 344, 345,
346, 347, 373,
488, 521, 531,
537, 542, 544,
575, 577, 578,
580, 584, 586,
587, 590, 594,
665, 717, 753;
adults in
parental home,
347; baby
boomers, 319;
Blacks, 340;
care, 307;
children, 342;
collaboration,
316; contact,
310; daughters,
327;
dependency,
315; Egyptian,
330; elder
abuse, 309;
filial
responsibility,
346; four-
generation,
341; generation
gap, 339;
grandmother,
321;
grandparents,
299; Hispanic,
332; immigrant,
306; kinship
interaction,
343; Korean
elders, 308;
Mexican-
Americans, 312;
mobility, 318;
Navajo Mexican,

329; public
policy 341;
Puerto Rican,
333; resource
redistribution,
302, 314;
remarriage,
304; teaching,
317; three-
generation
families, 296,
300, 323, 328,
336, 344;
women's group,
303;
Interpersonal
needs, 92
Irish, 530
Israel, 553

Japan, 377, 518,
533, 550

Kinkeepers, 715
Korean elders, 308,
531, 582, 762,
767

Labor force
participation,
109, 115, 162
Latin American
countries, 607
Lesbian
relationships,
88, 751
Libyans, 546
Life care, 617
Life cycle, 710,
730, 771, 778
Life events, 708
Life satisfaction,
86, 90, 151,
155, 172, 182,
185, 188, 679,
758, 761, 766
Living alone, 25,
52, 117
Living arrangements
(housing),
524, 531, 556,
563, 595, 596,
597, 598, 599,
600, 601, 602,
603, 604, 605,
606, 607, 608,
609, 610, 611,
612, 613, 614,
615, 616, 617,
618, 619, 620,
621, 622, 623,
624, 625, 626,
627, 628, 629,
630, 631, 632,
633, 634, 635,
636, 637, 638,
639, 640, 641,
642, 643, 644,
645, 646, 647,
648, 649, 650,
651, 652, 653.
654, 655, 656,
657, 658, 659,
660, 661, 662,
663, 664, 665,
666, 667, 668,
669, 670, 671,
672, 673, 674,
675, 676, 677,
678, 679, 680,
681, 682, 683;
assisted
living, 658,
671; Black
elderly, 610,
630; board and
care, 616, 677;
community
housing, 597,
601, 623;
continuing
care, 595, 617;
Denmark, 655;
depression,
615; emergency
housing, 614;
extended family
living, 607;
federally-
assisted
housing, 613,
619; financing,
660; frail
elderly, 614,
620; functional
capacity, 632;
home care, 618,
620, 631, 634,
637, 663; home
conversion,
602; homeless
elderly, 668,
669; housing
allowance, 603;
independence,
624, 649;
institutional-
ization, 631,

635; Latin
America, 604;
life care, 617;
living alone,
612;
loneliness,
615; long-term
care, 604, 611;
mobile home
parks, 645;
nursing home,
633, 636, 639,
646, 651, 652,
653, 654, 661,
662, 665, 669,
683; older
unmarried
women, 626;
options, 640,
641, 647, 650,
656, 657, 659,
660, 666, 670,
672, 673, 674,
675; parents
and children
interaction,
605;
preferences,
600;
psychological
well-being,
616;
psychosocial
processes, 622;
repair
services, 627,
628; research,
629; shared
housing, 596,
598, 599, 606,
648, 676, 680,
681, 682;
single-room
occupancy
hotels, 608,
638, 644, 667;
Spanish
elderly, 610;
suburban
elderly, 609;
unmarried
elderly, 632;
Loneliness, 52, 149,
161, 615, 716
Long-term care, 508,
604
Long-term marriages,
58, 74, 75, 76,

77, 78, 79, 80,
81, 82, 83, 85
Love, 56, 72, 84

Marital adjustment,
89
Marital attitudes,
65
Marital fairness, 71
Marital power, 93
Marital-role
expectations,
61, 67
Marital
satisfaction,
86, 500
Marital status, 69,
70
Marriage quality,
58, 60
Married elderly,
724, 759
Men, 760, 763
Mental health of
caregivers, 427
Mentally retarded
adults, 390,
412, 529
Mexican-American
elderly, 312,
516, 519, 520,
521, 522, 534,
535, 537, 538,
540, 543, 548,
551, 562, 563,
565, 566, 567,
568, 573, 574,
575, 584, 585,
586, 589, 591,
592, 610
Mexico, 770
Middle age, 1, 2, 3,
4, 5, 6, 7, 8,
9, 10, 11, 12,
13, 14, 15, 16,
17, 18, 19, 20,
21, 42, 44,
148, 154, 169,
177
Middle-aged family,
21
Midlife men, 10, 12,
13
Midlife women, 2, 3,
5, 9, 10, 11,
12, 17, 20, 42,
44, 148, 154,
169, 177, 759
Midlife stress, 701

Minority groups, 516, 517, 518, 519, 520, 521, 522, 523, 524, 525, 526, 527, 528, 529, 530, 531, 532, 533, 534, 535, 536, 537, 538, 539, 540, 541, 542, 543, 544, 545, 546, 547, 548, 549, 550, 551, 552, 553, 554, 555, 556, 557, 558, 559, 560, 561, 562, 563, 564, 565, 566, 567, 568, 569, 570, 571, 572, 573, 574, 575, 576, 577, 578, 579, 580, 581, 582, 583, 584, 585, 586, 587, 588, 589, 590, 591, 592, 593, 594; adult children, 589; American Indians, 523, 568, 569, 581; Blacks, 519, 527, 528, 529, 536, 542, 547, 549, 558, 559, 560, 564, 570, 571, 572, 576, 577, 578, 579, 583, 587, 590, 593, 594; Britain, 552; Chinese, 525, 557; cross-national eldercare, 532; Egypt, 526; ethnicity, 517; family support, 525, 526, 532, 533, 536, 545, 549, 574, 579, 583, 584, 585, 591, 593; filial responsibility, 588; Filipinos, 588; grandparents, 576, 577, 590, 592; health services, 555; housing, 524, 556, 563; intergenera-tional, 531, 542; Irish, 530; Israel, 553; Japan, 518, 533, 550; Korean, 531, 582; Libyans, 546; life satisfaction, 546; mental retardation, 529; Mexican-Americans, 516, 519, 520, 521, 522, 534, 535, 537, 538, 540, 543, 548, 551, 562, 563, 565, 566, 567, 568, 573, 574, 575, 584, 585, 586, 589, 591, 592; minority families, 539, 541; Pacific/Asians, 561; policy, 517; Polish family, 554; poverty, 564; Puerto Ricans, 555; reciprocity, 530; research, 517; rural, 530, 552; social relations, 547; widows, 568, 588; women, 548, 568, 573, 580, 588;

Mobile homes, 645
Morale in widowhood, 123

Native American elderly, 523, 568, 569, 581
Native American grandparent-hood, 215, 329

Never married, 40,
47, 48, 725
Nursing homes, 269,
452, 611, 633,
642, 646, 651,
652, 653, 654,
661, 679, 757
Nursing practice 57

Older couples 15,
18, 56, 57, 58,
59, 60, 61, 62,
63, 64, 65, 66,
67, 68, 69, 70,
71, 72, 73, 74,
75, 76, 77, 78,
79, 80, 81, 82,
83, 84, 85, 86,
87, 88, 89, 90,
91, 92, 93;
androgyny, 86;
bereavement,
88;
interpersonal
needs, 92;
lesbian women,
88; life
satisfaction,
90; long
marriage, 74,
75, 76, 77, 80,
81; love and
sexuality, 56,
57, 62, 63, 72,
73; marital
attitudes, 65;
marital
fairness, 71;
marital
quality, 58,
60, 67; marital
status, 69;
middle-
aged/older
couples, 87,
92; modern
marriage,
82;physical
attractiveness,
68; policy, 64;
remarriage, 66,
89; role
expectations,
61; role
strain, 91;
social
casework, 78;
types, 59;

working class
marriages, 93
Older women 26, 27,
28, 106, 108,
119, 126, 127,
128, 129, 130,
131, 133, 134,
136, 138, 139,
140, 141, 142,
151, 154, 161,
168, 197, 201,
209, 214, 222,
224, 228, 229,
230, 234, 236,
241, 242, 249,
559, 626, 685,
690, 693, 699,
718, 725, 739,
744, 750, 756,
758, 764, 768,
772, 773, 774,
777
Older women/younger
men, 4, 6, 16

Pacific/Asian
elderly, 561
Parenting, 266
Physical
attractiveness
(role of), 68
Polish, 554
Poverty, 564, 700,
778
Psychological well-
being, 616,
699, 745, 760,
764
Psychological well-
being
(widowhood),
168
Public policy, 695
Public services, 387
Puerto Rican
elderly, 555,
774

Recycling buildings,
621
Religious
perspectives on
grandparent-
hood, 195, 213
Remarriage, 66, 89,
116, 304
Repair services,
627, 628

Research (family
    life), 727
Research (housing),
    629
Residential
    mobility, 678
Respite services for
    caregivers,
    417, 418, 419,
    423, 497
Retirement, 528,
    706, 725, 744,
    760, 763, 766
Retirement
    communities,
    725
Role strain, 91
Rural, 123, 171,
    271, 276, 290,
    400, 401, 499,
    530, 552, 619,
    706
Rural widows and
    widowers, 123,
    171

Safe home
    environment,
    620
Self-care, 386
Services, 689
Sex-role
    expectations,
    61, 87
Sexuality, 56, 57,
    62, 63, 73, 746
Shared housing, 596,
    598, 599, 606,
    648, 676, 681,
    682
Sibling
    relationships,
    265, 383, 404,
    737
Siblings as
    caregivers, 404
Single elderly,34,
    35, 36, 37, 40
Singlehood, 22, 23,
    24, 25, 26, 27,
    28, 29, 30, 31,
    32, 33, 34, 35,
    36, 37, 38, 39,
    40, 41, 42, 43,
    44, 45, 46, 47,
    48, 49, 50, 51,
    52, 53, 54, 55,
    626, 632;
    childless

    elderly, 33,
    53; divorce,
    24, 31, 32, 41,
    43, 43, 44, 46,
    49, 54, 55;
    ever-single
    women, 30, 39,
    47, 48, 50, 53;
    family ties,
    22; finances,
    34, 37;
    friends, 26,
    27, 28; gay
    men, 23;
    isolation, 35;
    never married,
    40, 47, 48;
    poverty, 25;
    resources, 36;
    widowed, 55;
    women, 26, 27,
    28, 30;
Single room
    occupancy, 608,
    638, 643, 667
Single women, 22,
    30, 39, 47, 48,
    616
Social adjustment in
    widowhood, 148
Social networks,
    171, 691, 743,
    745, 764, 769
Social roles, 8
Social support 106,
    107, 110, 111,
    113, 114, 117,
    118, 120, 160,
    163, 167, 179,
    183, 262, 353,
    362, 367, 381,
    385, 387, 388,
    390, 403, 412,
    413, 414, 431,
    432, 442, 484,
    491, 492, 503,
    509, 725, 769,
    777
Spousal caregivers,
    427, 428, 500,
    503, 512
Stratification, age,
    735
Stress, 742
Stress among
    caregivers, 398
Stroke, 421, 503

Support for family
     caregivers,
     445, 446

Widowers, 123, 124,
     125, 132, 137,
     143, 187
Widowhood, 55, 94,
     95, 96, 97, 98,
     99, 100, 101,
     102, 103, 104,
     105, 106, 107,
     108, 109, 110,
     111, 112, 113,
     114, 115, 116,
     117, 118, 119,
     120, 121, 122,
     123, 124, 125,
     126, 127, 128,
     129, 130, 131,
     132, 133, 134,
     135, 136, 137,
     138, 139, 140,
     141, 142, 143,
     144, 145, 146,
     147, 148, 149,
     150, 151, 152,
     153, 154, 155,
     156, 157, 158,
     159, 160, 161,
     162, 163, 164,
     165, 166, 167,
     168, 169, 170,
     171, 172, 173,
     174, 175, 176,
     177, 178, 179,
     180, 181, 182,
     183, 184, 185,
     186, 187, 188,
     504, 568, 582;
     adjustment,
     100, 102, 108,
     113, 148, 163,
     177; African,
     167; age
     differences,
     154; American,
     96, 111, 112;
     bereavement,
     124, 127, 131,
     147, 150, 163,
     165, 166, 179,
     187; Blacks,
     182; Canada,
     116;
     construction of
     a day, 122;
     cross-cultural
     perspectives,
     121; divorce,
     180, 181;
     family
     interaction,
     114; finances,
     94, 119, 148,
     162; funerals,
     165; health
     status, 103,
     124, 129, 172;
     historical,
     184; identity
     loss, 154;
     institutional-
     ization, 150;
     labor force
     activity, 115,
     162; learning,
     155; life
     satisfaction,
     144, 155, 172,
     182, 185, 188;
     live alone,
     117;
     loneliness,
     149, 161;
     longitudinal
     analysis, 169;
     phenomeno-
     logical
     framework, 186;
     remarriage,
     116;
     Renaissance,
     146; research,
     105; rural,
     123, 126, 158,
     159, 171, 185;
     self-esteem,
     170, 180; sex
     differences,
     101, 175;
     social
     relations, 104,
     157, 171, 178,
     182, 183;
     stress, 178;
     support
     systems, 97,
     106, 107, 110,
     111, 113, 117,
     118, 120, 144,
     160, 163, 167;
     teaching coping
     skills, 174;
     transition,
     145, 156, 162;
     use of
     physicians,

109;
volunteering,
180; well-
being, 101,
106, 119, 168,
175; widow in
fiction, 152,
153, 173, 176;
widowers, 123,
124, 125, 137,
143, 175, 186;
widowhood
mortality
technique, 164;
widow-to-widow,
99;
Widowhood research,
105
Women, 2, 3, 4, 5,
6, 22, 24, 26,
27, 28, 30, ,
33, 38, 39, 42,
44, 46, 47, 48,
50, 53, 94, 95,
96, 97, 98, 99,
100, 101, 102,
103, 104, 105,
106, 107, 108,
109, 110, 111,
112, 113, 114,
115, 116, 117,
118, 119, 120,
121, 123, 124,
126, 127, 129,
130, 131, 133,
134, 135, 136,
138, 139, 140,
141, 142, 144,
145, 146, 147,
148, 149, 150,
151, 152, 153,
154, 155, 156,
157, 158, 159,
160, 161, 162,
163, 164, 165,
166, 167, 168,
169, 170, 172,
173, 174, 175,
176, 178, 179,
180, 181, 182,
183, 184, 185,
186, 187, 188,
197, 201, 209,
214, 222, 224,
228, 229, 230,
234, 236, 241,
242, 249,
370, 371, 373,
377, 413, 450,

483, 488, 496,
497, 500, 504,
505, 513, 548,
559, 560, 578,
586, 616, 685,
690, 691, 693,
699, 710, 715,
718, 725, 739,
744, 750, 756,
758, 759, 760,
763, 764, 765,
766, 768, 772,
773, 774, 776,
777
Work, 756
Working class
marriages, 93

About the Compiler

JEAN M. COYLE is Director of The Institute for Gerontological Research and Education (TIGRE) at New Mexico State University. She is a founder and president-elect of the Southwest Society on Aging and is President of the New Mexico Association for Gerontological Education. Her numerous publications include *Women and Aging: A Selected, Annotated Bibliography* (Greenwood, 1989).